WINTON (BARNWELL) COUNTY SOUTH CAROLINA MINUTES OF COUNTY COURT AND WILL BOOK 1 1785–1791

BY
BRENT H. HOLCOMB
CERTIFIED GENEALOGIST

HERITAGE BOOKS
2011

HERITAGE BOOKS
AN IMPRINT OF HERITAGE BOOKS, INC.

Books, CDs, and more—Worldwide

For our listing of thousands of titles see our website
at
www.HeritageBooks.com

Published 2011 by
HERITAGE BOOKS, INC.
Publishing Division
100 Railroad Ave. #104
Westminster, Maryland 21157

Copyright © 1978 The Rev. Silas Emmett Lucas, Jr.

Copyright © assigned to Brent H. Holcomb, 1989

All rights reserved. No part of this book may be reproduced or transmitted in any form or by any means, electronic or mechanical, including photocopying, recording or by any information storage and retrieval system without written permission from the author, except for the inclusion of brief quotations in a review.

International Standard Book Numbers
Paperbound: 978-0-7884-3510-2
Clothbound: 978-0-7884-8921-1

INTRODUCTION

    Winton County was one of four counties formed in Orangeburg District in 1785. Like other circuit court districts, Orangeburg District was not a court of record until 1781, when it was made a court of ordinary, or probate court, handling wills and estates. This situation continued until 1787. However, in 1785 counties were formed within these circuit court districts and held county courts, recorded deeds, handled small court cases, etc. The counties set up in Orangeburg District were Lewisburg County, Orange County, Lexington County, and Winton County. Winton County is what later became Barnwell. It is the only county of Orangeburg District which has any eighteenth century records extant. We have Winton County Court Minutes, 1786-1791, and deeds for the same period, with the wills beginning in 1787, when the circuit court districts ceased that function. However, there was great dissatisfaction with the county court system in general in South Carolina, and particularly in Winton County. In fact, there was a riot at the court house, and the minute book of the Winton County Court was actually thrown out in the rain (the water stains can still be seen on this volume). The county court in Winton County was abolished and the area reverted to be again part of Orangeburg District. In 1800 all counties in South Carolina became districts, and Winton County was revitalized as Barnwell District with some slight boundary changes. It was renamed Barnwell County in 1868. Because Orangeburg District records were burned in 1865, there is a gap in the Winton/Barnwell records: the probates 1781-1787, and the deeds, probates, and other records from 1791-1799 are not extant. This volume contains a transcription of the court minute book, which includes a tax list for the year 1787, and abstracts of the instruments in Will Book 1. The original loose wills and estates papers for the period 1787-1791 have not survived. They probably perished with the Orangeburg District records in 1865.

    It is with great pleasure that this volume is being reprinted. The new and improved index should make this a more valuable research tool for this difficult time period in Barnwell County research.

                                         Brent H. Holcomb
                                         January 5, 1989

Winton Court Minute Book from Oct. 1786 to Feby 1791

William Christie, Defendant on the Part and behalf of the Plaintiff herein fail not on Pain of the Penalties that will fall thereon, as well as the forfeiture of Ł 10 proc. money. Dated at Charleston 20 Mar 1787. Holmes, Pltffs Atty.

Fees, on the Probat of a Will, &C &C &C Altered Feb. 29, 88.

	Ł	S	D	
Probat of a Will		14	. . . . .	1/0
Letters Testamentary		14	. . . . .	1/6
Warrant of appraisement		7	. . . . .	1/6
Qualifying Exexr. or Admr.		2	4	2/4
Coppy of the Will for every 90 words) or figures)			6	3
Citation		6		1/6
Letters of Administration &) Warrant for appraisement)	1	4		1/6
Administration Bond		7		1/6
Dedimus		14		1/0
Letters Guardian Bonds & C	1	4		
Ordinary Licence	3			10.00
Clerks Fees for Bond & C		11	8	
Marriage Licence & C	1	3	8	2 Dollars for a poor person 9/4

SOUTH CAROLINA, ORANGEBURG DISTRICT, WINTON COUNTY
17th. October 1786.

1 PURSUANT to an Act of the general Assembly of this State, intitled "An Act for the establishment of County Courts and for regulating the proceedings thereof," Aaron Gillett, John Caraway Smith, Daniel Green, Thomas Knight, James Farr and William Buford, Esquires, being a majority of the Judges appointed and qualified to carry into execution the said Act met and assembled themselves together for that purpose at a place called and known by the name of the Big House on the plantation of Charles Brown in the said County.
  After the opening of the Court and Proclamation thereof made according to Law--the Court proceeded to the choice and election of a Clerk when a majority of the Court appointed Mr. William Vince for one year from this time. Ordered that Mr. Vince give Bond and Security according as the Law directs. Ordered unanimously that there shall be an election and choice made of a Clerk for this Court once every year.
  The Court proceeded to the election and choice of High Sheriff for this County, accordingly ordered that he produce his Commission from the Governour at the next Court and that he give Bond and Security according to Law.
  The Court then proceeded to the Choice of their County Attorney when William Shaw, Esq. was appointed unanimously, having been previously admitted to practice the Law in this Court.
  The Court then proceeded to the Choice of a Treasurer for this County When it was ordered that the Clerk of the Court for the time being should be Treasurer to receive all Fines and monies coming due to the County for the use of the County and that he keep a proper Book for that purpose.
  The Court proceeded to the Choice of a Coroner for this County, when Aaron Smith, Esq. was unanimously appointed, ordered that he produce his commissions from the Governour at the next Court.

Mr. William Vince appointed Clerk for this Court proposed Mr. George Robinson, Captain Joseph Vince and Mr. Joseph Harley as his Securities for the true and faithful performance of his office which the Court approved of.
The Court Ordered the Minutes to be read.

        A. Gillett
        Jno. C. Smith
        Daniel Green
        Thos Knight
        James Fair
        Wm. Buford, J. P.

The Court adjourned to nine o'Clock to Morrow morning.

Wednesday 18th. October the Court met according to Adjournment.
        Present
        Aaron Gillett)
        John C. Smith)
        Daniel Green   )
        Thomas Knight) Esquires
        James Fair   )
        William Bufort)

Ordered that the Clerk employ a proper person to make a Jury Box for the use of this County to contain six divisions each division to be four inches square, to have covers for each division and to have two good locks with keys, that the same be compleated against the next Court & the cost to be defrayed by the County.

The Court proceeded to the choice of Constables for this County when Henry Cannon, James Halcomb, Henry Mills, James Montgomery, William Creech, John Ward, William Woodcock and Charles Wheeler were appointed to act as Constables for one year and that the Clerk issue summonses for each of them to appear at the next Court to be qualified for that Office.

Henry Mills and Charles Wheeler appeared personally in Court and qualified for the Office of Constable for one year. Ordered that Henry Mills and Charles Wheeler serve the processes issued out of this Court until the meeting of next Court.

Ordered that the Clerk employ a proper person to make six staffs for the Constables and for the use of this County, that they shall be six feet in length and the cost defrayed by the County.

Mr. William Vince delivered into Court the Bond and Security required by Law which was acknowledged in open Court by all the parties and Ordered to be recorded. Ordered that Mr. William Vince take the Oath of Office prescribed by Law which was done accordingly.

Whereas Joseph Vince, Esq., has declined acting as a Magistrate for thie County, the Court proceeded to appoint another to act in his place when the Court appointed Nathaniel Abney.

Ordered that all the Magistrates of this Court meet at this place on the first Monday in December in order to fix on a proper place in this County to erect a Court House and other public Buildings.

The Court proceeded to the choice of Grand and Petit Jurors for the next Court, when John Wyld, Colonel William Davis, Absolam Best, Robert McElworth, Joseph Vince, Jacob Swicord, George Robinson, Joseph Harley, Richard Vince, John Parkinson, Stephen Smith, Thomas O'Brian, Jonathan Clarke, John Collins, William Dunbar, Captain William Wheatley,

Robert Hankerson, Robert Lark, Ezekiel Williams, Richard Creech Senr. were appointed to serve as Grand Jurors and Bartlett Brown, Solomon Owens, Thomas Owens, George Kersh, Alexander Newman, William Newman, Reubin Newman, Alexander Kennedy, John Bates, Samuel Way, Moses Collins, Richard Jackson, Benjamin Odom, Thomas Morris, Joseph Brooker, George Collins, Henry Coker, William Mason, William Carson, Arthur Davis, Reubin Rountree, Richard Creech Junr., Amos Way, Frederick Brant, George Cope, Henry McMillian, Isam Cleaton, James Giddons, John Drummond & Joseph Collins were appointed to serve as petit Jurors.

4 Ann Foreman   )
      vs   )   Attachment.
   William Conway)

It appearing to the Court by the return of the Constable to whom the sd. Attachment was directed that he had attached one Horse, the property of Sd. Conway & he not appearing to replevy the said Horse or any other person for him and in Consideration that the property attached is perishable property, on the Motion of Mr. Shaw, Attorney for the Plff. Ordered that the said attached property be immediately exposed to public sale according to the directions of the Sheriffs Sale Law and that the money arising therefrom remain subject to the Plaintiff's Recovery by the Verdict of a Jury.

On mature consideration of the above Order and the County Court Law relative to the proceedings on Attachments, the Court are of Opinion that an Order of Sale of perishable property where the absconding or absent debotr does not appear to replevy the property attached according to Law would in many instances be just and reasonable and highly beneficial to injoined creditors, but conceiving the Law to be inexplicit judge it will be safe and proper in all cases to postpone all Orders of Sale until after the Plaintiff hath obtained Judgment, Ordered that for the reasonsabove ment., the Order of Sale in the Case of Ann Foreman against William Conway shall be & is Hereby rescinded so far as it relates to a sale of the property attached. It is Ordered nevertheless under the particular circumstances of the Case that upon the Plaintiff giving security to indemmify the Office attaching the property be delivered to her remain in her Custody until her right to recover damages agt the absent Debtor be determined by the said Verdict of a Jury and that she shall be answerable for the forth coming of the property or the value thereof.

Ordered that the Clerk do advertize & publish throught this County that the Judges of the County Court will meet at the Big House on the plantation of Charles Brown on the first Monday in December

5 next and will be ready to receive all Applications of persons inclinable to undertake the Building of the Court HOuse and Public Buildings for thie County on the lowest terms.

Ordered that the Clerk apply to the several Assessors and Collectors of the public Taxes for an Account or list of the several persons who paid a tax for the support of Government the last year and in case of refusal to serve each of them with a Copy of this Order which requires them severally to appear at the next Court held for this County to shew Cause for their refusal.

Ordered that the Minutes be read.

[To conserve space, the names of the Justices will appear only once for each day of court, although in the original they appear at the beginning and end of each day.]

The Court adjourned till nine o'clock tomorrow morning.

Thursday 19th October the Cort met according to Adjournment.
Present   Daniel Green   )
                    Thomas Knight   )
                    James Fair   )   Esquires.
                    William Buford.)

Ordered that a road be laid out from Silver Bluff to Matheses Bluff and that Capt. Richd. Kirkland, John Wickly, Capt. Joseph Vince, Stephen Smith Esqr., Stephen Boyt and William Holmes are appointed Commissioners of the said road and that they lay it out as near the corse of the old road as they find most convenant.

Ordered that a road be laid out and opened from Hamptons Ferry on Savannah River on a direct cors to orangeburgh as far as the limits of this County and that Jonathan Clark, Tarlton Brown, Joseph Harley, Benjamin Odom, Thomas o'Bannon, Edward Miles be & are appointed Commissrs. of sd. road.

6   That a road be laid out from the lower Bridge on the old Three Runs on a direction for Saltcatcher Bridge and to continue as far as the limits of this County that Capt. Wm Weekly, Colo. Wm. Davis, Joseph Brooker are appointed Commissioners for the Said Road.

Ordered that a road be laid out the nearest and Best way from Parkers Bluff to Williamses foard on the Saltcatcher, thence to continue the nearest way to the Green Pond on Edisto; that Bartlett Brown Senr., John Wyld Esqr (stricken), Richd Creech Jr., Robert Jordon, James Brabham, Arthur Jenkins is appointed Commissioners for the said Road.

Ordered that a road be laid out from the lower Bridge on the new three runs to the uper Bridge on the lower three runs from thence down the old Saltcatcher road to Whippey Swamp, that Robert Hankinson, William Dunbar, John Bates, Richard Creach and John Cox (stricken) Wm Roberts Senr is Appointed Commissioners for the said Road.

Ordered that a road be laid out from Williamses foard to Big Saltcatcher to the old Savannah foard on Little Saltcatcher and that Isom Cayton and Moses Distoe is Commissioners for the Said Road.

Ordered that a road be laid out from David Jacksons on the Charleston Road to cross Edisto at the mouth of Shaws Creek, from thence to Benjamin Kirklands foard on Edisto and that Nathaniel Abney, David Gibson, John Rivers and Wm. Jones is Appointed Commissioners for the Said Road.

Ordered that the orphen children in possession of Richd. Tradaway, Esq. and Zadock Woolly Remain in their care till the next cort in cors.

7   Ordered that the minutes be read which was done.

The Cort adjourned till the Cort in cors which is the third tuesday in January next at the plantation of Charles Brown.

Tuesday 16 January 1787. The Court Met according to Adjournment.   Present   Esqrs.
                    Wm. Robinson
                    Aaron Gillett
                    Wm Buford
                    Richd. Threadaway
                    Thos. Knight

Ordered the Sheriff's Commission be read in open Court which

was done accordingly.
   Also ordered that he should be qualified as the Law directs.
   Proposed that Henry Cannon should swear in Sheriff, and was also sworn according to Law.
   Propsed that the Grand Jury being called and no business being to be transacted and dismissed.
   Ordered that the Minutes be read which was done.
                                                    Wm Robinson.

8   The Court adjourned untill the 17th of this Instant and then to attend @ nine O'Clock.

    Wed. 17th.   Court met according to adjournment. Present:
                                (Wm. Robinson
                                (Wm. Buford
                      Esqrs.   (Richd. Treadaway
                                (Thos. Knight

9   Ann Foreman   )   Executed one Horse the property of Wm.
N18   N/S   )   Conway by Henry Mills, Conble. this 5th
     Wm. Conway   of Sept. 1786.

The Court find for the   Ord. of Court is issued that sd.
plaintiff Ł 40 and cost   Horse should be sold to satisfy
of Suit   the plaintiffs Debt and cost of Suit.

10 Winton County.   No. 27
    Wm Davis   )   Case of Attachment.
       vs   )   Executed by Wm. Wise 16th Oct 1786. This
    Wm McKensie   )   Attachment Satisfied and the Plaintiff
                          pays the cost

    No. 15
    Wm Robinson, Esq   )   Case of Attachment.
       vs   )   Executed by James Mongomery.
    Timothy Hollingsworth   )   That the Court finds for the
                                   Plaintiff 50 Ł award that the
                                   sd. property attacht may be
                                   sold to satisfie Debt & Cost
                                   of Suit.

    No. 16
    Thomas Obanion   Case of attachment.
       vs   Executed on a Negro Woman the
    Jeremiah Joiner   name of Fillis, one negro boy
                             the name of Saul one bay Horse
                             Benj. Odom, Avr. Newman, Gd.
    Ordered that the attachment be dismissed the plaintiff pays
    the cost.

11 No. 17
    John Wyld   )   Case of Attach. Executed on a negro man
       vs   )   named Will. Executed by CVD Wyld, 1st
    Maj. __?__)   Jan. 87. Ordered by the Court that the
                        above property be sold to Satisfy the
              plaintiff's debt for Ł 50 and Cost of Suit.

    No. 17   )   Case of Attachmt.
    John Wyld   )   Executed on a Blind Wench & Two
       vs   )   Children 1st Jany. 1787
    Maj. Robinson   )   Clw D Wyld.
    Ordered taht the above property be sold to satisfy the plaintiffs
    debt and cost of Suit.

No. 1
Alexandr Kennedy   )   Writ.
Josias Wallace   )   Executed on the body of Josias
                          Wallace the 28th Decmbr. 1786 by
Henry Mills. The return of the indictment between Alexander
Kennedy and Josias Wallace, we the Jurors find in favor of
the plaintiff Ł 14 0 0 With Debt & Cost.

No. 21   )
Col. Wm. Davis   )   Attachmt.
    agt   )   Executed on the Body of a negro, the
Isaac Cuthberd   )   property of Isaac Cuthberd by one
                         Thos Cox Ad. Domn 1786
                         Ordered that the above negro be sold
                         to satisfy the debt & cost
that the Court finds for the Plaintiff Debt & Cost.

No. 2
12 Absalom Causey   )   Writ.
        agt   )   Served on the Body of James Mirick the
    James Mirick   )   28th day of Demr 1786 by Henry Mills
Postponed untill the next Court by reqr of the defts.

No. 4
Thos.   )   Writ.
Henry Frederick   )   Served on the Body of Jno. Young the
    agt   2nd of January 1787 Henry Coker Secur-
Jno. Young   ity by Henry Mills.
Postponed until next Court.

No. 5
Jno Wyld Esqr   )   Writ
    agt   )   Copy left at the House of Wm. Brown
Wm. Brown   )   the 4th of January 1787 by Henry Mills
                          The jury after mature deliberation
thinks proper to bring in verdict in favour of the defendant.
                                    Jos. Holly, foreman

No. 6
Jno Wyld, Esqr.   )   Writ.
    agt   )   A copy left at the House of Wm. Davis
Col. Wm. Davais   )   the 4th of January 1787 by Henry Mills
January 1787;
Plaintiff and defendant both present the plaintiff nonsuited.

13 No. 7
Jno. Wyld Esqr   )   A copy left at the House of Wm Davies
    agt   )   the 4th of January 1787 by Henry Mills
Col. Wm Davies   )   the plaintiff and defendant both prest

By Ord. of Court Wm Woodcock Sworn in Constable for Winton
County to serve for one year.

Sheadrick Goodwin & Wm. Davis do acknowledge themselves to
be indebted to the State of South Carolina in the sum of Ł
200 ster. money for the appearance of Wm. Stringer at the
next court.

14 Absalom Causey
    No. 8   )   Writ.
    Col. Wm. Davies)   Trespass and abuse.
        agt   )   Damage 20 Ł
    Jno Wyld, Esqr.)

6

Wm Buford
Jno. Grady, Witnesses) Executed on the body of Jno Wyld the
4th Jan. 1787 by Henry Mills.) The jury do after mature con-
The plaintiff Defdndt.   ) sideration think proper to
both presnt. ready for   ) give averdit in favor of the
Trial   ) Defendt. one Shilling Sterling.
                                    Joseph Holly, foreman.

Moses Odom   No. 9   ) Writ
   agt   ) Damage 60 ₤
Wm Brown   ) Copy left at the House of Wm
Dismissed the plaintiff   Brown 4th Jan 1787 by Henry
pay cost   Mills

No. 22   ) Deld. mt.   Attachment
Wilson Carroll   ) One Horse property of Jno Hill
   agt   ) Ordered for Sale the above
Jno Will   ) property discharge debt & cost.

15 No. 10
    Moses Odom   )   Writ   Transferred
       agt   )   Damage 50 ₤
    Wm. Brown   )   Copy left at the house of Wm
    Dismissed the plaintiff pays Brown the 4th Jany 1787 by
    cost   Henry Mills
              [entire above entry stricken]

    No. 19
    Adam McNealy)   Detach.mt.
       agt   )   Executed 200 Acres of Land the property
    Micl. Odom   of Mcl Odom by Wm Creech, constable.

    No. 20
    Absalom Causey) Attachmt. on the property of Micl Odom
    Micl. Odom   ) One feathr bed, one Side Saddle, one
                     Looking Glass, one hand saw, Excd. by
                     Moses Duesto.
    Ordered that the above articles be sold to satisfy the plain-
    tiffs Debt and Cost.

16 No. 13
    Arthur Fairman)   Writ
       agt   )   Debt ₤ 24
    Jno Hicks   )
    Served on the Body of John Hicks the 4th January 1787 by
    Henry Mills. Laid over to next Court as the defendt. did not
    apr.

    No. 17
    Stephen Smith   ) Writ
       agt   ) Debt 12 ₤
    James C. Murphey)
    A Copy left @ the House of James Murphey 8th Jany 1787 by
    Henry Mills. Laid over to next Court as the defendant wants
    a witness.   it is to be at his cost.

17 No. 10
    Moses Odom   )   Writ
       agt   )   Damage ₤ 50
    Wm. Brown   )

    Wm. Robinson, Esq.)   A copy left at the House of Wm.
    Witness for the Plaintiff

                    the 4th day of Jany 1787 by
                    Henry Mills.
The jury considers that there is
no cause of action against the
Defendt.   Jos. Harley, foreman.

Ord. that the minutes be read which was done.   Wm. Robison.

Ord. that this Court be adjd. until tomorrow 9 o'clock which
will be the 18th Instant.

Thursday 18th.   Court met according to adjmt.
            Prest.   (Thos. Knight
                     (Wm. Buford
                     (Richd. Threadaway
                            Esqrs.

The Court after examining into the conduct of Henry Mills
have order'd that he should pay the cost of three Writs
which he neglected to execute.

Ordered that Charles Wheeler pay a fine of 40/ for neglect
of duty.   Ordered that Charles Wheeler's fine be remitted.

18   Ordered that all the Grand Jurors that did not give
    their attendance at this Court shall pay the sum of 20/
    and Pettit Jurors 10/ on not producing or giving lawful
    excuse for not attending.

       Approved by the Court that Francis Bassett as Deputy
    Clark for this County.
       Ordered that Capt. Jno Fitts be overseer for the Road
    and that he take all the hands between Jacksons Branch and
    Six miles on the opposite side of the Road leading from the
    Branch at his mills to the Buford line and keep the same in
    good repair, Also Solomon Owens & Benjm. Allen to take all
    the hands within six miles of the Road on this side leading
    from the three runs to the Road leading from Capt Fitts'
    Branch to his Road and keep the same in repair and act as
    overseers for said Road for the space of one year.
       Ordered that the Clerk furnish the Sheriff with summons's
    for the Overseers of the high Roads in order that they may
    be worked upon as speedy as possible and that the Clerk ap-
    point a certain day for their meeting.
       Ordered that the Minutes be read which was done.
       Ord'd that the Court adjourn till the next Court in course.
                              Thos Knight, Snr. Justice.

20 Blank

21 Tuesday. Court met according to adjournment 17th Apl 1787.
    Those Present.   Thos Knight   )
                      Wm Buford   )   Esqrs.
                      Richd. Threadaway   )
    Ordered that the Grand Jury be drawn.
         Grand Jurors drawn to serve at this our Court
    held for the   ) Jno Parkinson, Foreman
    County of   ) Jno Bates
    Winton.   ) Henry Koker, Godfrey Lee, Micl. Swycard,
                      Jno. Green, Jno. Bush, Jacob Buxton,
    Joseph Vince, Jno Wyche, Wm. Dunbar, Jno. Cochram, and
    sworn accordingly.

                                8

Pettit Juriers drawn to serve at out Court held for
the County of Winton
Wm. Bryan, Foreman. James Roberts, Noe Turner, Wm. Ashley,
Moses Plummer, Simon Bryan, George Kersh, Henry Dyas,
Wm. Mason, Levi Long, Wm. Moore, Nathan Koker.
Order'd that the minutes be read, which was done.
Ord'd that the Court be adjourned till nine O'Clock.
tomorrow.   Thos. Knight, JP

Wednesday Court met according to adjournment Aprl 28th 1787.
Then Present   Thos. Knight   )
                  Wm. Buford   )   Esqrs.
                  Richd. Threadaway   )

22 The Court hath taken it into consideration that the Road
    which was granted by ordr. of Court from Perkins Bluff, to
    widow Well's foard, be altered and that said Road be carried
    the nearest and best way from Thos Burton's ferry on Savan-
    nah River to Sd. Widow Williams foard on Big Saltketcher.
    Capt. Wm Weekley is appointed Overseer of said Road in place
    of Capt. Richard Creech Junr. who has moved out of the
    settlement.
        Mr. Sheadrick Goodwyn appeared and made oath the he could
    not safely come to tryal in behalf of Wm. Stringer, his evi-
    dence's appearing.

    Absalom Causey   ) Writ
         agt   ) The verdict of the Jury that the defendant
    James Myrick   ) the plaintiff 10 ₺ with cost of Court
    No. 2

    No. 17
    Stephen Smith   ) Writ. The jury finds for the Plaintiff
         agt   ) s 10 d 8 with cost of Suit.
    James C. Murphey)   Wm Bryan, foreman.

    No. 12
    Stephen Smith   ) Writ. The Jury finds for the Plaintiff
         agt   ) debt & cost of Suit.
    Edward Miles &   )   Wm Bryan, foreman
    David Shipes   )

    No. 13
    Arthur Foreman   ) Writ. The jury finds the plaintiff
         agt   ) 12 ₺ with cost of Suit.
    Jno. Hicks   )   Wm. Bryan, foreman

        Ordered that the minutes be read which was done.

23   Ordered that the Court be adjourned till tomorrow @
    9 O'Clock.

        Court met according to adjournment April 19th 1787,
    Thursday.
    Then Present   Wm. Robison   )
                      Thomas Knight   ) Esqrs.
                      Wm. Buford   )
                      Ricd. Threadaway)

    No. 17
    Richard Kirkland) Writ. The defendant being sworn postpons
         agt   ) tryal on acct. of a witness wanting in
    Whitmill Odom   ) his favour.

No. 4
S- William Brown) Writ. at the request of plaintiff
   agt) postponed untill next Court.
Moses Odom)

No. 2
Absolam Cuasey) Writ. The defendant swears that he
   agt come to tryall for lack of
Wm Goode witnesses Ord'd to be laid
over till next court.

No. 14
Moses Odom) Writ. Ordered to be postponed till
   agt) next court the defendant not
Bartlett Brown) being ready.

24 Robert Hankerson) Petition the court adjudges for the
   agt plaintiff a note of Six pounds and
Jno Hicks Cost of suit.
No. 13

No. 3
Hammond & Hankerson) Petition the Court adjudges for
   agt) the Plaintiff Six Pounds Ster and
Jethro Wood) Six Pence with cost of Suit

No. 1
Thomas Knight, Esq.) Petition, Postpond till next Court
   agt) Plaintiff could not attend on account
Benjamin Odom, Junr.) Of being called to Orangeburg Court.

No. 45
Milly Hill) Writ. case of Trover & Conversion
   agt) We of the jury do find for the
Richard Kirkland) defendant one shilling Ster. with
cost of Suit for the plaintiff to
pay. Wm. Bryan, foreman.

    Whereas Lark Robison is appointed as Deputy Sheriff for this County and sworn in accordingly
    Ordered that a dedimus be issued from the County of Winton for to take ye deposition of Benjm. Matthews in ye State of Georgia before two justices on behalf of Patrick McLemurry agt and James Pitote.

25 Ordered that a Dydemus be issued from the County Court of Winton to take the deposition of Wm. Walker in the State of Georgia before two Justices in the behalf of Wm. Stringer. Likewise Joshua Jumand.

No. 46
Aaron Gillett, Esqr.) Writ. Plaintiff has made appear that
   agt) he is not able to attend and put over
Stephen Collins) untill next Court

No. 47
Aaron Gillett, Esqr.) Writ. The Plaintiff has made it ap-
   agt) that he is not able to attend, and
Nicholas Nobles) put over untill next Court

No. 5
Aaron Gillett, Esqr.) Writ. Plaintiff acknowledge that
    agt   )   he is satisfied.
Savannah Bass   )

No. 33
Aaron Gillett, Esqr.) Writ. mutually agreed to be put off
    agt   ) till next Court.
Arthur Jenkins

26 No. 14
Francis Davis   ) Petition The Court find for the defendant
    agt   ) the Cost of Suit
James Brown   )

No. 48
Robert Handkerson   ) Writ the Plaintiff doth accnowledge
    agt   )   satisfaction
Henry Dyas   )

No. 10
Jessee Carney   ) Writ. plaintiff satisfied and actions
    agt   )   dismissed
William Miner   )

No. 49
James Pitote   ) Writ ordered to be laid out to next
    agt   )   court
Patrick Macklemurry)

No. 2
Zadock Woley   ) Petition the defendant made oath that he
    agt   ) could not come to trayll for lack of
Jno. Green   ) evidence

No. 50
Aaron Gillett   ) Writ laid over till next Court
    agt   )
Joshua Williams   )

No. 6
Aaron Gillett, Esq.) Writ satisfied
    agt   )
Jno. Lears   )

27 No. 15
James Montgomery   ) Writ. Ordered to be laid over
    agt   )   until next Court
Arthur Turner &   )
Joel Anthony   )

No. 1
William Dyches   ) Writ. Ordered to be laid over until
    agt   )   next Court
James Collins   )

No. 7
Frank Stone   ) Writ. The plaintiff nonsuited, and
    agt   ) the Court for the defendant five
Moses Odom   ) shillings with Cost of Suit.

11

No. 4
Mathias Bentley   )   attachmt. Laid over till next court
  agt   )
James Bently   )

No. 1
Jno Collins   )   atachment this Suit laid over until
  agt   )   next Court, the Court also orders that
Jno. Clayton)   Mr. Stephen Smith detain the property
                  in his hands until next Court

No. 25
Charles Wheeler)   Atachment-- ordered to be laid voer
  agt   )   untill next Court and that property
Sabrad Odom   )   be detained in the Constables hands.

Ordered that the minutes be read which was done. Ordered this Court be adjourned till 9 o'clock tomorrow. Wm. Robison.

28   Court met according to adjournment April 20th 1787.
     Then Present   William Robinson)
                    Thos. Knight   )   Esqrs.
                    Wm. Buford   )

Ordered that Jonathan Clark shall be overseer of the Road leading from Jno. Hamptons Ferry on Savannah River to Wm. Harleys Bridge on the lower Three Runs, and that he keep the same in good repair, that Joseph Harley as overseer of sd. Road, from said Bridge on the Thre Runs to the Big Saltketcher and keep the same in good repair unto the middle of sd. Saltketcher Swamp that Benjamin Odom overseer of said Road from the Big Saltcatcher to the County Line & keep the same in good repair.
Ordered that Wm. Vince and Amos Way lay off the Road from the Upper Three Runs Bridge to Pen Branch, and that Robert Hankerson be overseer of said Road to the lower side of pen branch including the swamp and that he open and keep the same in good repair, that Mr. Dunbar be overseer on sd. from pen Branch to Neds Branch and keep the same in good repair. That Mr. John Bates be overseer of said Road from Neds branch to Mr. Harleys Bridge and keep the same in good repair. that Mr. Tarlton Brown be overseer of said Road from Mr. Harleys Bridge to a pond called fiddle pond and keep the same in good repair. the Reuben Golikely be overseer of said Road from the fiddle pond to the cart ponds and keep the same in good repair. that Mr. Wm. Roberts Senr be overseer from said cart ponds to the County line and keep the same in good repair.
Ordered that in case any dispute should arise between any two overseers of the Road that he make application to the next Justice for said County, who shall determine the matter.

29   Ordered that no Executions be given by this Court till further orders.
Ordered that the Minutes be read which was done.
Ordered that this Court be adjourned untill the next Court in Course.

Tuesday. Wm. Robison   )
) at a Court held for the County
                          of Winton on Tuesday the 17th
                          July 1787,

12

Present: Wm Robinson, Richd Threadaway, Aaron Gillett, Jno. Co. Smith, Wm. Buford.

Ordered that the Grand Jury be called which was done accordingly: namely Jno Wyld, Esqr. Foreman. Wm. Weekly, Joseph Brooker, Ricd. Kirkland, Solomon Owens, Bartlett Brown, Wm. Newman, Alexn. Newman, Sampson Griffin, Jno. Collins, Absalom Best, Ricd. Creech, Lewis Weathersby, which was sworn accordingly.

Ordered that the Pettit Juriers be called which was done accordingly: Jno. Joyce, foreman. Tal Odom, James Giddins, Benjm. Odom Junr., Bid Vince, Benj. Buxton, Edward Miles, Dav'd Shipes, Wm. Causey, Jno. Caves, Saml. Way, Wm. Goode, Charls Bailes.

Ordered that the minutes be read which was done accordingly.

30 No. 28
Joseph Dick agt Moses Cree   Attachment   Ordered that the property be sold which was attached to discharge Debt & Cost
Ordered that the court be adjourned to 9 O'Clock tomorrow.

Wednesday. Court met according to adjournment 18th July 1787.
Present: Wm. Robinson, Aaron Gillett, Jno. C. Smith,
          Wm. Buford, Ricd. Threadaway, Thos. Night, Esqrs.

No. 11
Vincent Rene Alexander)
          agt   )   Attachment. A negro wench in the
Peter Randolph   )   hands of Micl. Swicord by Lark
                            Robison, D. S.
Ordered that the Sheriff expose the property attcht to public Sale and retain the produce arising therefrom in his hands for the further order of the Court.

31 (Blank)

32 and order of Court that the property be Sold Joseph Dick agt Moses Cree   which was attacht
Ordered that the Court adjourn to 9 O'Clock tomorrow.

33 No. 12 1787 22nd Jany)   Writ. Executed 11th April 1787
   Stephen Smith   )   by Henry Cannon, D. Shff.
        agt   )
   Edwd Myles & D. Shipes)

   No. 15
   Richd. Kirkland)   Writ. By copy left 31st March 1787
        agts   )   By Henry Cannon, D. Shff.
   Whitmil O'Dom   )

   No. 4
   Wm. Brown   )   Writ. Executed 1st March 1787
      agt   )   By Henry Cannon, D. Shff.
   Moses ODom   )

   No. 3
   Hammond & Hankinson) Writ. Executed 28th March 1787
          agt   )   By Henry Cannon, D. Shff.
   Sarah Wallace   )   Postponed till next court
                                 Stephen Smith

13

23rd
No. 2
Absalom Causey) Writ. Executed 19th April 1787
   agt   )   by Henry Cannon, D. Shff.
Wm. Goode)
Thos. Moses Security.

24th
No. 14
Moses ODom) Writ. Executed 1st February 1787.
   agt   By Henry Cannon, D. Shff.
Bartlett Brown Junr
Lewis Johnston and Rachael Moore, witnesses for the Plaintiff.

34   24th Jany 1787
No. 13
Robert Hankinson) Petition. Executed 20th March 1787.
   agt   )   By Henry Cannon, D. Shff.
John Hicks)

No. 3
Hammond & Hankinson) Petition. Executed 20th March 1787
   agt   )   By Henry Cannon, D. Shff.
Jethro Wood)

25th Jany
No. 1.
Thomas Knight, Esq.) Petition. Executed 11th April 1787
   agts.   )   by Henry Cannon, D. Shff.
Benjamin Odom, Junr.)

No. 45
Milly Hill) Executed 10th February 1787.
   agts   ) By Henry Cannon, D. Shff.
Capt. Richd Kirkland)

15th Feby
No. 46
Aaron Gillett, Esqr.) Writ. Executed 28th March 1787
   agts   )   by Henry Cannon, D. Shff.
Stephen Collins)

No. 17
Aaron Gillett, Esq.) Writ. Executed 2nd April 1787
   agts   )   By Henry Cannon, D. Shff.
Nicholas Nobles)
Purl Johnston
Joshea Cannon
&   (?)

No. 35
Aaron Gillett, Esq.) Writ. Executed 29th March 1787
   agts   )   By Henry Cannon, D. Shff.
Mrs.   Bass)

35   15th Feby 1787
No. 33
Aaron Gillett, Esq.,) Writ. Executed 28th March 1787.
   agts   )   By Henry Cannon, D. Shff.
Arthur Jenkins)

26th March
No. 14
Francis Paris) Petition. Executed 10th April 1787.
   agts) By Henry Cannon, D. Shff.
Jos. Brown)

No. 48
Robert Hankinson) Writ. Executed 28th March 1787.
   agts) By Henry Cannon, D. Shff.
Henry Dyas   The above action Satisfied.

No. 10
Jesse Carney) Writ. Executed 5th April 1787.
   agts) By Henry Cannon, D. Shff.
William Minor) Plaintiff satisfied and action dismissed.

No. 49
James Pelot) Writ. Damage ₤ 50
   agst) Executed 28th March 1787, By Henry Cannon,
Patn. McLammuray) D. Shff. Ordered to be laid over till next court

No. 2
Zadock Woolley) Petition Executed 29th March 1787
   agts) By Henry Cannon, D. Shff
John Green)
Witnesses for the Plaintiff:
   John Red, Lars Woolley, Hezekiah Williams

1787 28th March
No. 8
Lucy Wood) Writ.
   agst) No to be found. Henry Cannon, D. Shff
Absalom Causey)

29th
No. 50
Aaron Gillett, Esq.) Writ. Executed 5th April 1787
   agts) By Henry Cannon, D. Shff.
Joshua Williams)

No. 6
Aaron Gillett, Esq.) Executed 5th March 1787
   agts) by Henry Cannon, D. Shff.
John Lears)

29th
No. 15
James Montgomery) Executed 11th April 1787
   agts) By Henry Cannon, D. Shff.
A. Turner & Joel   Edward Miles, Security.
Anthony

No. 1
William Dikes) Writ. Executed 28th March 1787,
   agt) By Henry Cannon, D. Shff.
James Collins)

No. 7
Francis Stone) Executed 22d March 1787
   agt) Wt. By Henry Cannon, D. Shff.
Moses Odom)

37 No. 12 Aaron Gillett, Esq.)   Not to be found in the
            agt   )   County, Henry Cannon, D.
         John Davis   )   Shff

   No. 4
   Martha Bentley) Attachment on a horse in the hands of
       agt   ) James Bentley 6th April 1787
   James Bentley) By Henry Cannon, D. Shff

   No. 1
   Jno Collins   ) Attachment in the hands of Stephen Smith
      agt   ) as much property as will satisfy Debt and
   Jno Clayton   ) cost 31st day of January 1787
                                        Henry Cannon, D. Shff.

   No. 25
   Charles Wheeler) property executed according to Law, on
       agt   ) Horse, Bridle and Saddle, the property of
   Sabrad Odom   ) Sabrad Odom by Wm. Woodcock, D. Shff.

   Miss'd to be put on the Docket last Court.

   No. 2
   Robt Hankinson) Attacht. One negro fellow named Cesar
       agt   ) also money in the hands of Henry Coker
   Fredk. Francis) Ordered that the attachment be laid over
                     till next court 20th.

38 18 Jy 1787.
    No. 8
    Lucy Wood   ) Writ. Executed 19th April 1787
       agt   ) By Henry Cannon, D. S.
    Absolam Causey) Nonsuit

    No. 16
    Robt Hankerson   ) Writ. Executed 15th Apl 1787
        agt   )   By Henry Cannon, D. S.
    Frederick Goodwyn)
    Peter Coms, Atty for Df.

    No. 21
    Arthur Jenkins) Writ. Executed 11th July 1787.
        agt   )   By H. Cannon, D. S.
    Joseph Collins)

39 No. 7
    Wm Wise   )   Petition. Executed 17th Apl 1787.
       agt   )   By Lark Robison, DS.
    Bartlett Brown)

    Wm Smith   )   No. 8 Petition Executed July 9, 1787
    agt   )   by Lark Robison, DS.
    James Kirkland)

    No. 5
    Frans Bassett) Petition Executed 12th July 1787.
        agt   )   By Henry Cannon, D. S.
    Josias Wallace)

    No. 10
    William Parker) Petition. Executed 3rd June 1787 By
        agt   )   Lark Robinson, D. S.
    Alexn. Newman)

16

appeared Wm. Newman and made oath that the above acct. was paid on which the Court gave Judgt. for the Deft.

40 No. 411
Absalom Causey)   Petition. Executed 8th June 1787 by
    agt   )   Lark Robison. D. S.
Jno. Weekley   )

No. 51
Michael Swicord.   ) Writ. Executed 4th July 1787 by
    agt   ) Lark Robison, D. S.
Laurence Fibiger   ) action withdrawn by consent of the
                       parties.
Received this 29th Novem. 1787 of Aaron Smith Clerk Winton County a Note. of hand from Lars.Fibiger to Michael Swicord for Seventy five pounds Sterling & also One Note of hand from the same dated the next day being the 22d March 1787 for Seventy eight pounds Six Shillings Sterling __ P me.
Michael Swicord.
Test. Thos. Wyld.

No. 6.
Thos. Filpot) Petition Executed 10th June 1787 by
    agt   )   Lark Robison, D S
Henry Mills   )

41 No. 52
John Montgomery   ) Wt. Executed 8th June 1787 by
    agt   ) Lark Robison, D. S.
James Montgomery) Suit with Drawn by consetn of the
                     parties.

Henry Peoples.   ) No. 18 Wirt. Executed 8th June 1787
    agt   ) By Lark Robison, D. S.
James Montgomery)

The Court met according to adjournment 18th July 1787. Present Wm. Robison, Aaron Gillett, Jno Smith, Willm. Buford, Ricd. Threadaway, Thos. Night, Esqrs.

No. 11
Vincent Rone Alexander) Attachment
    agt   ) a negro wench called Sarah in the
Peter Randolph   ) hands of Ml. Swicord.
                                    Lark Robison, D. S.
ordered that the Sheriff expose the property attacht to public sale and retain the produce arising there from in his hands for the further ordr. of Court.
    Ordered that Jno Gill serve as Constable for this County for one year.
    Ordered that Henry Mills be dismissed from serving as Constable in this County

42 No. 29
Wm. Buford, Esq.   ) Attachmt. Executed a horse
    agt   ) Dismissed by the approbation of the
James Prendargast   ) Court.

Entered in Book of fines Page (18)
Ordered that Jno. Ward pay the sum of twenty shillings, that the Sheriff immediately levy and execute and also sell to satisfie the same

17

ordered that a citation be issued by the Clerk of this
Court to the next of kindred & creditors whereby letters of
Administration may be granted Ann Cunningham for the Estate
of Joseph Neather late of this County deceased.
ordered likewise that the said Ann Cunningham act as
Guardian to an Orphan Child now undr. her care.

The State   )   Larceny. July 18th. 1787.
  agt   )   We the Pettit Jurers for this County of
Benjm. Odom   )   Winton held at the Big house after due
Consideration have found the prisoner guilty. Joseph Harley,
foreman. The prisoner was brought to the Bar by ordr. of
the Court and asked if he had anything to offer why __ Judgt
should not be passed on him, having nothing to offer the
Court unanimously determined that the Prisonr should
immediately be taken from the Bar and Carried to the most
Public Place in the Courtyard and that he should on his
bare Back receive thirty nine lashes well laid on by or
undr. the directions of the Sheriff and should be discharged on paying his lawfull Fees.

43   Ordered that John Bates, the son of Wm. Bates, deceased
and Sarah his mother, shall have it in his power to appoint
Jno. Bates to be his guardian to act and Transact his
affairs till of age
    ordered that Rich. Creech & Ann Creech that they shall
have a citation to warn all kindred & creditors to appear
and give in reason by letters of administration should not
be granted
    ordered that the minutes be read which was done
                              Wm. Robison
                              Richard Threadaway
                              Thos. Knight.

Court met according to adjournment
        Present   19th July 1787.
            Wm. Robison   )
            Ricd. Threadaway   )   Esqrs.
            Wm. Buford.   )

44 No. 30
Wm. Williams   )   Attachmt. Executed a sorrel mare Branded
  agt   )   I O and said to be the property of sd.
James Lewis.   )   James Lewis.   Clevers D. Wyld.

Court met according to adjournment 19th July 1787.
            Present
                        Wm. Robison   )
                        Ricd. Threadaway)
                        Wm. Buford   )   Esqrs.
                        Thos. Night   )
                        Aaron Gillett   )

No. 46
Aaron Gillett, Esq.)   continued till next Court.
  agt   )
Stephen Collins   )

No. 47
Same   )
  agt   )   Contd till next Court
Nicholas Nobles   )

No. 5
Same   )
   agt   ) discont. at Defts Costs.
Susanna Bass   )

No. 33
Same   )
   agt   ) continued till next Ct.
Arthur Jenkins)

No. 50
Same   ) referred by mutual consent to the
   agt   ) Arbitration of Aaron Smith & Joseph
Joshua Williams) Vince with power of umpirage to return
                  their Award next Court.

No. 8
Lucy Wood   )
   agt   ) Plaintiff nonsuited
Absalom Causey)

No. 4
Absalom Causey) Plff nonsuited Mr. Bisset to pay the
   agt   ) costs.
John Weakley   )

No. 49
James Pilote   ) Ordered that this cause stand over
   agt   ) till next Court on the application of
Patrick McElmurray) the defendant & that the affidavit
                    of Miss Henny pilote Michael Swicord
                    and Elizabeth pilote be read as evi-
                    dence to the Jury at the Trial of
                    the Cause by the consent of the
                    Defendant.

No. 3
Hammond & Hankerson)
   agt   ) ordered that this Cause stand over
Sarah Wallace   ) till next Court by consent of the
                      parties.

No. 4
Wm. Brown   ) ordered that this Cause Stand over till
   agt   ) next Court by consent of the parties to
Moses Odom   ) the Cost of the Defent.

No. 4
Absalom Causey) ordered that this cause stand over till
   agt   ) next Court by mutual Consent of the
Wm. Goode   ) parties

No. 1
Thos. Night, Esqr.) Judgment for the plaintiff of 2 L-
   agt   ) 18 S-4½ D with interest from the 26
Benj. Odom   ) March to the present time. The de-
                     fendant as error pleaded no effects
                     the defdt. to be pd out of the
                     effects of Michl Odom deceased
                     that comes to the hand of the Deft
                     the Plaintiff paying cost of Suit.

46 No. 2
Zadock Wooley) ordered that Judgment shall pass agt the
   agt   ) Defendant 19th July 1787 for Debt & Cost
Jno. Green   ) ₤ 3. 10S..2 D and the cost that may amount
                 of day the plaintiff allows 6 weeks to
                 the Defendant to pay Debt & Cost Execution
                 to be delivered immediately.

The Grand Juriers return in their present. to the Court,
the Court return their thanks to the Grand Juriers, ordr.
their presentments be entered on the Records.

We present a great grievance for the want of a Court house,
Goal &C in this County
We present it a great grievance this County labours under
for the want of a Jury List and a Regular Draught of the Same
for the Different Jurers
We present a grievance the Want of the Laws of this State
not being able to proceed to business for the want of the
Same.
  We return our hearth thanks to Wm. Shaw, Esq. States
Atty. for the County of Winton for Charge given us.
     17th July 1787)   John Wyld, Foreman.

The State   )
   agt   ) Larceny July 19th 1787.
Jno. Red   )
We the Pettit Jurers for the County of Winton held at the
Big House after due consideration have found the prisoner
Guilty. Edward Miles, Foreman the prisoner was brought
to the Bar by ordr. of the Court and asked if he had anything to offer why Judgment should be passed on him having
nothing to offer the Court unanimously determined that the
prisoner should be immediately be take from the Bar &
carried to the most public place on the Court yard and that
he should on his bare Back receive thirty nine

47 nine lashes by or undr. the direction of Sheriff and should
be discharged on paying his lawful fees.

The State   )
   agt   ) Larceny. July 19th 1787.
Stephen Blackman)
We the pettit Jurors for the County of Winton held at the
Big house after due consideration have found the prisoner
Guilty. Edwd. Miles, foreman, the prisoner was brought to
the Bar by ordr. of the Court and asked if he had anything
to offer the Court unanimously determined that the prisoner
should be immediately taken from Bar and carried to the
most public place on the Court yard and that he should on
his bare back receive thirty nine lashes well laid on under
the direction of the Sheriff and should be discharged on
paying his lawfull fees.

No. 1.
Jno. Collins)
   agt   ) Atachment
Jno. Clayton) Ordered that it Stand over till next Court

By ordr. of Court that Wm. Southwell Shall have letters of
Administration by giving Bond & Security to the Clark.

No. 30.
Wm. Williams) Attacht. The Court after hearing/evidence/
   agt   ) on part of the Deft. gave Judgment in his
James Lewis   ) favor for Seven Pounds Sterling and ordered
              the property attached to be sold to satisfy
              the Clevers D. Wyld pays cost of Suit.

No. 53
Margt. Canniers) action of Wm. Shaw, Esq. ordered that
   agt   ) Theadorick Goodwyn and Wm. Davis
Wm. Stringer   ) become special Bail in this action

ordered that the Court be adjourned to 9 O'Clock tomorrow
which was done.
ordered that the minutes be red which was done accordingly.
                              W. Buford
                              Thos. Knight
                              Jno. C. Smith.

Court met according to adjmt.
Present   July 20th. 1787
Wm. Robison   )
Aaron Gillett)
Jno. C. Smith) Esqrs.
Thos. Night   )
Wm. Buford.   )

Ordered that Elij. Gillett /Esqr/ shall be granted letters
of administration on the Estate of Wm. Jacamiah Smith,
Deceased

Ordered that the Sheriff apply to the different Tax Collectors for a List of the Taxables of the County of Winton.

No. 18
Henry Peoples   ) Writ. Judgment confess'd /by the Deft/
   agt   ) Staying execution three months for 13
James Montgomery) Guineas   the Deft paying Cost

No. 2
Robert Hankerson) Attachment A negro man named Caesar
   agt   ) and money in the hands of Henry Coker.
Frederick Frances) Ordered that this attachment be laid
                    over till next Court.

Ordered that the County Atty. shall be entitled to 10/ℒ/
quarterly, to be paid from money arising from fines

No. 15
Wm. Wise   ) Petition.
   agt   ) Ordered that the plaintiff should be
Bartlett Brown) nonsuited with cost

Ordered the Court House be established at the head of cedar
Branch, waters of Savannah River near the plantation of
James Mitchel where he now lives)
                              Wm. Robison, J. P.
                              W. Buford, J. P.
                              Thos. Knight, J. P.
                              Jno. C. Smith, J. P.
                              A. Gillett

No. 6
Thos. Telput) Petition. Judgment confessed. for Debt &
   agt   ) Cost with stay execution for
Henry Mills)

No. 17
Richard Kirkland) Writ. Judgt. confessd. with stay
   agt   )   execution for three months
Whitmill Odom   )   with cost of Suit.

Ordered that Dedimus be granted Threaderick Goodwyn and Pat McLemurrey both of the State of Georgia that the deposition of Sarah Bassett, Eliz. Turner, Luke Dean for Mr. Goodwyn James Weatherford for Mr. McLemurry before two Justices of the aforesaid State

No. 1
Wm. Dyches   ) Writ. Ordered that the cause be admitted
   agt   ) to the arbitration of Thos. Morris &
James Collins) Saml. Way they having liberty to chuse an
                Umphire if wanted

50 Wm. Smith   ) Petition Suit withdrawn by consent of
       agt   ) both parties the plaintiff paying Cost.
    James Kirkland) No. 8

Ordered that William Robison, Wm. Buford, Thomas Night, Aaron Gillett, Esqrs. be Commissioners to let the Public Buildings at the Head of Cedar Branch near the Plantation of Mr. James Mitchell on the first Friday in August.

   Ordr. that Mr. Sheriff take a Bond of Henry Mills for his appearance next Court.
   Ordered that Capt Ricd. Creech and Ann Creech shall have letters of Administration be giving Bond and Security to the Clerk.

No. 54.
Thos. Garnett   ) Writ. Judgment confessd. and Execution
   agt   ) Stay'd for t___ months, the Deft paying
Sampson Griffin) Costs.
Dec. 1, 1787. Execution for ₤ 12, or 4 Cows & Calves & 4/6 Costs delivered to Henry Cannon.
   Ordered that Capt. Joseph Vince & Mr. W. Vince lay of the Road from Harleys Bridge on the lower runs to the Bridge on the upper Runs the nearest and best way & that they divide the hands between the three overseers and lay off their bounds to work on also from the Upper Run Bridge leading to fort Moore Bluff as far as the Ninety Six line the nearest and best way Wm. Eve/re/t. Benj. Heath lay of and open the same and keep it in good repair

   Ordered that /Mr./ Thead. Goodwyn shall have a citation in ordr that he may obtain letters of Administration against next Court on the Estate of Roland Walker, deceased

51   Ordered that the minutes be read which was done

   Ordered that the Court be adjourned/ to the next/ Court in Course.
         Wm. Robison   Thos. Knight   W. Buford

22

52 Blank

53 Blank

54 Tuesday 16th October 1787.
Court met according to adjournment.)
    Present William Robison   )
               Ricd. Threadaway   ) Esqrs.
               Aaron Gillett   )
               Daniel Green   )
               Jno. C. Smith   )

Ordered that the Grand Juriers be called.

Thomas Morris
James Collins
Thomas O'Bannon
Nathaniel Sanders
Moses Collins
William Dunbar
John Hall
William Green
William Boyet
Stephen Smith
John Parkinson, foreman
Jonathan Clarke
Alexandr. Newman - Silver Bluff

The Court appointed John Parkinson foreman.
    Ordered that the grand Jury be Sworn, which was done.

The Court appointed Dr. Aaron Gillett president, who delivered the charge to the Grand Jury.
    On motion of Mr. Shaw, Ordered that J. P. Carnes, Esqr. having produced his Commission should act as Attorney in this Court.
    Ordered that Peters Carnes, Esqr. to admitted as an Attorney of this Court by producing his admission next Court.
    Ordered that Robt. Stark Esqr be admitted as Atty. of this court by producing his admission next Court.

55 Mr. Justice Robison having moved to the Court that Mr. Shaw should be discharged from the office of County Attorney, all the Justices upon the bench (except Mr. Robison) approved of Mr. Shaw's Conduct, as County Atty. and negatived the motion
    Ordered that the Pettit Jury be call'd.
James Myrick
James Morris
George Collins
Edward Nix
Thomas Enox
Thomas Matthews
James Matthews
John Drummon
John Harrington
John Fitts
William Tuton
William Coker
    Ordered that the Pettit Jury be discharged till 9 O'Clock tomorrow

Ann Collins came into Court and swore that James Hammilton is father of a base Born child, born of her Body.

The Court ordered her to give security to indemnify the County and also for the payment of five pounds fine proclamation money to be paid for the use of the County.

Mr. Elijah Threadaway was sworn in Constable for one year.

Thos. Cox, acknowledge this Deed of Conveyance to Wm. Brooker for 45 Acres of land ordered to be recorded.

Thos. Cox acknowledges this Deed of Conveyance to George Kersh 200 acres of land ordered to be recorded.

Jeremiah Joyner's Bill of Sale to Sarah Southwell proved by the oaths of Thomas Morriss and Nathl. Saunders.

56 Robt. Smith and Ricd. Threadawat proved a Deed of Conveyance from David Odom to Thos. Weathersby for 150 acres of land, ordrd to be recorded.

Tarlton Brown acknowledges Lease and release, to Tob Red for 640 acres of Land orderd to be recorded.

John Wyld acknowledges his lease & release for 200 acres of land to Solomon Owens, ordered to be recorded.

William Dunbar Acknowledges his lease & release to Rolley Williams for 500 acres of Land. Ord'd to be rec'd.

John Wyld acknowledges his lease and release to Henry Cannon for 294 acres of Land ordered to be recd.

Ordered that the minutes be read which was done.

Ord'd that the court be adjourned to 9 o'clock tomorrow morning.

       Jno. C. Smith
       A. Gillett
       Richard Threadaway

Wensday 17th Oct. 1787 Court met according to adjournment
Present Aaron Gillett)
     John C. Smith)
     Wm. Buford) Esqrs.
     Wm. Robison)

The State   )
 agt   )
Henry Mills, Edwd Bentley,) Pettit Larceny.
& Rob'n Smith   ) On the affidavit of Mrs. Derisee that her husband is unable to attending as a witness for the State, Ordered that the several recognizances in this prosecution be laid over till next Court.

John Wyld acknowledges his lease and Release to Arthur Jenkins for 100 acres of land. Ordered to be recorded.

57 John Parkinson acknowledges his Lease & release to James A. Murphey for 200 acres of Land ordered to be recorded

Wm. Robison & Wm. Vince, Esqrs. proves a Lease and Release from James Barringtine & Wife to Arthur Symkins, Esq. for 198 acres of Land order'd to be recorded

William Vince acknowledges his Lease and Release to Wm. Dunbar for 200 Acres ordered to be recorded

William Thomas acknowledges his Lease and Release to James Joyce 640 acres of Land Ordered to be recorded

William Thomas acknowledges his Lease & Release to James Joyce for 100 acres of Land ordered to be recorded

Dan'l Green, Esqr. acknowledges his lease & release to Jesse Winburn for 200 acres of Land ordered to be recorded

John Mitchel and Michael Franch prove Lease & Release from William Southwell to Edward Jackson for 200 acres of a Land ordered to be recorded

Verdeman Clemens acknowledges his Lease and Release to George Kirkland for 200 acres of Land ordered to be recorded

Jesse Wynbourn and Jesse Rogers prove Lease & Release from Danl Odom to Zadock Woolley for 100 acres of Land ordered to be recorded

Danl Green Esqr. and William Woodcock proves Lease and Release from Edwd Miles & Pricilla his wife, to Xadock Woolley for 101 acres of Land ordered to be recorded.

Simon Briant and Ann Bryant proves Lease and Release from John Williamson to William Bryant for 100 acres of Land ordered to be recorded

Simon Bryant and Ann Bryan proves Lease and Release from John Williamson & Rebecca his wife to William Bryan for 100 acres of Land ordered to be recorded.

Redden Fields acknowledges Lease & Release to William Bryan for 198 acres of Land ordered to be recorded.

58   Ordered that Alexn Newman open the Road from the Red /hill/ agt Jesse Southwell's Old field to cross at his Mills and come in the old Road on the top of the Hill, below the Creek

Ordered that Letters of Administration be granted Cathrine Baxter on the Estate of Wm. Baxter deceased, and that she give Jno. Collins and Moses Collins Security for the Administration in a Bon__ of One Thousand pounds

At the request of Elizb. Clarke & Henry Sap, ordered that Elizb. Olive, daughter of said Elizb. aged two years and a half old be Bound to said Sap till she comes of age of sixteen and that the said Sap give Security to the County for his maintainance of the said child in the sum of Twenty pounds Sterling and that Richard Jackson be Security.

Ordered that Letters of Administration be granted Ann Cunningham on the Estate of Joseph Nat///cher, deceased and that she give William Newman and Robert Bradley security for the Administration in a Bond of Twenty pounds Ster.

The County against Elizabeth Myrick Bastardy
Elizb. Myrick came into Court and swore that Dennis Murphey of the Congaree is father of a Bastard child called Lany; that the father of John another Bastard child is Edward Southwell, deceased; that the father of Mary another Bastard Child was also the said Edward Southwell and that the father of Sarah, another Base Born child is William Southwell. The Court fined the said Elizabeth Myrick fifteen pounds proclamation money to be paid within nine months.

The Court have ordered that Sieri facias be issued against Dennis Murphey of the Congaree and William Southwell of Winton County, to show cause why fines should not be levied on their Estates.

The Grand Jury returned the following Bills.

The State	)	
agt	)	Assault
Danl. Shingleton, otherwise	)	True Bill
D. D. Shingleton	)	

59
The State	)	Indt. for Branding a Heifer.
agt	)	True Bill
Henry Mills	)	

The State	)	Pettit Larceny
agt	)	True Bill
John Elkins	)	

The Court then returned their thanks to the Grand Jury for their services this term and ordered them to be discharged which was done accordingly.

David Edenfield acknowledged his Deed of Conveyance unto John Gill 100 acres of land.

Ordered, that the order entered Concerning Elizabeth Myrick be suspended untill next court by giving Security for her appearance.

The Court proceeded to Election of Clark. agreeable to Law, when Aaron Smith, Esq. by a majority of the Court was appointed Clerk of this Court during his good behavior on which he immediately took the Oath prescribed by Law and proposed as his Securities Aaron Gillett and John Carraway Smith, Esqrs. as his Securities which the Court approved of and ordered the Bond to be Executed to morrow

Ordered that Mr. Vince, the late Clerk of the County deliver to the present Clerk, all the records, books, papers and Manuscripts appertaining to the Court or Office of Clerk

State vs John Elkins   Petit Larceny   the Grand Jury having found a Bill of Indictment agt. John Elkins, Ordered that he give Security for his personal appearance at the next Court to Answer the sd. Indictment and that John Martin Strozier, the prosecutor, give Security to prosecute   and that David Dennis and Mary Strozier to give Bond to appear as witnesses

State v. Henry Mills. For marking and branding a Heifer. Ordered that he give Security to answer the said indict. And that Mr. Holmes give Security to presecute.

60   State v. Daniel Shingleton, otherwise Singletary. Assault & B. Ordered that sd. Shingleton give Security to answer sd. Indict- the next Court in the sum of thirty pounds Sterling and that Thomas Knight, Esq. give Security to prosecute.

Daniel Shingleton, otherwise David Singletary, and James Sims acknowledged themselves bound to this County /each/ in the sum of Twenty five pounds Sterling for the personal appearance of the sd. Shingleton, otherwise Singletary to answer the indictment depending agt. him
                    Daniel Shingleton
                    James Sims

Thomas Knight, Esq. and Danl. Green, Esq. acknowledged themselves indebted to this County in the Sum of Twenty five pounds Sterling for the personal appearance of Mr. Knight to prosecute an Indict. agt Danl Knight.
                    Thos. Knight
                    Daniel Green

   Mr. Deas and Patrick McElmurray having delivd. up Edmund Bentley to this Court The Court ordered other security.

   Edmund Bentley, Charles Wheeler and Sampson Griffin severally acknowledge themselves to be indebted to the County of Winton in the Sum of fifty pounds Stg. for the personal appearance of sd. Bentley at the next Court to answer a charge of petit Larceny.
                    Edmund his mark Bentley
                    Charles Wheler
                    Sampson Griffin.

Mary Southwell and Francis Basset came into Court and acknowledged themselves indebted to the County in the sum of Twenty five pounds Sterling to be void on the personal appearance of the sd. Mary Southwell to answer the charge of the Court.
                    Mary her mark Southwell
                    Frans. Bassett.

Elizabeth Myrick and James Myrick came into Court and acknowledged themselves indebted to the County of Winton each in the of Twenty five pounds Sterling to be void on the pensl. appearance of the sd. Elizabeth Myrick at the next Court to answer the charges of this Court.
                    Mary her mark Myrick
                    James his mark Myrick

61 On the Application of William Williams, Nephew and Heir at Law of Nathan Williams deceased, Ordered that a Citation be issued directed to Mary Davis the Widow of the said Williams to shew Cause why Letters of Administration sd. not be granted to him on the Estate of the sd. Williams deceased & that a return thereof be made next Court.
   On the application of James Jackson ordered that a citation be issued directed to the widow next of kin and creditors of Geo_ Fallas deceased to shew cause at the next Court why Letters of Administration shd. not be granted to him on the Estate of the said George Fallas.
   Tester agt Bates On an appeal from a single Justice ordered that this appeal stand over till next Court at the applicant's cost.
   Leandor Tester and William Green acknowledge themselves Security for the costs.

No. 42
Reubin Hargrove) James Mathews enters himself as Security
      agt   ) for the Costs in this action, the plain-
John Crow   ) tiff living out of the State

Same) (NB to ask Mr. Shaw if this is antoher suit)
 agt) Ordered that the Writ in this action be amended
Same) it appearing a clerical mistake that the plea of
the Defendt be over ented and pleads a substantial plea

No. 9.
John OHerd (?)) Judgment for the Plaintiff Ten pounds
agt) ordered that John Redd be summons as a
Moses Johnston) Garnishee to state what he has in his
hands the property of sd. Johnston.
A. Gillett

Issued for)
Garnishee to)
appear)

The Court adjourned till 9 O'Clock tomorrow.
W. Buford
Thos. Knight

Thursday the 18th October 1787.
The Court met according to adjournment.

Aaron Gillett)
Wm. Robinson)
Richard Threadaway) Present.
Wm. Buford)
Daniel Green)

Ordered that the public Buildings be erected at the head of Cedar Branch near the plantation of John Mitchell pursuant to an Order of last July Court - it appearing to the Court that the Com
for letting the public Buildings had postponed carrying their powers into Execution on Account of an apposition which was

reported was to be made to the said Order by petition to the Governor and Council and no such Petition having been preferred.

Ordered that one eighth part of the Tax paid by the Citizens of this County/ for their property within the County/ for the use of the State be assessed on all the Inhabitants of this County for the purpose of defraying the Expence of the public Buildings that the Sheriff apply to the different Tax Collectors of this County for exact copies of their respective tax lists and that the Sheriff levy and assess the same immediately, according to Law.

Ordered that if it appears on the general Tax list that any person or persons have included in their return to the Tax Collector of this County any part of their taxable property which is situated in any other County that the Sheriff is at liberty to deduct so much of the tax on the property situated in another County on the person or persons conceiving himself aggrieved producing an affidavit made before any Justice of Peace in this County proving the fact, which affidavit the Sheriff will return to this Court.

Ordered that the Sheriff be allowed five pounds per cent for collecting the above Tax

State) For marking and branding a Cow. A jury
agt) being called Paneld and sworn Viz
Henry Mills) James Myrick, James Morris, George Collins, Edward Nix, Thomas Enox, Thos. Mathews, James Matthews, John Drummond, John Garrington, John Fitts, Wm. Tuton, Wm. Coker.

Ordered that the jury do seal up their verdict and return the same to the Court tomorrow.
Ordered that this Court adjourn till 9 o'clock tomorrow morning.

Wm. Robison
Daniel Green
Richard Tradaway
A. Gillett

63 No. 55
Cave   ) Friday Court met according to adjournment
   agt   )   Wm. Robinson
O'Bannon   ) Contd. by Consent -- cont.   Red Tradaway
                                                 D. Green

No. 11
John Vincent Alexander) Ordered that a Commission into
         agt   ) Georgia Burk County directed to
Peter Randon   ) John Green and Thomas Burton,
                         Esqr. to examine Francis Parris
Issued 30th Oct.   on the part of the Defendant.

Deed of Conveyance from Owen Odom to Andrew Bates proved by the Oaths of Wm. Ashley and Richd. Bates and ordered to be recorded.

John Wyld, Esq.) No. 14. Attcht. levied on Land-Ordered
     agt   ) that notice be given in the Gazette for
Jeremiak Webb) the Deft. to appear within twelve months
                 from this day and plead to Plff's Declar.
                 otherwise Judgt. will be entered agt him
                 by Default.

No. 13.
Same   ) Attacht. on Land - Ordered that like Notice
     agt   ) be given for Deft to appear and plead within
Wm. Gilbert   ) Nine months from this date otherwise Judgt.
                by default.

State   ) The Jury to wit the same as yesterday,
    agt   ) returned the verdict not guilty. John Fitts,
Henry Mills   )   foreman
     The Court discharged the petit jury.

No. 7
Cd. Wm. Davis) Ordered that the Deft. have nine months
     agt   ) to plead to the Plff's Decln. otherwise
Benj. Brown   ) Judgt. by default.

No. 15
James Montgomery) Discontinued but the costs to wait
     agt   ) the determn. of the Arbitrators to whom
Arthur Turner Law) this Cause is referred.

No. 16
Lear Brooker   ) This case having been referred to
     agt   ) Arbitration and their award having
James Collins   ) been determined and returned to this
                   Court ordered that the same be entered
                   on record & Judgt. entd. accordingly-

the award of the Arbitrators are in the following wards. We are of opinion that the defendant James Collins pay to the plaintiff Lear Brooker one Cow and Calf and Costs given under our hands this 27th day of July 1787.
Thomas Morris
Samuel Way - Judgt. is given accordingly

64 Aaron Smith, Esq. having resigned the Office of Coroner to this County, Joseph Vince, Esq. is by the Court appointed to succeed him. Issued 3rd Nov. 1787.

No. 2
Robert Henkerson) Attacht. The Sheriff having attached
   agt   ) a Negro Fellow called Caesar, ordered
Frederick Francis) that the said Negro Fellow be sold and the money arising therefrom remain in the hands of the Sheriff until the Plff obtain a Judgt of this Court.

Henry Coker having been summoned as a Garnishee confesses he has the Sum of Seventeen pounds three Shillings in his hands due and belonging to Frederick Francis.

Ordered that all the recognizances not carried into Execution shall be laid over till the next Court.

No. 23
Wm. Causey   ) Attacht. Ordered that the perishable
   agt   ) property attached be exposed to public
Redden Fields) sale and the proceeds to remain with the Sheriff until the Plff obtain a Judgt. of this Court. Issued Nov. 3, 1787.

David Drennon) Attachment. Ordered that the property
   agt   ) attached by the Sheriff in this Cause be
John Harrison) exposed to Public Sale and that the money arising from the sale remain in the hands of the Sheriff till a Judgt. be obtained by the Plaintiff.
Issued 3 Nov.

Sarah Wallace, Executrix of Michael Wallace, Deceased, having delivered to this Court all the Books, papers & accounts of her late Husband that remain in her hands,
Ordered that the Clerk of this Court examine the same & report a true state thereof to next Court.
NB the Books & all the Papers were returned to the Widow by April 8th, 1788. A. Smith, CWC

65 Lease and Release for Five Hundred and forty acres of land from William Nibbs to John Wyld, Esq. proved by the oaths of Aron Smith and Cleviers Wyld, and ordered to be recorded.
Ordered that the road leading from the white ponds to the runs leading to Richd Tradaways be put in proper repair and that Charles Wheeler be overseer of the said road from the white ponds to Mrs. Tradaways, and that Elkanah Green be overseer of the road from the three runs to the County line. And that all hands within five

Miles of each side of the road be summoned to work on the said roads.

Bargain and Sale from William Christie to John Collins proved by the Oath of Steven Collins only and ordered to lie over for further proof.

Ordered that/ there be a new/road/laid off/ leading from Somerills Ferry along an old path until it intersections a new road which Mr. Clarke has cleared as an overseer and that the road leading thro the plantation of Wm. Robinson, Esq. be discontinued the above order is postponed till next Court and Mr. Clarke to be cited at the next Court to shew Cause why he did not pursue the directions of this order of Court.

Shaderick /Reed/ comes into Court and acknowledges his Deed of Leas & Releas to Hardy Reed for 100 acres of Land.

Elija Gillett, High Sheriff of Winton County came into Court and acknowledged his conveyance for 100 to Richard Vince.

No. 22
John Brooker) Discontinued at plffs Costs the Deft having
    agt   ) agreed to delivered up the negro in question
John Kersh   )

Wm. Robinson
Richard Treadaway
Daniel Green.

The Court then adjourned to James Mitchells Plantation at the head of the Cedar Branch

66   Blank

67   At a Court held for Winton County on the Third Tuesday, on January the 15th. 1788 at the Plantation of James Mitchels, on the Head of Cedar Branch, by Adjournment from the Bigg House.

Present   William Robinson)
          Richard Tradaway)
          Thomas Knight   ) Esquires.
          William Buford   )

A List of the Grand Jury   A List of the Petit Jury

Daniel Odom   William Price discharged
Leavin Collins   1   Joseph Geater Do
Joseph Collins   2   1 William Davis
Joseph Obannon   3   2 Isaac Tool
Charles Nix   4   3 Frans. Roberts
Benjamin Odom Junr   Joseph Youngblood
William Miles   5   4 Robert Nix
Thomas Morris   6   5 David Mills
George Collins   7   6 Job Redd   And. Nimmons
Ephrai. Picket   7 William Daniel James Sims
Adam Lard   8   8 John Griffin Willm. Goode
                                    foreman
James Gideon   9   9 Nathl. Saunders

John Cave	10	10	J̶e̶s̶s̶e̶ R̶o̶g̶e̶r̶s̶ Saml. Simms
Tarlton Brown	11	11	William Johnson
W̶i̶l̶l̶i̶a̶m̶ S̶c̶a̶r̶b̶o̶r̶o̶u̶g̶h̶			J̶o̶h̶n̶ N̶e̶w̶m̶a̶n̶
A̶l̶e̶x̶a̶n̶d̶e̶r̶ N̶e̶w̶m̶a̶n̶		12	Robt. Jourdan
Reuben Newman, foreman	12		W̶i̶l̶l̶i̶a̶m̶ G̶o̶o̶d̶e̶
John Wickley	13		

On the Motion of Aaron Smith for the Approbation of a Deputy Clerk.
Ordered that Thomas Wyld be appointed Deputy Clerk of this Court during his good behavour and was Qualified accordingly.
 Richd. Tradaway ackowledged his Deed to John Green for 300 Acres of Land & ordered to be recorded.
 Robt. Lark acknowledged his Deed to Robt. Adoms 100 acres,
 Appriasement of Wm. Baxter's Estate returned by the Apprai O. to be Rd.
 Hezekiah Nobles proved a Bill of Sale from Wm. Christy to John Collins O. R.
 Moses Plummer proved a Deed to Charity Reed from Shadrack to lay over for further proof.
 Joseph Harley acknowledged his Deed of Leas Releas to Emelia Matthews - Ordered to be Recorded.

68 Nathaniel Abney's Will was proved by Thos. Wyld & Clevers D. Wyld and admitted to Record.
 James Jackson acknowledged his Deed of Lease & Release to Edward Jackson. Ord, to be Recorded.
 Ordered that Reuben Rountree have Administration on the Estate of Job Roundtree, Wm. Dunbar & Wm. Vince, Security in L 1000 Bonds Executed.
 Edwd. Jackson Acknowledged Deed L & Release to Tarlton Brown.
 Chas. Beck acknowledged his Deed to Wm. Dunbar O.R.
 Ordered that John Ambrose Obannon be appointed under Sheriff & took the Oath accordingly.
 Lucy Abney was Swore Executrix to her Husbands Will &C
 Ordered that Mary Williams have citation of Letters of Adm on Nathan Williams Estate & Abraham Richardson & Richd. Tradaway be her Surety in Fifty pounds.
 Ordered that William Vine Joseph Collins & Jos. Vince do Di__ the Estate of Wm. Baxter & return the same to next Court. Copy de__
 The Grand Jury being Sworn Reuben Newman was appointed Forman & discharted till tomorrow at 9 O'the Clock
 The Petit Jury discharged till tomorrow morning 9 O'the Clock

 The Orders of Court being Read the Court was adjourned till tomorrow Morning 9 O'the Clock.
Wm. Robison
W. Buford
Thos. Knight
Richard Tradaway

At a Court held at Cedar Branch & Continued by adjournment on Wednesday the 16th January 1788.
 Present: Aaron Gillett) William Buford) Esqrs.
     William Robison) Richard Tradaway)
     Thomas Knight)
          Copy delivered 30th.

The Jury Box being prepared a Boy ___ Drew in the presence of Court the following Persons to serve as a Pettit Jury for April Court:

David Shipes	1	James Arnold	4	Danl Price	7	
Patrick McLemurry	2	James Joice	5	Alex Newman Runs	8	
Abrm Cook	3	Jacob Surinoy	6	Wm. Goode	9	

James Morris
James Jackson
Wm. Price

69 Ordered that the Rates of Liquors &C be Settled at the following Prices for this year

Best Old Jamaica Spirits	2/Pr Pint
Good Jamaica Rum a P. the Pint	1/6
French Brandy, a P. Pint	1/6
Peach Brandy, if good a P. Pint	1/6
Continental or Taffia Rum a P Pint	7 d
Good Madeira Wine a P. Bottle	43/9 M
Teneriff or Port Wine a P. Bottle	3/
London Porter P Bottle	1/6 2/ - Bottle
For a good Hott Dinner 1/ & wth Turkey or Fowles & Good Ham	1/6
For a cold dinner	1/
For Breakfast & Supper without Tea or Coffee	/1
with good Tea, Coffee or Choco.	1/3
For a good Lodging with clean Sheets	1/6
For Stableage & Fodder for a Horse one Night	1/
For Indian Corn, P the Quart	2d
For Oats P the Quart	2d
or Rough Rice P the Quart	2d

Ordered that Elijah Gellett, Esq./Brand & Mark E + G & under heel in each ear be Recorded.

O. That Aaron Gillett Esq / Brand/& Mark AG & Cross in the right Ear and underheel in the left be Recorded.

0   That John C. Smith Esq./Brand &/Mark ICS & Cross in the Left underheel in the right be recorded

0   That James Mitchell be allowed to sell Liquors at his House untill the Court House is fully Established without County fee.

0   That the Clerk is impowered to record in his Office old Brands & Marks.

0   Wm. Robinson Esq. brand WR Cross & two Slitts in the Left & half cross in the Right - O.R.

0   John Parkerson Deed of Sale to Mary McNeely acknowledged OR

0   William Weekly obtained a Licence to keep Ordinary who with John Wickly became his Security

33

O   James Myrick obtained a Licence to keep Ordinary who with Thomas Morris became his Security

Testor vs Dabney. Appeal from a Justice-Judgmnt of the Justice recovered & Judgmt for the Plaintiff & Cost.

Mr. Jonathan Clark appeard agreeable to Citation & /was/ cleared of Censure & is released as Overseer & Wm. Vince appointed in his room.

The /Minutes being read/ Court adjourned till tomorrow morning 9 O'the Clock.

       Wm. Robison
       Thos. Knight
       A. Gillett.

70 At a Court held at Cedar Branch and continued by adjournment to Thursday the 7th Day of January 1788

    Present: Aaron Gillett)
         William Robinson)
         Thomas Knight) Esquires
         Richd. Tradaway)
         William Buford)

Joseph Vince acknowledged himself Security/ for Cases/ for Thos. Burton vs. Wm. Davis.

Burr Harrison Deeds of Lease & Release to Joseph Duncan was proved by the Oaths of Wm. Good & Wm. Davis & ordered to be Recorded.

Ordered that Henry Cannon have Citation against Wm. Green's Estate.

Joseph Merris Deed to William Goode was proved by the Oath of Joseph Duncan & ordered to lay for the other Evidence.

John Abston acknowledged his Deed of Lease & Release to Elijah Abston & ordered to be recorded.

State vs. Israel Walker, Jonathan Walker & Willm. Bassett for Affray. The parties come into Court & acknowledged their error & promised future better behavour & were discharged on paying fees.

State vs. Danl. Shingleton, alias Danl. Shingletarry)
Thos. Knight Evidences, Simms & Simms) Shingleterry)
& Jas. Kirkland, Evidences   ) Not Guilty)
                 Wm. Goode foreman
                 Wm. Davis, Wm. Tool
                 Fras. Roberts, Rob
                 David Mills, And
                 Nimmons, Jas. Simm
                 Willm. Thomson,Nathl
                 Saunders, Tom Sim
                 Rob. Jourdan.

Wm. Robinson, Esq. vs Jno. Randall Atty. Proved that the Negroes attacht Emanuel George be sold & the money be to remain in the Sheriff's Hands. that this Cause being omitted by the late Clerk it may be entered on the Docket.

John Redd Garnishee declares that he has trhee Cows & Calves on his hands the property of Moses Johnson.

David Drennon vs John Harrison. The acct. proved to the Satisfaction of the Court by two Evidences Judgment for PV 38-14-4 & Cost.

28   Mary Harrison vs. Md. Harrison Atty. Acco. proved Judgmt. for thirty Guineas - after David Drennon is paid & Costs.

1   Daviss-vs Burton - Contd.

2   Pendergast vs Odom   Discontd. Plff pay Cost.

3   Powell vs Odom   Contd.

4   Knight vs Singleton   Discontd. No Attorneys fees to be taxed

5   Singleton vs Knight   Contd.

6   Singleton vs Knight   Contd.

7   Brown vs Myrick   Contd.

8   State vs Dennis Murphy,

9   State vs Southwell-Ordered to give Security/in Off/ to Indemnify the County & pay Costs.
Ordered that a Subpoena & Copy be issued for every Witness Summond

71   Returns of the Grand Jury

11 State vs   ) True Bill. Order that Capias issue &
    Wm. Capps   ) that Derrl. Johnson give Security to Prose-
                     cute who with Elij. Gillett, Esq. his
                     Security acknowledged their Bonds for the
                     same.

State   )   True Bill.
vs   )   To give Security in ₤ 100
7 Edna Bently   )   Traverse to next Court.
8 Robert. Smith)
10 Henry Mills   )

State vs   )   True Bill. Traversed under
Benj. Odom 12   )   Recognizance.

State   )
vs   )   No Bill
Dl. Singleton   )

State, The   )
vs   )   No Bill
Adam McNeely   )

The State   )
   vs   ) No Bill
Hezekiah Williams)

The State   )
   vs   ) No Bill
Levi Long   )

State Attorney ordered Execut. to be issued against the above persons.

The State   )
   vs   ) No Bill
Joseph Duncan)

The State   )
   vs   ) No Bill
James Arnold)

The Grand Jurors were discharged with the thanks of the Court & C

Hankerson vs. Fred. Francis. The Acct. proved by the Oaths of John McLehany. Judgment for the Plaintiff ℔ 41 -8-9 & Cost.

Ordered that a Road from the main Road near Capt. John Weeklelys be made over Davisses Brach to Baldock Mills; from thence to Cedar Branch, where the Court now is or/ may be placed/ & that Thomas Wooton, John Mitchell & Owen Jones, be appointed overseers & that the Road/ shall be/ begin to be made the first Monday in February next & that Elijah Gillett, Esq. engages to make a good Framd Bride over Boggy Gutt & keep the same in Repair & also to find sufficient Slabbs to make a Good Crossway/& bring them in Places/ over Davises Branch & that all Hands within five Miles of the said Road shall work upon it & Mr. Gillett engages to keep the bridge/ and Causeway/ in Repair & Supply Slabbs for the Causeway for his Part of the Work.

Thomas OBannon is recommended as a Magistrate for the County.

On Compaint of the High Sheriff, that he was Assaulted, molested and insulted in his Office, in summoning a Guard to keep Edmd Bentley; by Robt. Shields, Ordered that he take the sd. Shields into custody till tomorrow.

72 Ordered the Minutes be read and then the Court adjourned /till/tomorrow morning 9 O'the Clock.
    Thos. Knight
    Richard Tredaway
    A. Gillett

At a Court held at Cedar Branch & continued by adjournment to Friday the 18th. January 1788.
Present, Aaron Gillett, Thos. Knight, William Buford, Esqrs.

On the Motion of/ Willm Shaw, Esqr./ County Attorney against Robert Shields for an Assault & Misdemeanour against the High Sheriff in the Execution of his Office   Copy sent
B S

Ordered that Robt. Shields now in Custody be brought to the Barr

O that Thomas OBannon, David Mills, Arthur Turner, Henry Cannon & Elijah Gillett, Esq. Evidences & John Gill & Robt. McLeworth Evidences be sworn & Aaron Smith
The prisoner at the Bar acknowledged his bad behaviour & promised future better behavour & resigned himself to the Mercy of the Court.

O. The Court therefore upon hearing the Evidences Order that be fined Seven pounds, Ten Shillings/Ster/ and pay all Costs & that he/give sufficient Security for his good behavour for 12 months in a Bond of L 500,
O that he remain in custody till he comply with the Orders.

John Parkinson & Moses Plummer proved the last Will & Testament of William Crostie 3/4 O. to be recored & John Parkinson provd the Codicil & O. be Recrd.

The Court ordered that the appearance dockett be called over for the last time.

10. Gillett vs Christie N E J - Judicial Attachmt.

11. Turner, Assignee - vs Jenkins - Dis. Pv Costs.

12. Burton vs Davis - Con. Security given for costs.

13. Putman vs James C. Murphey - Acct. provd by Seth Howard Judgt 8 b 1 cost.

14. Seth Howard proved his Attendance 5 Days at 2/6 & milage 100/mils/@ 2 d per Mil.

14. Weathersby vs Gross NE   Off

15. Harley vs McNeeley - Acct. Provd. Judgmt. 4-3-11 & Cost

16. Harley vs Davis   Contd.

17. Jenkins vs. Collins Odom   Contd.

18. Nix vs Randall   Contd.

19. OBannon vs Lee - Ruled to Bail Absalom Best Spec Bail

20. Miles vs Mills &   Continued

21. James Clark vs McNeely. Judt. Confsed. accordy to note s--ing Exec. 3-Marks.

22. Wallace vs McLeworth Contd.

23. Gillett vs Jenkins. Agreed to be dismissed. Plff to pay Costs.

73 24. William Brown vs Eli Williams, Dismissd Plff paying costs

25. Drummond vs Cannon. Settled, Costs to be paid by Cannon
26. C. D. Wyld vs Cannon. Dismissed at Deft Costs.
27. M. Odom vs. Morris - Contd.
28. Ann Odom vs Causey. N.E.
29. Crawford vs Carr   Judgt. wth Int. 7-9-4 Stay E. 3 months
30. John Sweat vs Carden   Contd.
31. Derrl. Johnson cs Capps - to be renewed the

Ord That Capt. JoVince be paid 4 Days Att. in the suit Pilote vs McLemurry.

Ord That Capt. Jo Vince be pd 4 Days attendance The State vs Bentley.

O State vs That/ Eli Myrick appear within one Month at the Clerks Office and give security to Indemnify the County for the maintenance and support of the following Illegitimate /children/ Amy, John, Mary & Sarah   fifty pounds each.
    That/State vs in/all the State Tryals agt the Delinquents/they/do / attend at/ the Clerk's Office in a Month & give Bonds accordingly & on failure Exps to be issued.
    O. That Wm. Vince, Esq. the late Clerk be paid by the Treasurer b   when Cash is in the Treasurery out of the Assemt
        The same order for the Sheriff
        The same order for the County Attorney
NB   (not being fully entered was alterd as below)

O. That the Clerk represent to the Members for this District that the Court Day may be altered to the third Monday & state the several benefits that will attend it. Issued & Copy

O   That the High Sheriff provide a pair of Strong Stocks and Whipping Posts.

O   That David Mills at the request of the High Sheriff be appointed Deputy Sheriff   and was sworn accordingly.

O   That the Minutes be read.

O   That this Court be adjourned to the Court in Course.

       On Motion of the Attornies
Ordered That all the Causes remianing on the issue Docket & undetermined be Continued over untill next Court   1786

No. 12 H. Mills vs Willis   Contd.

No. 14 Joseph Vince vs Fred. Frances   Contd.

1787 Causes
No. 1   Willm Dyches vs James Collins. Contd.

    2. Absom. Causey vs Willm. Good. Contd.

No. 3. Hammond & Hankerson vs Sarah Walla-ce. Contd.
4. Brown vs Odom - Contd.
10. Gillett vs. Davis - Off. Discontinued
11. Odom vs. Brown
13. Hankinson vs Goodwyn. Contd.
16. Kennaday vs Wallace. Contd.
17. Jenkins vs Collins - Contd.
20. Pendergast vs. Odom. Dismissed PDF Cost
21. Williams vs Moody - Dismissed Plff Cost.
22. Williams vs Myrick. Dismsd.
23. Wheeler vs. A. Newman - Contd.
24. Burton vs Trower - Contd.
25. Odom vs. Morris - Contd.
26. Gill vs Wallace - Contd.
27. Stedman vs Banner - Contd.
28. Gillett vs Jenkins & Uxor - Contd.
29. Odom vs. Causey - Dismissd.
31. Wallace vs. McLewarth - Contd.
32. Wyld vs Davis - Contd.
33. Ward vs Cannon - Contd.
34. Hargrove vs Crow - Contd.
35. C. D. Wyld vs Cannon - Dismissed at Deft Cost.
38. Gillett vs Collins - Contd.
39. Gillett vs Nobles - Contd.
41. Pilote vs McLemmurray - Contd.
42. Gillett vs Williams - Contd. for Arbitration Jor-Vince & Aaron Smith with power of Umpriage.
45. Conyers vs Stringer - Contd.
47. Cave vs Obannon - Contd.
48. Williams vs Myrick - Discontinued
49 Jackson vs Collins - Contd.

No. 50. Tester vs Dabney - Judgmt for Plaintiff
   51. Collins vs Clayton - Contd.

No.   Attachments
1. Collins vs. Clayton - Contd.
2. Hankinson vs Frances - Judgt for Plaintiff & Costs.
3. White vs Matthews - Contd.
4. Bentley vs Bentley - Contd.
5. King vs Trower - Contd.
6. Stone vs Odom - Contd.
7. Davis vs Brown - Contd.
8. Trower vs Mills - Contd.
9. Offord vs Johnson - Contd.
75 10. Banner vs Tuten - Contd.
11. Alexander vs Randon - Discontinued
12. Davis vs. Williams - Contd.
14. Wyld vs Gilbert - Contd.
15. Wyld vs Webb - Contd.
18 Foreman vs Conway - Contd.
19. McNeely vs Odom - Contd.
20. Causey vs Odom - Contd.
21. Davis vs Cuthbert - Contd.
22. Carrell vs Hill - Contd.
23. Causey vs Field - Discontinued
24. Drennon vs Harrison - Judgmt. ₺38 -- 14-4 & Costs
25. Wheeler vs Sabard Odom - Contd.
26. Cannon vs. Humphries - Contd.
27. Robison vs Randal - Orderd the Attacht. Property
             be sold.

No. Summons & Petitions
5 Frances Bassett)   ) January Court 1788
      vs   ) Sum & Petition)
   Josias Wallace) ₺ 6-0-0   ) Continued

40

10
Absalom Causey   ) Sum & Petition)   January
   vs   ) ₺ 2-6-8   )   Court 1788
John Wheekly & Aaron Gillett)   )   Continued

11
Henry Robertson) Sum & Petition) January Court 1788
   vs   ) ₺ 4-0-9½   ) Continued
Saml. Boyett   )

No. 36   Attachments.
Mary Harrison vs John Harrison. Att. Acco provd Judgt. for thirty Guineas after David Drennon is paid & Costs. Off.

38 Robt. Cook vs. Michl. Delon - Contd.

35 Edwd Washington vs Wm. Lamax - Contd.

37. Nehemiah Powers vs Willm. Turner - Contd.

           Adjourned
Ordered that the Court be to the next Court in Course.

                    A. Gillett
                    Thos. Knight
                    W. Buford.

76 Blank

77 By Virtue of an Act of Assembly, passed at Charleston on the 27th Day of February 1788 - Be it enacted by tghe Authority aforesaid, that the Court days for the County of Winton be alterd from the Third Tuesday in January, April, July & October, to the first Monday in February, May, August & November in Consequence of a Petition from the Justices of the Court of the said County/ presented by their Delegates to this Assembly/ & Agreeable to the above said Act of Assembly; the Court did meet Viz

At a Court held for Winton County on the first Monday the 5th Day of May/1788/ at the Plantation of James Mitchells on the __ of Cedar Branch
          Present   William Robison)
                   Richard Tradeaway)
                   Thomas Knight   )   Esquires.
                   William Buford   )

The County Attorney, Willm. Shaw being absent, the Court on his being Called Legally & not appearing/ appointed/ Robert Starkley Attorney/for this/ County pro Tempore.

Ordered that the Grand/Jurors be John Myers, Joseph Collins, Son of George, Joshua Smith, John Bates, Absalom Tyler/Issued/Thomas Owen, Sampson Griffin/ Michl. Swicord, Charles Boyl_?, Richd. Blalock, John Cochran, George Kirkland, Joseph Youngblood, Charles Pechman, Solomon Owen, James Brown, Jonathan Clark, Thomas Matthews, John Harrington.

      Ordered that the Petit Jurors be drawn & Downy Lane, Wm. Mason, Stephen Smith, Rowland Roberts, Simon Bryant,

Arthur Fo__er, Purlivan Johnson, Fred Brant, Reuben Mixon, Joseph Vince, Isaac Deeson, John Byles,/Issued/ Mocajah Matthews, William Vince, Willm. Newman, Joseph Lancaster, William Causey, Jacob Adams, William Hitchcock, John Dunn, Clement Clements, Rowley Williams, Nathan Coker, Thel. Enock, William Dyche, William Williams, Willm. Roberts, John Snealing, David Jackson, Robert Adams, Blanchard Coleing - 31

    The Petit Jury being Called according to Law the following Jurors Apperd David Shipes, William Good, upon a reasonable Excuse was discharged, James Morris, Willm. Price.

    The Jury failing to Appear, Ordered by the Consent of the Court and parties that the Sheriff Summons a sufficient number of the Persons at Court to make up a sufficient number of Jurymen.

78   The State vs Bentley. The Defendant's Attorney in this prosecution having notified to the Court and prosecutor that he was now and has been since this bill was found by the Grand jury ready for his trial & the Court having Called on the Clerk for the Indictment which he said was in possession of the County Attorney, By the Court therefore Ordered that Edmond Bentley be discharged on paying Costs & the Sheriff to keep him in Custody till the Costs are paid.

6   The State vs John Elkins. The same order as above & discharged on paying Fees & to be in custody of Sheriff till Paid.

NB 12.   The State vs Benj. Odom. The same order & dischargd on paying Fees and to be in custody of the Sheriff till Paid.

    Pannell of Petit Jury David Shipes, James Morris, Wm. Price, David Drennon, Tarlton Brown, Hezekiah Williams, Capt. Benj. Odom, John Wyche, Peter DePrushee, Robt. Brown, George Robison, Nichl. Nobles. The Jury Discharged bill to Morrow morning 9 of the Clock.

    Ruth Townsend vs Jno. Fox, Att. ordered that Saml. Hicks Deposition be taken and allowed to be read as Evidence

    Joseph Morris acknowledged his Deed to Willm. Goode for 102 acres of Land & Ordered to be recorded.

    John Wyche enterd himself as Security for Edmd. Bentley to pay the fees or deliver him up at the breaking of the Court.

0.   William Shaw Esqr. not having attended to the Duties of his office this Term, & having been this day Accused of Malpractice in his Office, by seven Persons, which information is satisfactory to the Court & sufficient in their opinion, to Warrant them in discharging him from Exercising the duties of County Attorney; therefore Ordered that Willm Shaw, Esq. be and he is hereby discharged from the Office of County Attorney, Also that the Court proceed to the Appointment of County Attorney to Morrow to succeed Willm. Shaw, Esq. who is discharged.

    Ordered. That Robt Stark, Esq. be appointed County Attorney pro Tempore.

79   Ordered that the Road by Wm. Robison/Esq/ from Jonathan Clark be turnd by the lower end of Mulberry Savanna to Somerlines ferry & that Willm. Vince/be/overseer of the Road do turn the same

    Ordered that the Minutes be read.

The Court adjourned till to Morrow Morning 9 of the
Clock.
                    Wm. Robison
                    Richard Tradaway
                    Thos. Knight.

   At a Court held for Winton County, /on Tuesday/ the
6th May at the Plantation of James Mitchells on the head of
Cedar Branch, the Court met according to adjournment.
Present, William Robinson,
Richard Tradaway)   William Buford)
John Wyld   )   Thomas Knight) Esqrs.
Thomas Obannon) Esqrs.   Daniel Green)
William Sissen)

   The Court considered the order of Yesterday relative
to the Choice of a County Attorney to succeed Willm. Shaw,
Esq. whereupon Thomas Peters Carnes, Esq. be, and is appointed Attorney for this County, Unanimously.
   Ordered that the County Treasurer give bond and
security in the Sum of five hundred pounds Ster & for the
faithful discharge of his duty as Treasurer and that he be
allowed the sum of two & one half percent on receiving and
the same on paying away all monies as Treasurer.
   Ordered that the Sheriff do without delay payninto
the hands of the Treasurer all monies that are in his hands
Collected for the use of the County by a County tax fines
&C
And collect no more till further Orders.
   Ordered that Walter Robinson have Licence to keep
Tavern
   John Wyld, Esq. being appointed a Magistrate by the
Honbl. the General Assembly this Day took the Oath according
to Law/in Open Court/

No. 17.
Arthur Jenkins   ) The Deft. plead that the Declara-
       ovs   ) tion was not filed in time agree-
Jos. Collins & A. Odom.) able to the County Court Law &
if he should be overuled he pleads that

80 If the note was signed by the Deft. that it was for money
won at Gaming   The Court then ruled that the Deft. should
please Substantially   The Jury being called & Sworn to
Wit David Shipes, James Morris, David Drennon, Tarlton
Brown, Hezekiah Williams, Benj. Odom, Jno. Wyche, Peter
DeRushee, Nichl. Nobles, Robt. Brown, Patrick McLemurry,
James Collins. Wee find for the Plaintfiff that Judgmt of
the Deft. pay to ₺2-17-6 with Costs of Suit/according to
Instalment Law ₺ 17-6   Jno. Wyche, Foreman.

P. 10 Causey vs Wickly & Gillett - Nonsuit - Dismsd.
No.12 Henry Mills vs Wm. Willis - Nonsuit - Dismist

   Thomas OBannon Esq being appointed Magistrate by the
Honbl. the Gen. Assembly, this Day took the Oath according
to Law in Open Court.

14 Joseph Vince vs Fred Frances - Nonsuit - Dismist

1   Wm. Dyches vs. James Collins - Judgt & Cow & Claf

    2   Absalom Causey vs Wm. Good - Nonsuit - Dismist

    3   Hammond & Hankerson vs Wallace - Nonsuit - Dismist

    5   Brown vs Odom - Nonsuit - Dismist

   11   Odom vs Brown - Nonsuit - Dismist

   13   Hankinson vs Goodan - Nonsuit - Dismist

P   5   Bassett vs Wallace - Judgt. ₤ 10 & Costs Instalment Deft.

   11   Robinson vs Boyett - Nonsuit - Dismist

   16   Kennaday vs Wallace - Nonsuit - Dismist

   23   Wheeler vs Newman - Nonsuite - Dismist

   22   Benj. Burton vs Levi Thraver - Nonsuit - Dismist

   25   Odom vs Morris - Nonsuit - Dismist

   27   Steadman vs Banner - Nonsuit - Dismist

   28   A. Gillett vs Jenkins & Uxor - Abated by death of Plff. Dismist

   31   Wallace vs McLeworth - Nonsuit. See No. 22, the suit being renewed - Dismist.

NB
NB
       NB
   26   John Gill vs Wallace - Judgment by Default & the Jury sworn the same as before to Execute a Writ of Inquiry. We find for the Plaintiff 10 D. 8 & Cost & Interest till paid.
              Jno Wyche, Foreman.

   34   Hargrove vs Crow - Judgmt by Default   )
                             Contd for Writ of Inquiry)

   38   Gillett vs Collins - abated - Dismist

   39   Gillett vs Nobles - abated - Dismist

   42   Gillett vs Williams - abated - Dismist

   45   Conyers vs Stringer - Nonsuit Dismist

81   The Last Will & Testament of Jno. Wood was proved by the Oaths of Stephen Smith & Mary Dee & Ordered to be recorded.

   32   John Wyld, Esq. vs Wm. Davis, Esq., The Jury being Called and Sworn to Wit: David Shipes, James Morris, David Drennon, Tarlton Brown, Wm. Carr, Benj. Odom, Jun., John Wyche, Peter DeRoussee, Nichl Nobles, Robt. Brown, Patrick McLemurry, James Collins, It is the Opinion of the Jury that the Defendant pay to the Plaintiff twenty Seven Pounds Ten Shillings with the Costs of the Suit. Jno. Wyche, Foreman.

James Crawford proved a Deed from Shadrack/Reed/ to Charity Reed. Joseph Vince, Garnishee Gillett vs Christy being sworn and saith that he owes William Christy the Summ of Fifty pounds five Shillings due by Note of hand due Jany. 1787.

On application of Elijah Gillett & Elizabeth Gillett for a Citation on the Estate of Aaron Gillett, Esq. Order the same to be Granted.

Ordered that the Road from Orange County Line to Kellys Cowpen be under the Care of Daniel Odom, from Kellys Cowpen to the White Ponds under William Myles, from the White Ponds to the Head of the Runns Under the Care of Walter Robinson, from the Runns to the County Line, under the care of Simeon Cushman.

Ordered that the Road be straightened from Harleys Bridge to Cross Steel Creek near Wm. Dunbarr, Esq. Mill, from thence to Thomas Philpott's Mill, from thence to Rutledges Mill on the three Runns. Mr. Rich. Vince & Willm. Dunbar, Esq. to be Overseers to Dunbarrs Mill from Harleys Bridge, Robt. Lark & Thos. Philpot from Dunbar Mill to Ruthledge Mill.

Mr. Wm. Buford Esq. acknowledged his Deed to James Myrick for 54 Acres of Land, Orderd to be Recorded.

33 Ward vs Cannon. The same Jury being Called & Sworn do Say. We find for the Plaintiff L5 & Costs.
John Wyche, Foreman.

49 Jackson vs Collins - Dismist.

35 Washington vs Lamax Moses Disto Garnishee being Sworn says he has no Effects having pd what he owed to Willm. Lamax since the Summons & Judgment for Plaintiff three pounds nineteen Shillings & Costs.

41 James Pilote vs Patrick McLemurray - Nonsuit - Dismist. Wm. Dias, Evidence attended 13 Day at 2/6. Jos. Vince 1 day 2/6 - Levi Thrower 10 days 25/& milage 45 three times 45/ 135 miles r d.

47 Jno. Caves vs. Obannon - Dismist

82 William Sissen, Esq. being appointed a Magistrate by the Worshipfull Court of Winton County, now sitting, this Day took oath according to Law in open Court to serve during the Recess of the Assembly,
Ordered That all persons who have taken up Strays do bring them to Court on Friday next to be Sold according to Law.

51 Collins vs Clayton. The Pleas pleaded by the Defendant being Considered as evasive, were overruled & he Ordered to plead Substantially. The Defendant was then called & disappeared whereupon judgment was had by default, and a Writ of Enquiry executed as follows, to Wit We, Jno. Wyche, Foreman & the same Jury do find for the Plaintiff L 18. 9 . 6½ with Costs & Interest.

Ordered that the Minutes be read.
The Court then adjourned till to Morrow Morning 9 of the Clock. Thos. Knight, Daniel Green, John Wyld.

At a Court Continued by Adjournment on Wednesday the 7th May 1788
Present Daniel Green   )
         Thomas Knight   )
         Thomas Obannon) Esquires.
         John Wyld   )
         Willm. Buford   )

Ordered that the Docket be Called & notice given.

47. Tamar Odom vs Dorcas Powell the Plaintiffs Attorney moved that the Petition & Summons/ be amended of a Clerical mistake that the name of the Husband be added to the Writ - Judgmt - for Plaintiff 20/all fees rembd.
  Ordered that the Sheriff make due return of all the Executions into the Clerks Office, that have/been/Executed by him.
  Ordered the Sheriffs pay 1/2 costs of the Old Causes dismissed on their Errors.
  Ordered that Eliza Tony be bound to James Gideon till she comes of lawful age.

83 No 1 Collins vs Clayton Att - Discontinued at Plaintiff's Cost
    3 White vs Matthews - Nonsuit - Dismist
    4 Bentley vs Bentley - Nonsuit Dismist
    5 King vs Trower - Nonsuit Dismist
    6 Stone vs Odom - Nonsuit Dismist
    7 Davis vs Brown - Continued Dedimus to be fowd to Theo.
              Buxton & Nathl. Miller to examiner Jno.
              Green Notice given the 20th May next.
    8 Trower vs Mills - Discontjnued
    9 Olford vs Johnson - Dismist
   10 Banner vs Tuten - Nonsuit - Dismist
   12 Davis vs Williams - Contd & Dedimus issued to Georgia
              to Thel Buxton & Nash Miller, Esq.
              to examine John Green, Esq. 20th May
   14 Wyld vs Gilbert - Contd.
   15 Wyld vs Webb - Contd.
   18 Foreman vs Conway - Discontinued
   19 McKeely vs Odom - Discontinued
   20 Causey vs Odom - Discontinued
   21 Davis vs Cuthbert - Dismist
   22 Carroll vs Hill - Dismissed
   25 Wheeler vs Odom - Discounted

Elijah Gillett, Esq. High Sheriff failing to bring the Buckle/that were put into his/Custody, by Virtue of an Affidavit, which prevented the Trial/Wyld vs Newm Ordered that he deliver the Buckles to the Clerk, & that/All such Articles be lodged for the future in the Clks Office.

   26 Cannon vs Humphreys - Discontinued at Plaintiff's Cost.
   30 Willm. Williams vs Lewis - Dismissd.
    7 Wm. Brown, Assignee Benj. Buxton vs Jas. Myrick - The Jury being Sworn to Witt David Shipes, James Jackson, Thos. Morris, Tarlton Brown, Robt. Bradley, Benj. Odom, Junr, Jno. Wyche, Foreman, Nichl Nobles, Robt. Brown, Patrick McLemurry, James Collins, Bartholomew Roberts. One of the Jury being withdrawn by Consent & the Plff. failed to Answer whereof a Nonsuit took to call - Nonsuit-Dismist.

- 31 Robison vs Randall Dismissd Deft Cost R. Stark, Atty Plff.
- 37 See Appearance Docket
- 38 Appearance Docket turn over 2 Pages
  References to Janu term.
- 1 William Davis vs Thomas Burton.
  Dismissed at Plffs Costs
- 3 Dorcas Powell vs Benj. Odom - Continued under Demurrer by Consent.
- 5 Singleton vs Knight - Dismissed
- 6 Singleton vs Knight - Dismissed
- 7 Nonsuit See above No. 7
- 10 Olaron Gillett vs Wm. Christy - Abatement by death of Plaintiff
- 12 Thomas Buxton & Wm. Davis, Contd for Award - referred to the Arbitration of John Green & Michl. Reeser with Liberty of Umpirage their Award to be returned to the next Court & to become a Judgment of the Same.

84 Ordered that the Estrays to be Sold on Thursday the 8th May 1788.
Ordered that the appearance Docket be Cald the Second Time.

- 59 Clevears D. Wyld vs Alex Newman, Dismissed at Mutual Consent of/the Parties to pay their own cost/
- 60 Cleavers D. Wyld vs Wm. Newman. Dismisd by the Consent of the Plaintiff.
- 61 Wilson & Wife vs Wm. Sisson   Non Est/Dismiss/ to be renewed in 6 Weeks.
- 62 Brown vs Rouse - Judgt by Default Cont. for Writ Enquiry
- 63 Jno. Clayton vs Jno. Wyld, Esq.   Dismist.
- 64 Jno. Clayton vs Jno. Wyld, Esq.   Dismist.
- 65 Crawford vs Clayton   Judgmt 7-7-9 Under Installment
- 66 Crawford vs McMillan Judgt. 6-6-0 Do Installt.
- 67 Crawford vs Alex McMillan, Judgt. 7-0-0 Do Installment
- 68 Turner vs Montgomery - Judgt. 4.13-5 & Costs.
- 69 Bowers & Adis vs Newman & Holmes - Nonsuit Dismist
- 70 Boils vs Bassett   Discont. at Plffs Cost.
- 71 Boils vs Williams   Judgt. 4.6.0. & Cost.
- 72 Newman vs Tradeway   Dismissed at Plff Cost.
- 73 Swicord vs Charity   Contd.
- 72 Beddingfield vs Jno. Petter - Nonsuit - Dismist
- 75 Brown Assignee Brown vs Dunbar - Contd.
- 76 Mitchell vs Newman   Contd.
- 77 Robinson &C vs Brown   Judgt. Confert for 25 Guineas the Deft. to pay Cost.
- 78 Williams vs Smith   Dismist
- 79 Williams vs Boyt   Contd.
- 80 Montgomery vs Turner   Contd.
- 81 Wickly vs Buxton   Judgt Batt 2/8 & Costs
- 82 Wickly vs Hicks   Judgt 9-18-0 Installmt.
- 83 Garnett vs Graves   Contd.
- 84 Harley vs Davis   Dismissd Davis
- 86 Townsend vs Fox   Judgt by Default
- 85 Thomson vs Millidge   Came too late.   Dismist
- 87 McNeely vs Cannon   Contd.
- 88 Brown vs Wickly   Contd.
- 89 Roberts vs Windam   Judgt. Default Contd.
- 90 Sum vs Christy   Contd.

The Minutes being read the Court adjourned till to

Morrow Morning 9 of the Clock.
                    Daniel Green
                    Thos. Obannon
                    John Wyld
         See the other Side

85   39 C. D. Wyld vs Wm. Newman - Contd.
     40 Sunn vs Newman Contd.
     41 Kersh vs Shields Contd.
     42 Causey vs Fields Dismissed Nonsuit
     43 Knight vs Singleton - Dismissed Non en
     44 Wickly vs Wm. Newman - Dismissd at Plff Cost
     45 Derrell Johnson vs Capps - Dismissd at Deft Costs.
     46 Williams vs Brown - Dismissd
     47 Benjy. Odom vs Dorcas Powell - Judgmt for 20/all fees
                                                 remitted
     48 Eliza Williams vs Eliza Myrick - Judgt by Default
                                                 ₺10 & Cost
     49 Gillett vs Christy -- Abates by Death of Plff.
     50 Pully vs Cargill - Dismissed at Plff's Cost.
     51 Newman vs Scarbrough - Dismissed at Plffs Cost.
     52 Turner vs Jno. Price - Nonsuit Dismist
     53 Roberts vs Windam - Nonst. Dismist & Att. granted No.89
     54 State vs Capps - Dismist
     55 State vs Mills - Dismist
     56 Fitts vs Wickly - Contd.
     57 State vs Smith - Dismist
     58 Wickly vs Reading Field - Dismist Nonest.

     NB Turn to the Appearance Dockett on the other Side for the
     /above Cause/

     16 Har/le/y vs Davis - Dismist at Plaintiff's Cost.
     18 Nicks vs Randall - Judgmet for Plaintiff ₺ 10 & Costs
                                                 same Jury.
     19 Obannon vs Lee - Dismist at Defendt Cost.
     20 Miles vs Mills - Discontinued Note taken out of the
                                Office/ by Plaintiffs Attorney/
     21 Wallace vs McLewrath - Nonsuit
     27 Odom vs Morris - Contd. by Consent.
     28 Sweat vs Cardin - Contd.
     31 Johnson vs Capps - Dismist at Deft Costs.
     32 Odom vs Causey - Nonsuit - dismist
     33 Rousee vs Wyche - Contd.
     34 Turner vs B. Odom Sen. - Contd.
     37 Nehemiar Powers vs Turner - Dismist at Plff Cost.
     38 Cook vs Delon - Dismissd
     8   State vs Smith - Discharged on Paying Fees
     10 State vs Mills - Discharged on Paying Fees
     11 State vs Capps - Discharged on Paying Fees.

     NB The above Causes were alled when the Jury were out &
     read with the other Minutes on the other Side but no Room
     to Sign them here.

86   At a Court held and Continued the 8th May 1788 by Adjourn-
     ment
             Present   Daniel Green   )
                       John Wyld   )
                       Willm. Beauford   )   Esqrs.
                       Thomas Obannon   )

                                  48

On motion of the County Attorney the Court proceeded to the appointment of a Coroner, when Tarlton Brown, Esq. was by the unanimous Consent of the Court Appointed as such. /Issued Copy/

Ordered that a Road from the White Pond to the Pine logg, from thence to Columbia, in a /direct/ Course as farr as the County of Winton extend be laid out, & Walter Robinson be appointed Overseer.

Ordered that a Road/be laid out/ from Morris Ford, over both the Saltketchers, by Joseph Collins, thence the nearest & direct Way to ghe Charleston Road, that Joseph Duncan & Joseph Jeeter be appointed Overseers.

Ruth Townsend vs John Fox, the Jury being sworn/on a Writ of Inuiry/to Wit, John Wyche, Nichk. Nobles, William Weakley, James Montgomery, Bartholomew Roberts, John Mitchell Tarlton Brown, Fras. Bassett, William Creach, Burrill Parker, Jesse Cournee, William Woodcock, do say We find for the Plaintiff Sixtynine pounds Eleven Shillings and eleven pence with Costs. Under the Instalmt Act.

Ordered that a Road be laid of the Directest & best Way from the /lower/ three Runs Bridge to Philip Ulmores old Place, and that Joseph Brooker & William Weekley & Solomon Owens, be appointed Overseers /and to lay/ off the same.

Order that a Dedimus be issued to Thomas Burton & John Green Esqrs. to examine Willm. Ashley in the Suit of Roberts vs Windham.

Order that Edmd. Bentley be allowed 4 Attendance in the Suit Williams vs Boyt - at the Plff Cost.

Ordered that Mary Southwell be allowed 11 Days attendance Williams vs Myrick at the Plaintiff Cost.

Ordered that James Montgomery be allowed 7 Days attendance Odom vs Bartley Brown Jun. at the Cost of Brown.

Ordered that Wm. Beauford Esq. be allowed 4 days attendance in the Suit of Dorcas Powell vs Benj. Odom at Plff Cost.

Ordered that the Tavern Keepers Licence fee be respited till next Court.

Ordered that Israel Walker & Jonathan Walker be summoned to appear at the next Court to show reason why they have not paid their fees.

Ordered that the Road from Charles Browns old Place on the three Runs to Sandy Run, be laid out by Joseph Brooker, William Weekley & Williams Roberts, the best and most convenient way, & they are hereby appointed Overseer of the Same.

Ordered that the persons, John Shaw, Charles Wheeler & Lazarus Wooley, who took up Stray Horses, be summonsed to Appear at the /Second Day of/ next Court with the Horses they have taken up & shew cause why they did not bring them to this Court to be sold according to law.

Order that Sarah Southwell be allowed for 8 days Attendance in the Suit of Williams vs Myrick at the Plff Cost.

Ordered that Lorana French be allowed 4 Days attendance in the Suit of Eliza A. Williams /vs/ James Myrick at the Suit of Deft.

Ordered that George Collins be appointed Overseer of the Road from the Saltketchers to Tobys Creek/ in the room of Benj. Odom, Senr/ & that Charles Nicks be Overseer of the Road from Tobys Creek to the County Line.

It appearing to this Court, that the People are dissatisfied with the present Place of Holding the Court. The Court have upon mature deliberation, concluded to Adjourn from the Plantation of James Mitchell on Cedar Branch to the Plantation of Benjamin Odom, Senr. & it is requested, that every Member of the Court will meet on the first Day of the next Court, the first Monday in August, to consider of & conclude on a Suitable Place to Fix & Erect the Publick Buildings for this County.

Ordered that the Minutes of the Day be Read.

Ordered that the Court be adjourned to the House of Benj. Odom Sen. on Turkey Creek unto the Court in Course.

       Daniel Green
       Thos. Obannon
       John Wyld.

88 Blank

89 August 4th 1788. The Court met according to adjournment. Present

    The Worshipfull
       Daniel Green)
       Thomas OBannon) Esquires
       Jesse Winburn)

The Minutes were read in due form and the Court Ordered to adjourn to tomorrow Morning 9 O'Clock.
       Daniel Green
       Thos. Obannon
       Jesse Windborne

At a Court held for Winton County on Tuesday the 5th August 1788, by adjournment Present

         (William Robison, Esq.
         (Daniel Green)
         (Thomas OBannon)
 The Worshipfull (William Sisson) Esqrs.
         (Jesse Winburn)

The Jury Box being produced, a Boy of about the Aged of Twelve drew in the presence of the Court, the following Persons to Serve for a Pettit Jury for November Court, viz James Kirkland, Jesse Rogers, Michl. Swicord, Daniel Howell John Williams, John Newman, John Rivers Sen., Charles Beck, William Matthews, Willm. Frazer, Daniel Philpot, James Neale, William Brooker, Reuben Likely, Nehemiah Powers, Absalom Best, Joseph Humphreys, Richard Jackson, John Wickly, Chas. Nix, Silas Rolls, David Reeves, Jacob Harley, Jacob Rountree, Isaac Bush, Thomas Shields, Richd. Creech, Moses Plummer & William Carr. -30-

The Grand Jury being impannelld were Sworn, Vizt Danl. Odom, Junr., Wilson Cook, Jos. Cave, Andrew Nimmons, Joseph Collins, Joseph Turner, Joshua Smith, John Bates, Absalom Tyler, Michl. Swicord, James Brown, Geo. Kirkland, Joseph Youngblood -13-
John Cave appointed Foreman
George Walker, Esq., having produced his commission as an Attorney, was admitted to practice as an Attorney in this Court Signed by the Honbl. John Ruthledge, Henry Pendleton & Adamus Bush, Esqr.

90 Ordered that a Deed from James Fair to Isaac Tool be recorded being proved by the Oaths of Reuben Rogers & Joseph Turner.
Ordered that Israel Walker on making due acknowledgement be discharged on paying fees & that No Attorneys Fees be charged to him & Jonathan Walker /from all fees/
The Attorney & Clerk relinquish their Fees Ardis & Bowers vs Newman & Holmes which was nonsuited last Court by Mistake by Consent of Parties Ord.
Ruth Townsend, Administratrix of Nathl. Hicks vs Jno. Fox-Atta. Stephen Smith summoned as Garnishee in this Cause came into Court and Made oath that to the best of his knowledge he is justly indebted to the said John Fox in the Sum of Seventy pounds Sterling.
John Collins vs. Jno. Clayton. Ordered that the Plaintiff pay no cost only in one Suit being mentioned by Mistake instead of One.
Ruth Townsend acknowledged satisfaction this Day received from Stephen Smith Garnishee in the Case Ruth Townsend vs Jno. Fox Ł 70 by a Note payable in January next for the sum of Ł 70.
Ruth Townsend

William Davis vs Benj. Brown - Judgmt by Default 10 Esg. 45 Ł 0.0, & Cost.
Ordered that all Persons who have take up Estrays bring them to be Sold on Wednesday the 6th August at 3 of the Clock in the Afternoon.
List of Pettit Jury Walker Robertson, Robt. Lancaster, James Geddins, Joseph Brooker, Benj. Odom, Junr., Adam McNeely, George Miller, Moses Collins, George Collins, Tho. Long, James Roberts, Robert Bradley   Benj. Odom, Junr. Foreman.
Jno. Green vs Wm. Table, /Contd/ Wm. Davis became Security for the Costs, Plaintiff.'
Davis against Asa Williams. We find for the Defendt. one Shilling & Costs/Benj. Odom, Foreman.
Ord. Thomas Enecks, Juryman in the Room of Walker Robison, who is discharged.
Ord. That David Chester be a Juryman in the Room of George Collins, who id discharged.
Ordered that a Road be laid of from Sykes Creek up Edisto River to intersect a Road from Charles& Town leading to long Cane, nead the Head of the Upper Three Runs, the best & most convenient Way & that Leven Collins be Overseer for the lower part, Zadock Woolley for the Middle Part & Jesse Rogers/of the Upper Part/ who are appointed Overseers & to lay off the same & that Danl. Green, Esq. is ordered to lay off the same in convenient Districts.

Ordered that the Minutes be Read, & the Court adjourned

to to Morrow Morning 9 of the Clock.
Wm. Robison
Daniel Green
Jesse Winborne

91   At a Court held for Winton County on Wednesday the 6th Day
of August 1788 & Continued by adjournment
    Present
        The Worshipfull   Willm Robison   )
                          Thomas Knight   )
                          Willm Sisson   ) Esquires
                          Richd. Treadway)
                          Willm Buford   )
                          Danl. Green   )

We the Grand jurors Present to the Worshipfull Court
as a Grievance John Latiers Son as his Father is not capable
to do for him, We request that he should be bound out to
a Trade that he may know how get his living in an honest
Way.
   Likewise that something should be done with Peggy
Welch's four Children.
   Likewise that Overseers should receive legall orders
from the Court, to keep the Roads in Good Repairs.
                               John Cave, Foreman
   Danl. Corbett acknowledged his Deed of Lease & Release
to Bunell Parker & ordered to be recorded
   Joseph Davis acknowledged his Deed of Lease & Release
to John Snelling & his wife being provately Examd. by W.
Robison Esq. acknowledged her right of Dower & also Mary
Davis acknowledged her right of Dower.
   On the Motion of T. P Carnes,/Attorney for Plaintiff/
Wm. Davis vs Asa Williams 1/ for/ a new Trial it /was/
granted.
   The Court thanked the Grand Jury for their diligence
& discharged them.
   That the Court forming themselves into a Court of
Ordinary Ordered that John Bush & Joseph Miller take the
Estate of Joseph Johnson out of the hands of Edmd. Bentley
as it is made appear to this Court that the sd. Bentley is
destroying the Same & that they give Bond & Security in
double the Sum of the Value /whereupon Danl. Green, Esq.
became Security.

Eleanor Welch) An appeal from the determination of Thos.
    vs   ) Knight, Esq. By the Court. Ordered that the
Looley French) proceedings in this Cause be Certified up
                  to this Court before next term. That it
continue over till then and That Looley French give Bond &
Security to the Clerk for the sum of Six Pounds to prosecute the appeal with effect and that the execution issued
in this Cause be Stay'd 'till the determination of this
Court can be had.

Thomas Crawford) Ordered that a new trial be granted till
    vs   ) next Court & that exception be Staid
William Cary   ) till the determination thereof.

92 Ordered that William Hall, Esq. is appointed a Magistrate
in the room of James Fair, and took the Oath according to
Law in open Court.

List of Pettit Jury Robt. Lancaster, James Geddins, Joshua Walker, Benj. Odom, Jacob Swicord/ Adam McNeely, George Miller, Moses Collins, Thos. Long, James Roberts Wyld/ Robt. Bradley, Thos. Enecks, Davis Chester & Sabard Odam Thos. Sheild - 12-

Jno. Wyld, Esq. vs. Willm Gilbert - Judgment by Default.
Jno. Wyld, Esq. vs Joseph Webb - Judgmt by Default, Contd for Writ of Enq.
Alex. Newman vs Reuben Newman Acknowledged their Deed to Jno. Mitchell. Ordered to be recorded - with platt annexed Jno. Mitchell vs Reuben & Alex Newman. Dismiss Agreed to pay half Legal Fees.

Ordered that Wm. Dunbarr, Esq. do Sell the perishable part of the Estate of John Disharoon, Decd. now in his Possession as Admr.
    Ordered that Stephen Smith, Jno. Parkinson & Jos. Vince Esq. be appointed Comn. to divide the Estate of Job. Roundtree, Dec. amongst the Heirs of the said Decd.
Robt Prawley Foreman

Jno. Wyld vs Wm. Gilbert. A Writ of Enquiry. We of the Jury do find for the Plaintiff nine hundred & forty three pounds Ster with legal interest for the Same & Cost of Sale. Robt. Bradley, Foreman.

Ordered. Alexander Newman acknowledged his Deed to Saml. Way and ordered to be Recorded.
    John Wyld vs Wm. Davis on a Motion for an Appeal by the Deft. Attorney & Solomn Agreements by each Party being waged, the Court determined that no Appeal be Granted. By consent of parties, Ordered that the Sale of the property now Levied on in the /cause/ Wyld vs Davis be suspended for fifteen days and if one third of the execution is not paid by the Defendant on or before the expiration of the sd. fifteen days, that the Officer proceed to sell the property to discharge one third of said execution; and that the balance be Levied agreeable to Instalment Law, provided the Defendant /dont/ give Security pursuant to the sd Law after being Cited to so do.
    Ordered that the Estrays be sold to the highest bidder on Three Months Creditt, giving Bond & Security to the Treasurer & property not moved until Security given. Aaron Smith & McC. Smithd bond was proved by Thos. Wyld, a Witness.
Orderd to be recorded

3. Dorcas Powell vs Benj. Odom, Senr. The Defendt Plea overruled. Trial ordered by Jury. N. B. Jacob Swicord & Thos. Shields, Jurymen in the room Benj. Odom & Sabard Odom objected to by the parties We of the Jurry do find for the Plaintiff Five Pounds & Cost of Suit Robt. Brandley, Foreman.

Ordered than Ann Collins on giving Bond & Security in Fifty pounds do Indemnify the County to maintain her Child that her Bond for her Fine be cancelled.

    The State vs Thos. Pully, taken up by the Vagrant Law before Thomas Knight, Esq. Order that he Certi the Proceedings to the next Court.

12 Ordered that Richd. Creech, Arthur Jenkins & William Roberts being first Sworn do View both the Roads from the Lower three Runs to Phillip Elmores old Place & to view the Conveniency & Inconveniency of the same &/ make their/ report to the next Court.

Ordered that the Minutes be read & the Court adjourned to to Morrow Morning 9 of the Clock.
                                            Wm. Robison,
                                            W. Buford
                                            Jesse Winborne

At a Court held for Winton County on Thursday the 7th August 1788, by adjournment   Present

    The Worshipfull   William Robison)
                       Willm. Buford)
                       Thos. Obannon) Esq.
                       Thomas Knight)

Ordered that William Robison, John Wyld & Thos. Obannon, Esq. or any two of them/ be appointed Commissioners to let the Building of a Jail & Stocks upon the two Acres of Land given by Willm. Robison Esq. to the County at the Head of Cedar Branch, adjoining the Land of James Mitchell to the Lowest bidder to be finished by the next Court.

94   Ordered. The Appearance Dockett be called for the Last Time.

91 Saml. Earl vs Danl. Shaw - Contd.
92 Bentley vs DeRoussee - Dismist Nonsuit
93 Bartlett Brown, Jr. vs Sampson Obannon. Judgt by
                                            Default - Contd.
94 Jos. Wallace vs Robt. McLewrath - Dismist
95 Geo. Miller vs Vet Turner - Contd.
96 Leah Brooker vs Jos. Brooker - Contd.
97 Leah Brooker vs Jos. Brooker - Contd.
98 Jos. Morris vs Jos. Duncan - Nonsuit. Dismist.
99 John Green vs Wm. Tutle - Contd. Plan. Cost
100 Jno. Green vs Richd. Creech, Admr. Ow Williams,
                                Contd at Plaintiff Case
101 Jno. McFail vs Wm. Turner - Contd.
102 Henry Robison vs Saml. Boyet - Contd.
103 Abram Boyet vs Reub. Newman - Contd Plaintiff Cost.
104 Patrick Cunningham vs Thos. Cargill. Dismist
105 Wm. McKinley vs Reuben Newman - Contd.
106 Wm. Shaw, Esq. vs Jos. Brooker Contd. at Plff Costs.
107 Jno. Davis vs Richd Creech - Contd.
108 Christopher Hall vs Jacob Swicord - Contd.
109 Levi Thrower vs Jno. Wyche Judgmt. for ₺ 6.5.0 & Cost
110 Celia March vs. Rich. Kershe. Judgt by Default -
                                            Contd.
111 Richd. Aldridge vs Jno. Gill. The Jury Pray'd at the
                                            Plaintiff Cost.
The Jury being Called & Sworn, Vizt. /Wm. Roberts/ James Geddins, Jacob Swicord/Bartlett Brown/George Miller, Moses Collins, Thos. Long, Robt. Bradley, Thos. Enocks, Davd. Chester, Arthur Turner, James Kirkland,/Benj. Odom/ Richd. Jackson, Robt. Bradley, Foreman.

112 Wilson & Wife vs Wm. Sisson N Est. J. Obannon to pay
    fees. Dismist pd 6/
    /We find for the Plff Ł8 with Cost of Fees/

113 Elijah Gillett & Eliza Gillett, Ex. of Aaron Gillett
    vs Wm. Davis - Contd.

114 The Same vs Willm. Christy - Contd.
114 The Same vs Arth. Jenkins - Dismist at Defts Costs.
116 Jno. Mallett & Wife vs Geo. Dyches - Judgt by Default - Contd.
117 Jno. Buford vs Jno. Cone - Contd.
118 Thos. Moore vs Gill Thomas - Dismissal Plff Cost
119 Richd. Kirby vs Thos. Cargill - Dismist Non St.
120 Saml. Way vs Reub & Alex. Newman - Contd.
121 John Wickly vs Michl. Swicord - Cont. under Arbitration
122 Benj. Odom vs Wm. Ashley - Judgt by Default - Contd.
124 Aaron Smith vs Henry Cannon Disstress. Order for
    Sale of Land given 30 days Notice

125 Thos. Long vs Henry Cannon, Judgt by Default tisement.
    Do-Contd.
127 Wm. Taylor vs James Fair, Esq. Judgt by Default -
    Contd.
128 Fras. Boyle vs Benj. Byrd - Nonsuit Dismist

95 William Taylor Garnishee, being Sworn Says that he has
    Twelve pounds one shilling on Hands of the Estate Benja.
    Byrd, which James Fair/was/as Administrator of the sd.
    Estate & took his Note for the same to the said Farr.

129 Thomas Jones vs Benj. Byrd Nonsuit Dismist.
130 David Chester vs James Fair, Esq. - Judgment by Default
    Contd.
131 David Chester vs Jas. Fair - Judgment by Default -
    Contd.
132 Jno. Wilsher vs Jos. Fair, Esq. - Judgmt by Default,
    Contd.
133 Geo. Robison vs Wm. Griffin - Judgt. for Ł 6-0-0 &
    Cost ordered that all of the property/attached be
    sold to pay the Plaintiffs debt & costs.
134 Benj. Odom, Junr. vs Jas. Fair, Admr. of Wm. Byrd,
    Esq. judgment for Ł10, The Lands of Benj. Byrd Deed
    to be exempted
135 Nathl Walker vs Burr Harrison - Contd.
134 Reuben Hargrove vs Jno. Crow - Dismist at the Deft.
    Cost
27 Moses Odom vs Thos. Morris - Nonsuit Dismist.
30 Jno. Sweat vs Chas. Carden - Nonsuit Dismist.
33 Peter DeRoussee vs Jno. Wyche - Dismist at Deft. Cost.
34 Wm. Turner vs Benj. Odom - Dismist at Plaintiffs Cost.
Ord. Richd. Creech acknowledged his Deed of L. & Release
    to Thos. Pulley for 100 /acres/ of Land/to be recorded.

39 Clevears D. Wyld vs Wm. Newman - Contd at Defedt Cost
40 Fred Sunn vs Jno. Newman - Dismist by Consent, each
    paying their Costs.
41 John Kersh vs Robt. Shields - Contd.
56 John Fitts vs John Wickly - Judgmt/confessed/ P Note
    according to Installmt. Dismist by/agreement./

62 Bartlett Brown vs Rouse - Dismist at Deft. Cost.
73 Jacob Swicord vs Willm Christie - Rules to Tryall. Judgment by Default.

Writ of Inquiry/We the Jury do find for the Plaintiff Ł 10S 2-0 With costs & Interest & Order that negro/attached be sold to satisfy the Judg/   Robt. Bradley, Foreman
vs Wm. Dunbarr/
75 Wm. Brown, Admr. of Bartlett Brown,/Rt. Lark & Geo. Robison, Dismsit, at the Plffs Costs.
76 John Mitchell vs Reub & Alex Newman, Dismist by Consent paying each half the Legall Fees.

Ordered that Susannah Nicks be allowed 3 Days attend.
   Aldridge vs Gill

79 Willm Williams vs Boyt-Contd.

80 James Montgomery vs Arthur Turner & Thos. Obannon - Contd. at Deft Costs.

O. The appraisement of Nathan Williams Estate returnd & Ord. to be recorded.'

83 Thos. Garnett vs Thos. & Humphrey Graves, Verdict Ł25. 13.0 & Cost. Robt. Bradley, Foreman

87 Adam McNeely vs Henry Cannon - Contd.

88 Bartlett Brown vs John Weekley - Contd.

89 Wm. Roberts vs Isaac Windam - Contd.

Ordered that Joseph Tuten be allowed 4 days attendance.
   Garnett & Graves.

96 Jno. Gill vs Josias Wallace.) -man Execution issued the Sheriff Robt McLewarth vs. Josias Wallace) returned that he had Levied on a Trass. Bassett vs Jos. Wallace) Negro in the Hands of Thos. Shields & that the sale was forbid   Ordered that the Sheriff go on to Sell the Property, except it is replevied according to Law.

Fred Sunn vs Wm. Christie. Judgmt. confessed for Ł20 & Cost,
Staying Execution 3 Months.
   Ordered that Wm. Buford be allowed 4 Days attendance Dorcas Powell vs Benj. Odom Also 4 Days for Wm. Shaw vs Jos. Brooker.
   Ordered that Wm. Robison & Wm. Buford, Esq. do visit the Clerks Office & Examine the State of it & make their reports to the next Court.
   Ordered that the Com. for letting/the building/the Prison 7 Stocks, do give Notice by Advertisement to let the same on Saturday the 16th at/the Court House at/ the head of Cedar Branch to the lowest bidder.

   Ordered that the Minutes be Read & the Court adjourned to the next Court in Course.
                        Wm. Robison
                        W. Buford
                        Thos. Obannon

97 At a Court held by adjournment for Winton County on
    Monday, the Third Day of November 1788, Present
    the Worshipfull
                    William Robison
                    Richd. Tradaway
                    Thos. OBannon
                    William Sisson
                    Jesse Winbourn
                    Wm. Buford
                    Thos. Knight, Esqrs.

The Jury Box being prepared a Boy about the Age of Twelve
drew in the Presence of the Court the following Persons to
serve as Grand Jurors for February Court, Viz

         1   2   3   4
William Weekly, Jno.McNight Johnson, Jos.Brooker, Joseph
         5   6   7   8   Jeter
Bathl Roberts, Robt.Bradley, LevenCollins, Thomas Tuten
         9   10   11   12
Arthur Jenkins, Benj. Corbett, Richd. Creech George Robison
        13   14   15   Junr.
Fras. Bassett, Willm Creech, Bartlett Brown, Senr.
                         16   17   18
J̸o̸h̸n̸ A̸s̸h̸l̸e̸y̸ S̸e̸n̸.Willm. Carr John Parkinson, Joham Clayton
        19   20   21
Saml. Way, John Drummon, F̸r̸a̸n̸s̸. B̸a̸r̸k̸e̸r̸

                                                         1
The Pettit Jurors were also Drawn, Viz. Reuben Harrison
         2   3   4   5
Matthew Cone, Charles Boiles, Jonathan Gregory, Elisha
                          6   7   8 Abeton
J̸n̸o̸. H̸a̸t̸t̸, Zadock Woolley, Reuben Roudtree, Isham Jourdan
         9   10   11   12
Abram Deeson, John Tabor, Verdemon Clements, Arthur Turner
        13   14
Abraham Johnson, T̸h̸o̸m̸a̸s̸ P̸h̸i̸l̸p̸o̸t̸, L̸e̸w̸i̸s̸ C̸l̸a̸r̸k̸, Jno. McCane,
        15   16   17   18
Benj Buxton, George Crossley, Henry Wood, Willm Jones
        19   20   21   22   23
Benj. Blunt, Danl. Crocket, Wm. Adams, James Walker, George
        24   25   27   Coupee
Jno. Platt, Nickl. Nobles, Anth. Leach, Robt. McLewarth,
        28   29   30
Saml. Dennis, William Tooten, Nuden Dunn

        The Last Will & Testament of Stephen Smith was proved
by the Oaths of Jno. Collins & Richael Walker, who also
swore they saw George Wiggins Subscribe & Sign his Name as
Witness/therefore/ & was orderd to be recorded.

        The Last Will & Testament of Robt. Hankinson was Proved
by the Oath of James Symes who Swore that he Signd the
same as a Witness & also Saw John McLehaney, Jun. Zachries
Garner Sign the Same as Witnesses to the same & ordered to
be Recorded.
            Copy delvd.
Wm. Hommer, Susannah Hankinson took the Oaths of Executor
& Executrix of the Estate of Robt. Hankinson, Decd.

98 Wm Vince and Martha Smith took the Oaths of Executor &

Executrix to the Last Will & Testament of Stephen Smith, Decd.

Ordered that Wm. Dunbar, Esq., John Collins, Robt. Lark, & Henry Cocker, or any three of them do Appraise the Estate of Hephen Smith, Decd.

Ordered that John Wyche, William Boyet, Noah Tanner & Ezekiel Williams do appriase the Estate of Robt. Hankinson or any three of them.

Ordered that the Sheriff be paid Seve Pounds, Ten Shillings and that a former order be complied with of Seven Pounds Ten Shillings.

William Davis & John Davis Acknowledged their Bonds in open Court for ℔ 1000 & ordered to be recorded as Tax Collector.

Ordered that the Minutes be Read.

Orderd that the Court be adjourned till tomorrow morning Nine of the Clock.   Richard Tradaway
                                    Jesse Winburn
                                    W. Buford.
                                    Wm. Sisson

The Worshipfull Court met according to adjournment on Tuesday the Fourth Day of November 1788,

Present
Thomas Obannon   )
Richard Tradaway)
Thomas Knight   )
William Sisson   )   Esqrs.
Jesse Winbourn   )
Wm. Buford   )

Ordered that Robt. Shields fine be remitted, on paying all other fees.
Alex Newman/& John Parkinson/ took the Oaths of Executors to the Last Will & Testament of Stephen Smith.
The following persons were appointed Constables to Serve for 12 Months & ordered to qualify themselves, Thomas Sheriff, Chas. Wheeler, Wm. Woodcock, Elijah Tradaway, David Adkinson, James Montgomery,

Ordered that Thomas Wyld be allowed for Attending 8 Days in the Suit of Docr Sunn vs Wm. Christie on behalf of the Plaintiff.

The Pettit Jury being Calld as appeared as follows- Jesse Rogers, Jno. Rivers, Chas. Beck, Wm. Matthews, Wm. Frazier, James Neale, Reuben Golikely, Richard Jackson, John Wickly, Chas. Nix, William Carr, Jno. Nimmons.

A List of the Delinquents James Kirkland, Michl. Swicord, Danl. Howell, Jno. Williams, Danl. Philpot, Nehemiah Powers, Joseph Humphreys, Silas Rolls, David Reeves, Jacob Harlor, Jacob Roundtree, Thos. Shields, Moses Plummer, to be sumnd. by Seice Facias.

Levi Trower by order of Edm. Bently vs Jno. Wyche. New Triall & the Costs to be Suspended on Affidavit ℔ 6-0-0 Georgia Money lodged in Office.

Richd. Tradaway acknowledged his Deed to Thos. Weathersby & Ord. be Recorded.

On Inventory & Appraisement of Andrew Tester Estate returned & orderd to be Recorded & Acco & Also.

180   Attachmt. Charles Wheeler vs Hezekiah Coleman Ł 11-17-5. All property be sold. Contd.

Ordered that the Estate of Andrew Tester be sold by the Admr.

Ordered that Wm. Christie give Bond & Security to deliver up Dick Sarah & Prince in double the Sum of the Judgment & to remain in Custody till the same is complied with.

Jno Wyld vs Jos. Webb dismist at Defendts Cost.

39   Clevears D. Wyld vs Wm. Newman, that the Property in Contest belongs to the Plaintiff. Decreed that the property be delivered to the Plaintiff & that the Defendant pay the Costs.

That Eliza Chisman be allowed two Days Attendance Wyld vs Newman.

That Lucy Wyld be allowed two Days Attnednate.

112   Burton vs Davis - Contd.

William Shaw, Esq. having appeared in Court & justified himself against the Accusation/ laid against him, The Court having taken the same into Mature consideration, are clearly of the Opinion that the said orders were improper & are to be expunged & have reversed the whole & reinstated him in the office of County Attorney.

Tarlton Brown, Esq. was by the Majority of /the/ Court Elected High Sheriff & Ordered that he give Bond & Security according to Law produce his Commission to the Next Court.

Joseph Harley, Esq., was unanimously Chosen Coroner for this County & Ordered that he give Bond & Security & produce his Comm. to the Next Court.

William Shaw, Esq. having resigned the Office of County Attorney, The Court unanimously made choice of Thoms. Peters Carnes as County Attorney & he is accordingly appointed.

Appraisement of Dannet Abney, Esq. was returned by order to be recorded.

81   Attachmt Arthur Turner vs Nicholas Cain 272 Guineas, the Accot. being Proved & Judgmt for Debt & Costs Ord the Attachd property be Sold. Contd.

182   Arthur Jenkins vs Ezekiel Harling, Ordrd that the property be Sold & remain in the Sheriff's hands till next Court. Contd.

Margt. Bluntin appointed Guardian to her Grandson, Ruben

Blunton, Richd. Creech & Ruben Golikely her Security.

100 Ordered that the Stray Horses be Sold on Three Months Creditt to Morrow. Ordered that the Bonds due for the Stray Horses Sold last Court be put into Execution if not paid by Thursday.

The Minutes were read in due form and the Court adjourned to tomorrow nine of the Clock.

       Richard Tradaway
       W. Buford
       Thos. Knight
       Jesse Winbourn
        Wm. Sisson

The Worshipful/Court/met according to Adjournment on Wednesday the 5th day of November, 1788.
 Present

      Willm Buford)
      Richd. Tradaway)
      Jesse Winbourn) Esqrs.
       Wm. Sisson)
      Wm. Robison)

William Davis & John Davis acknowledged their Bond for ₤1000 Ster as Collector of the Tax for this County & Ordered to be recorded.

Ordered that Sabard Odom be appointed Constable & was Qualified accordingly.

The appraisement of the Estate of Job Roundtree was returned into Court & Ordered to be recorded.

183 Attachmt. Thomas Obannon vs. Benj. Byrd and his Administrator Jas. Fair. Levied on the Goods & Chattels in Hands of Wm. Taylor - Contd.

John McCarral vs Bartlett Brown on Replevy/ The Judgmt be reversed &/ a new trial ordered, & a Dedimus to issue into Georgia to John Green & Thos. Burton, Esq. or any other two Justices.

Ordered that James Montgomery be alowed 2 Days attend. Wyld vs Newman for the Plaintiff.

        1   2
The Jury for to Day. John Wickly, Foreman, Jesse Rogers,
 3   4   5   6
Chas. Beck, Wm. Matthews, Wm. Frazier, James Neal, Reuben
 7   8   9   10
Golikely, Richd. Jackson, Arthur Turner, Micajah Matthews,
 11   12   12
Wilson Cook, Wm. Newman, Geo. Miller,
     Mer. Plummer.

No. 41.
John Kersh vs Robt. Shields - We of the Jury find for the Plaintiff ₤20 & Costs. Jno. Wickly, Foreman.

Ordered that in the Case of Sales of the Estrays, if any,

Persons shall bidd for any & not comply with the Terms - The Property shall exposed to Sale to the next highest bidder on the same Terms, & the deficiency to be made up, by the person who faild to comply before.

101 Wm. Robison & Thomas Obannon, Esq. have made their report that the Jail is finished according to Agreement & they have recd. the Same - & that an Acct. for some Surplus work not mentioned in the Agreement, Amounting to ₤ 2-1-10½ which is ordered to be paid by the said Thomas Wooton.

The Last Will & Testament of Wm. Myser being duly proved before Thos. Obannon, Esq. by the oaths of John Cook & Susannah Wood was ordered to be recorded.

Thomas Wyld made Oath that he Saw Aaron Smith & John C. Smith Sign Seal & Acknowledge their Bonds which is ordered to be recorded.

Orderd that the Clerks Fees for Tolling & Certificate of Estrays be paid out of the Sales of the Estrays.

On Motion Ordered that a Dedimus potestation issue directed to two of the nearest Justices to Mrs. Sarah Ferguson to examine her as a witness in the case of John Green, Esq. vs. Richard Creech, Plaintiff giving the Defendant legal notice of the time & place of examination.

Ordered that a Depo. issue directed to Thomas Burton & Nathaniel Miller, Esqrs. to examine Joseph Allison as a witness in the case John Green, Esq. vs William Tutle, Plaintiff giving the Defendant legal notice of the time and place of examination.

Ordered that The Sheriff do Settle immediately with The Treasurer fro the Execution & all Moneys recd by him in the Execution of his Office & all Taxes.

William Robison vs John Randal Judgmt. by Default Writ of Enquiry Executed. Wee of the Jury do find for the Plaintiff ₤ 238-2-9 & Cost & Orderd the Attachd property be Sold to pay Debts & Cost.

79 William Williams vs Wm. Boyet - Contd.

87 Adam McNeeley vs Henry Cannon - Contd.

80 James Montgomery vs Arthur Turner & Thos. Obannon - Contd. at the Plaintiff Cost.

80 Bartlett Brown, Sen. vs Jno. Wickley. Judgment/confessd Agreed/ by Installment for the Debt & Costs, according to Bond

Ordered that Ded. issue to Jno. Green & Thos. Burton, or any two in Burk County, to take the Deposition of Shadrack Minky & Wm. Black, Jno. Carroll vs Brown.

Copy. Ordered that Isaac Bush, John Wyche & Richd. Tradaway, or any two of them do examine & State the Acct of Edmd. Bentley & Wife, Admr. of the Estate of Joseph Johnson, Decd. & make their reports to the next Court.

102 89 Wm. Roberts vs Isaac Windam Att Judgmt by Default
Writ of Enquiry Executed. We of the Jury do find for the
Plaintiff Ł 44 with Interest & Costs. Jno. Wickly, Foreman.
91 Saml. Earl vs Danl. Shaw - Contd.
93 Bartlett Brown, Junr. vs Sampson Obannon - Abated by
the death of the Deft.

The Jury discharged till tomorrow morning 9 of the Clock.

The Hoggs now under Execution & the Cattle under Execution, Eliza Williams vs Eliza Myrick, are ordered by the Court to be returned, the Property being Proved the Hogs the Property of John Myrick, Son of Eliza Myrick & the Cattle to Sarah Southwell.

Jno. Green, Esq. vs Willm. Christie, came into Court & acknowledged themselves Indebted to Elijah Gillett, Esq. High Sheriff in the Sum of Two Hundred & Fifty pounds to be Void on the Delivery of the Negroes, Viz. Sarah Prince & Dick. taken by the Virtue of Execution at the suit of Jacob Swicord.

Joseph Obannon Qualified by a Constable.

The Minutes being read the Court adjourned till to morrow Morning nine of the Clock.
                            Wm. Robison
                            Richd. Tradaway
                            Jesse Winborne

The Worshipful/Court/met according to adjournment Thursday the 6th Novem 1788. Present
                            William Robison)
                            Richd. Tradaway)
                            Willm. Buford   )   Esqrs.
                            Jesse Winbourn)

Appearance Docket Orderd to be Called the Last Time.

Ordered that George Davis be committed to Jail till he give Security for his Appearance at Next Court on Motion of County Atty.

Ordered that Ded. be issued into Georgia Absalom Causey vs Jno. Fitts Directed to Jno. Green & Thos. Burton, Esqr. to Exam. Thomas Burns & Jonah Roberts on Part of the Deft. Given Lawful Notice.

123 Jno. Weekly vs Wm. Ashley Judgmt. by Default Contd.
124 Aaron Smith vs Henry Cannon - Settled
125 Thos. Long vs Henry Cannon - Attachmt. Judgmt by
Default Order for Sale to Remain in Sheriffs
Hands Contd.

126 Peter Banner vs Henry Cannon Judgmt. by Default.
Order for Sale. To remain in Sheiff's Hands, Contd.

127 Jno. Cone vs Jno. Buford   NE   Off   Dismist

128 Wm. Davis vs Wm. Christie   Continued

129 Thos. Jones vs Benjy Byrd, Decd   Nonsuit Dismist
103 130 David Chester vs James Fair - Judgt by Default Contd.
131 David Chester...Jas. Fair   Judgt. by Default, Contd.
132 John Williams vs Jos. Fair   Contd.
133 Geo. Robison vs Wm. Griffin   Contd.
134 Benj. Odom, Jr. vs Jos. Fair   Contd.
135 Nathl. Walker vs Ben Harrison   Contd.
136 Wm. Taylor vs Jas. Fair   Judgt by Default
137 Fras. Boyle vs Benj. Byrd   Nonsuit Dismist
138 Jos. Dick vs Thos. Galphen   Contd.
139 Jos. Dick vs Thos. Golphin   Contd.
140 J. Ardis vs Bowers & Newman & Holmes Contd.
141 Arthur Turner vs Jos. Turner & Grace Tool - Dismist
      at Plaintiffs Cost
142 Moses Johnson vs John Redd & Job Redd - Judgt by
      Default   Contd.
143 Absalom Causey vs Jno. Fitts - Contd. Ded ord
144 Benj. Odom Junr. vs Wm. Davis - Contd.
145 Willm. Davis vs Jno. Wyld   Contd.
146 Sabard Odom vs Wm. Woodcock - Contd.
147 Wm. Davis vs James Jones - N E renewed
148 Wm. Davis vs Thos. Jones - N E renewed
149 Eleanor Welch vs Looly French - Contd under Aribtration
150 Thos. Crawford vs Wm. Carr - Contd.
151 The State vs Thos. Pulley - Dismist
152 Wm. Davis vs Asa Williams - Discontd at Mutual Costs.
153 Jos. Obannon vs Arthur Turner - Contd.
154 Moses Diesto vs Abram Cook - Kept off by force of
      arms J. Obannon D S
    Ordered that a Bench Warrant be issued & sufficient
    assistance to take him.

155 Wm. Turner vs Benj. Odom - Dismist at Defendt Cost.
156 Wm. Turner vs Jno Green - Contd.
157 John C. Smith vs Willm Davis - Contd.
158 Arthur Jenkins vs Ezekiel Harding - Judgmt by Default
      Contd.
159 Thos. Garnett vs James Ingram - Settled by the Plain-
      tiff - Dismist
160 Do   vs   Do   Settled by the Plaintiff - Dismist
161 Do   vs   Do   Settled by the Plaintiff - Dismist
162 State vs Pemberton - Dismist
    Do vs Tradaway - Dismist
    Do vs Jno. Redd - Do
    do vs Jno. Rivers - Do

163 Wm. Buford vs Fred Brant - Contd.
164 Wm. Buford, Esq. vs Jacob Cone - Contd.

	165	Michl. Swicord vs Lars Fibiger - Judgment 8-1-0 & Cost
	166	Wm. Hancock vs Christopher Hall - Contd.
	167	Mary Rivers vs Elijah Gillett, Esq. Not Served for Want of a Coroner - Renewed after Feb. 7 Term.
104	168	Rudolph Swohacker vs Saml. Buxton N E - renewed Buston
	169	Alex Newman vs Thos. Wooton - Settled by Consent of Parties
	170	Aaron Smith, Esq. vs Jno. Wickly - Contd.
	171	Moses Odom vs Richd. Creech - Nonsuit Dismist.
	172	Moses Odom vs Thos. Morris - Nonsuit Dismist
	173	Moses Odom vs Bartlett Brown - N E Dismist
	174	Moses Odom vs Jno Green, Esq. N E Dismist
	175	Sarah Davis vs Benj. Odom, Senr. Contd.
	176	Adam McNeely vs Wm. Creech - The Sheriff kept off by force of arms - renewed.
	177	Wm. Williamson vs Wm. Newman - Returned by the Plaintiff Renewed
	178	Nich. Clark Co. Do Dismist
	179	Jennet McKay vs Jos. Brooker, renewed at the Sheriffs expense for neglect of Duty.

Appearance Docket finished

No. 95 Geo. Miller vs Arthur Turner - Dismist at Plffs Cost.
96 Leah Brooker vs Joseph Brooker - Contd at Defts Cost
97 Leah Brooker vs Joseph Brooker - Contd at Defts Cost
98 Jos. Morris vs Jos. Duncan - Nonsuit Dismist
99 Jno. Green, Esq vs Willm. Tutle - Contd at Plffs Cost on Affidavit
100 Jno. Green, Esq. vs Richd. Creech   Do   Do.
101 Jno. McFail vs Wm. Turner - Contd.
102 Henry Robinson vs Saml. Boyet - Contd.
103 Abram Boyd vs Reub. Newman) Judgmt. 9-3-0 & Interest & Cost
105 Wm. McKinley vs Reub. Newman) Judgment by Default - Writ Enq. Judgmt by Bond.
106 Wm. Shaw vs Jos. Brooker - Settled at the Defts. Cost except Attys fees.

108 Christopher Hall vs Jacob Swicord. We of the Jury do find for the Deft.

110 Celia Marsh vs Richd. Kershee - Dismist at Deft to pay Cost with liberty of Umpriage.

113 Elijah & Eliza Gillett vs William Davis. Arbitration Jno. Fitts vs Jno. Wickly.

115 Elijah & Eliza Gillett vs Wm. Christie, Atty. We of Jury do find for the Plaintiff ₺30 & Costs - Jos. Harley, Foreman.

116 Jno. Mallett & Wife vs George Dykes - Contd.

Moses Plummer, Juryman in the Room of George Miller & Jos. Harley

117 Jno. Buford vs Jno. Cone - Contd.

120 Sam. Way vs Reub & Alex Newman - Contd.

121 John Wickly vs Michl. Swicord - Dismist at Plaintiffs Cost

122 Benj. Odom Sen vs Wm. Ashley - Judgment by Default

Ordered that Aaron Smith, Esq. as Clerk be paid his salary for Extra Services ₤ 5 when Cash is in the Treasury for the last Year & Services.

Ordered that Elijah Gillett, Esq. produce his Acct. in the Office & they so be recd & recorded.

105 The Sheriff objected to the Sufficiency of the Jail - Ordered that he employ some Person to make the necessary amends & bring in his Charge to the next Court.

Order that Scire Facias be issued /Jo/Vince to shew cause why he does not appear at Court with the Money Attached in his Hands for Dod Sunn and Doc. Gillett.

The Minutes being read the Court was adjourned to the Next Court in Course.
      Wm. Robison
      W. Buford
      Richard Tradaway
      Jesse Winborne

106 At a Court held for Winton County at the Court House on James Mitchell Plantation Monday the 2nd. February 1789.

  Present, the Worshipfull Willm. Robison)
              Thomas Obannon) Esquires
              Jesse Winburn)

  The Jury box being produced a Young Person drew in the Presence of the Court the following to Serve as Pettit Jurors at Next Court, Viz. Jacob Powell, Robert Adams, Edwd. Nix, John Cooke, James Lee, George Robertson, Jacob Rivers, Lionel Lee, Joseph Bradham, Shadrack Quinley, Joseph Redd, Geo. Kersh, Henry Creech, Richd. Vince, William Ashley, Runns, William Briant, Robt. Lancaster, Benj. Kirkland, Laurens Teaser, James Matthews, Zachariah Griffin, Alex Canady, John Randoll, William Smith, Rifh, Kirkland, Robt. Brown, Nathaniel Walker, William Freeman, Arthur Davis, Joshua Williams -30-

              1   2
The returns of the Grand Jury - Willm. Weekley, Jos. Brooker
   3   4   5   6
Bath Roberts, Frans. Bassett, Bartlett Brown, Jno. Parkinson,
  7   8   9   10
Saml. Way, Rob. Bradley, Thos. Tooten, Benj. Corbett,
  11   12
George Robison, Jun. Jn⌀. H̶a̶m̶m̶o̶n̶d̶, Richd. Leech

The Grand Jury were discharged till tomorrow morning 10 of the Clock.
                1   2
  The Petit Jury return - Elisha Abston, Reuben Roundtree

          3   4   5   6
Henry Wood, Benj. Blunt, Wm. Adams, Willm Tooten, J̶o̶h̶n̶
                 7   8
G̶r̶e̶g̶o̶r̶y̶, George Crosley, John Platt.

    The Petit Jury were discharge till tomorrow morning 10 of the Clock.

The Appraisement of Stephen Smith's Estate was returned & ordered to be Recorded.

James Kirkland, Michl. Swicord, John Williams, Moses Plummer not appearing to serve on the Petit Jury and were on hearing their Excuses their Fines Remitted

The last Will & Testament of William Everet was proved by the Oath of Thos. Dyes & Ordered to lay over for further Proof V. by cash 4/8 & the said Ann D̶y̶e̶s̶ Everet & Wm. Dyes were Qualified as Executors.

107 George Miller acknowledged his Lease and Release to Rich. Bates & was ordered to be Recorded.

Silas Rolls acknowledged his Deed to Micajah Rice & ordered to be Recorded.

Ordered that the Minutes be Read & the Court adjourned till tomorrow morning 10 of the Clock.

Wm. Robison
Jesse Winborn
Thos. Obannon.

The Court met according to adjournment on Tuesday the 3rd Day of February 1789.

Present the Worshipfull Willm Robison)
                                Willm Dunbar   )
                                Thos. Obannon) Esqrs.
                                Thos. Knight   )

On the Application of William Weekley his Ordinary Licence was renewed.

On the application of Jas. Myrick his Ordinary Licence was renewed.

On the application of Jno. Gill his Ordinary Licence was renewed.

The Worshipfull Court confirmed the rates of Liquors for 1789 with the alteration of Continental Rum from 7d the Pint to 1/P Int.

Bowers & Ardis vs Newman & Homes. Judgmt Confest for 60 ℔ Sterl. & Interest from 8th Oct. 1787, Staying Execution 6 weeks.

The appraismt of Robt. Hankins Estate was returned & O. to be Recd.

Jno. Randall vs Jno. Reed & Jno. Glass/ on Motion of the

Plaintiffs Atty/ being a Clerical mistake Ordered that the name of Glass be altered to J̶n̶o̶ Goss

Jno. Parkinson, Foreman Grand Jury, Wm. Weekley, Jno. McKnight Johnson, Joseph Brooker, Bartho. Roberts, Robt. Bradley, Benj. Corbitt, Richd. Creech, George Robinson, Jun. Fras Bassett, Bartlett Brown, Sen., Wm. Carr, Isham Clayton, Saml. Way

Tarlton Brown, Esq. having produced a Commission from his Excellency, Thomas Pinkney, Esq., Governour & Com. in Chief for this State, as High Sheriff for this County Gave Bond & Qualified according to Law.

A̶r̶t̶h̶u̶r̶ J̶e̶n̶k̶i̶n̶s̶ / John Bates/ was offered as his Under Sheriff & approved by the Court & was Qualified accordingly.

Samuel Simms was appointed Constable & Qualified accordingly

The Appearance Docket was calld the first time.

Ordered that all the Defaulters on the Grand & Petit Jury be Sumd to appear at next Court & make their Excuses otherwise they will be fined.

The Grand Jury's Presentments.

The State vs Henry McMillan - Misdemeanor A True Bill.

Gill vs Wallace   )   A Negro named Primus, being taking
Bassett vs Wallace   )   in Execution the Property being
McLewrath vs Wallace)   claimed by Thos. Shields, Ordered
                           that the Cause by Tried tomorrow to
determine the Property.

Henry McMillan, Thos. Morris & Moses Diesto Acknowledged their Bonds for the appearance of Henry McMillan at the next Court to ans. an Indictment State vs Simon Yoan, Charge of Bastardy - discharged for want of the Oath & Warrant being Produced by the Justice.

Leah Brooker vs Jos. Brooker Trover - We of the Jury do find for the Defendt.
Wm. Tuten, Foreman, Elisha Abston, Reuben Roundtree, Henry Wood, Benj. Blunt, Wm. Adams, George Cope, Isham Jourdan, George Crossly,, Jno. Platt, Silas Rowls, Danl. Philpot.   Motion made for a new trial/ by the Plaintiffs Attorney/ & Granted.

The State vs Jno. Buford. Tresspass Indictment. A true Bill. Ordered that John Buford give Bond & Security for his Appearance at next Court to answer the sd. indictment. Wm. Robison, Esq. became his Security in the Sum of 25 ₤

Ordered the Traverse be tried to Morrow - Contd.

We the Grand Jury for the County of Winton do present Capt. Duncan for neglecting to open & not helping in Repair a Road laid out from Morris Ford on the Saltketcher over Toby's Swamp on the Information of Benj. Corbitt. Excused being Sick.

We recommend their Worships of the County of Winton to appoint new Overseers for the several Roads within this County as the Roads in general are in a bad State of Repair oweing as we apprehend to the want of Overseers being so appointed.

We present as a General grievance the want of doing Patrole duty in the Company commanded by Capt. John Weekly/ ordered to be summond to next Court/ and also of the want.

of the Vagrant Law put in force against certain persons living below the Runs comeing under that description on the Information of Doc Sunn, John Parkinson, Foreman, Bartlett Brown, Geo. Robison, Jun. Robt. Bradley, John McNight Johnson, Rich. Creech, Barth. Roberts, Fras. Bassett, Wm. Carr, Isham Clayton, Saml. Way, Benj. Corbitt, Willm. Weekley.

The Grand Jury were then discharged with the Thanks of the Court.

Joseph Duncan made his Excuse for not doing his duty as Overseer of the Road occasioned by sickness & was Excused.

Jno. Collins vs John Adam Neister Ruled to Special Bail Richd. Creech & Jno. Wickly entered as Special Bail.

Ordered that the Minutes be Read &/ the Court/ was adjourned till tomorrow morning 10 of the Clock.

      Wm. Robison,
      Wm. Dunbar
      John Wyld
      W. Buford

The Court met according to adjournment on Wednesday the 4th Day of February, 1789.

Present the Worshipful Willm. Robison)
          Willm. Dunbar) Esqrs.
          Willm. Buford)

On the application of John Fitts to have his Ordinary Licence renewed - Granted.

Ordered that the Estrays be Sold on Thursday.

By Virtue of a Certificate from Reuben Sanders Clerk of Johnson County in the State of North Carolina, with a Certificate annexed from his Excellency Saml. Johnson, Esq. Governour of North Carolina, the Last Will & Testament of Robert Lee was annexed thereunto & Ordered to be Recorded.

The State vs Geo. Davis - Discharged on Paying fees.

Leah Brooker vs Jos. Brooker Detinue - Continued

On Application from Henry Peoples for Judgmt against Elijah Gillett, Esq. the former High Sheriff, for not Settling the Execution Peoples vs James Montgomery. Ordered that Judgmt. be entered up against the sd. Sheriff for ₤ 7 15-0 & Costs.

110 Ordered that Administration of the Estate of Jno. Brown be Granted to Wm. Brown, Tarlton Brown & Robt. Stark, Sen. Bartlett Brown, Benj. Blunt & Absalom Best, Appraisers.

Ordered that Elijah Gillett, the late High Sheriff, do repay the several Person that paid him the Tax levied for Building the Public Buildings agreeable to their Receipts & the former Order by the Consent of the sd. Gillett be revolked.

On motion of Robt. Stark, plaintiffs Atty. Ordered that the property of Benjamin Brown, attached at the suit of Wm. Davis, Esq. be sold Agreeable to Law.

Wm. Williams vs Wm. Boyet Dismist at the Plaintiff's Cost.

Levi Febiger vs Jesse Griffin & Noah Tanner proved their Attendance 3 Days each. Ordered that the same be allowed.

By Consent of both Parties an amicable Suit is Entered Chas.

Jos. Duncan proved his Attendance 6 Days, Jas. Montgomery vs Turner for Deft.

29 Jno. McCarrol vs Bartlett Brown Judgment for Plaintiff ₤ 5 & Costs.

100 Green vs Creech - Contd at Plaintiffs Cost

101 Jno. McFail vs Wm. Turner. Judgment ₤ 3 & Costs.
Jury. Stephen Collins(1), Foreman, Wm. Dykes(2), Wm. Davis(3), Wm. Good(5), David Edenfield(5), Jno. Mitchell(6), Geo. Collins(7), Jno. Craddock(8), Joseph Duncan(9), Jno. Hardin(10), Jno. Redd(11), Jno. Green(12)

102 Henry Robertson vs Saml. Boyet - Dismist.

112 Rates for Liquors 1 altered to 1/P Pint for Continental Rum & Confirmed.

Ordered that Benj. Odom be appointed Overseer in the Room of Danl. Odom.

Way vs Alex & Reub Newman. Judgt for Plaintiff Conferd. Stay Exec. 6 Weeks P No. 2.

Ordered John Harrison be appointed Overseer in Room of Jno. Wickley & Make the Road good below the Mill of Doc. John Crocker & keep it in repair according to Law.

Ordered John Heyward for the upper part of the Road & Moses Collins for the /Lower/ be Overseer of the Road from the Bridge by M. Harley to the White Ponds.

William Buford   ) Referred to Isham Clayton, Henry
   vs   ) McMillan, Richd. Creech, Moses Disto,
Frederick Brant   ) with Powers of Umpriage.

William Buford,) Referred to the persons above with the
   vs   ) same Power & that the Return there
Jacob Cope   ) award to the next Court & their award
                 be a Judgment of the Court & their
award be under hand & Seal.

Gill & others vs Shields. Trial of Property. Verdict against the Deft. An appeal prayed & granted on giving Bond with Alex Newman & Absolom Causey Security in the Sum of Fifty Pounds to Prosecute the appeal with effect to pay all Costs & Damages in case the Judgment or verdict shall be confirmed.

The State vs Jno. Buford, & Jno. Cone the Prosecutor agreed to pay all the Cost which according to Jno. Beauford on the sd. Prosectuion.

Jno. Buford vs. Jno. Cone, Dismist at Defendants Costs.

Ordered that the Sheriff does not proceed to the Sale of the Land Attached,

Davis vs Brown if good & Sufficient Deeds & Titles are produced to him on or before the Day of Sale.

The Order being Read the Court was adjourned till tomorrow morning 10 of the Clock.
                        Wm. Robison
                        Thos. Knight
                        John Wyld.

Jones Brown vs Jno. Green, Esq. in Trover, for a Negro Edy & her Child Brutus, Damg. ₤ 50 to be tried next Term. Willm. Robison, Esq. Special Bail for the Defendt.

No. 12
Thos. Burton vs Wm. Davis - Judgmt P Award - Dismist
80 Jos. Montgomery vs Arthur Turner, Thos. Obannon,
              Dismist at Plaintiff's Cost
89 Adam McNeely vs Henry Cannon - Contd on Affidavit
91 Saml. Earl vs Danl/Shaw continued/ by Consent.
96 Leah Brooker vs Jon Brooker Trover Ruled new trial
                        next Court.

99 Jno. Green, Esq. vs Wm. Tutle - The Defent Prays a Jury Granted

The Jury being sworn to wit 1 Jas. Giddins, 2 Elisha Abston, 3 Reuben Roundtree, 4 Henry Wood, 5 Benj. Blunt, 6 Wm. Adams, 7 Geo. Cope, 8 Isham Jourdan, 9 Geo. Crossley, 10 Jno. Platt, 11 Silas Rolls, Foreman, 12 Danl. Philpot,

We find for the Defendant ₤ 3, 2-2 & Costs.

The State vs Jno. Buford for Hog Stealing on Traverse.
The Jury, to wit: Wm. Dykes(1), Wm. Davis(2), Wm. Goode(3), Wm. Causey(4), Wm. Tutle(5), David Edenfield(6), Jno. Mitchell(7), Chas. Matheny(8),, Hephen Collins(9),/Foreman/, Jno. Craddock(10), Rich. Creech(11), Abram Toney(12)

We of the Jury do say he is not Guilty. Dismist.

Ordered/that Absolom Causey be allowed 7 Days attendance Green vs Tuten.

111 On an interpleader
Thomas Shields & Sarah his Wife vs John Gill, Frances Bassett & Al the Jury being sworn to wit James Gedden, Elisha Abston, Reuben Roundtree, Henry Woods, Benj. Blunt, William Adams, George Cope, Isham Jordan, George Crossey, Jno. Platt, Silas Roles, and Daniel Philpot, returned a verdict. We find the Deed made by Josias Wallace to Sarah Wallace now Sarah Shields, a fraud.
Silas Rowls, Foreman

Wm. Robison
Wm. Buford
John Wyld

The Court met according to adjournment on Thursday the 5th Feby. 1789.
Present the Worshipful
William Robison)
William Buford)
Jno. Wyld) Esqrs.
Thomas Knight)
Thomas Obannon)

Ordered that John Fitts Tavern Licence be renewed.

Tarlton Brown, Thos. O'Bannon & Bartlett Brown acknowledged their Bond as High Sheriff & Security/ who were/ approved by the Court & ordered to be recorded.

Ordered that Wm. Causey be allowed 9 days Attendance Green vs Tutle, for Defts.

113 The Court met by adjournment on Firday the 6th February, 1789.
Present the Worshipfull   John Wyld)
Thomas Obannon) Esqrs.
Thomas Knight)

The Appearance Docket was called for the Last Time.

No. 1 Jno. Randall vs Jno. Redd. Contd. Renew vs Goss.

2 Ebenez Platt vs Danl. Shaw. Contd.
3. Wm. Womack vs Jno. Wych - Non suit.

4 Wm. Womack vs Henry Coker - Nonsuit
 5 James Robertson vs Jno. Watson. Nonsuit. Renew
 6 Levi Thower vs Jno. Wyche - Nonsuit.
 7 Adam McNeley vs William Creech
    Dismissed each paying his own Costs.
 8 Bartlett Brown, Jun. vs William Miner, Contd.
 9 Burel Harrison vs Frederick Sunn. Judgt. by Default
    Confessed for ₺ 3 0-0
10 Mical Odom and Wife vs Moses Disto & Absolom Cossey.
    Contd. Absolom Cossey made a party by consent.
11 Saml. Willison vs James French - Nonest renew
12 Robt. Montgomery vs Jno. Wickly - Contd.
13 Thos. Griffin vs Wm. Dunbar, Exors of George Golphin,
    vs Benj. Odom, Admr. of Mical Odom - Contd.
14 Andrew Rodgers vs John Craddock - Contd.
15 Benj. Harris vs Jno. Wyld, Contd. Jno. Wyche, Security
    for Cost.
16 Henry Furguson vs Alexander Newman, Dismist
17 Fedt. Sunn & Elijah Gillett vs Joseph Vince - Settled.
18 Delinquents - Settled by the Court.
19 Wm. Davis vs James Jones, - Dismist.
20 Wm. Davis vs Thos. Jones - Dismist
21 Geo. Miller vs Lott Loe, Judgmt by Default
22 Moses Disto vs Absolom Cook Non Est renew
23 Randolph Stoaker vs Saml. Buston, Non est.
24 Wm. Withorson vs Wm. Newman. Contd.
25 Jennett McKoy, vs Joseph Brooker. Dismist
114 26 Henry Hampton Esq. vs Henry Best, Judgt by Default.
27 Jacob Swicord vs John Wickly, Contd.
28 John Collins vs Jno. Adams Nestor - Contd.
30 Jno. Obannon vs John Prommunger - Contd.
31 Jno. Obannon vs Adam McNeley - Contd.
32 Peter DeRousee vs John Wyche, Contd.
32 Thomas Pulley vs Stephen Creech - Contd.
34 John Grimes vs William Newman - Contd.
35 Wm. Hancock vs Christopher Hall, dismissed
36 John Gill vs Manning Gore - Judgmt by Default.
    Judgment by the Court for ₺ 4 with Cost the property
    attached ordered to be Sold.

    The Court proceeded to call the Trial Dockett.

107 John Davis vs Richard Creech, Admor of Owen Williams
    Continued under Arbitration. Referred to Wm. Murray,
    Isham Clayton and others, their award to be returned to
    next Court & to become a judgment thereof.

113 Elijah & Eliza Gillett vs William David - Contd. under
    Arbitration.

116 John Mallett & Wife vs George Dykes - Continued.

120 Samuel Way vs Reuben & Alex Newman, Judgt confesd
    agreeable to Note Stay Ex. 6 weeks.

123 John Wickly vs Wm. Ashley, referred to the determination
    of Col. Davis, Contd.

122 Benj. Odom vs Wm. Ashley - Verdict for 10-17-6 Credit
    on the note to be allowed.

125 Thomas Long vs Henry Cannon - Settled at Defts Costs.

126 Peter Banner vs Henry Cannon - Settled at Defts Costs.

128 Wm. Davis vs Wm. Christie - Continued

130 David Chester vs James Fair - Contd.

131 The Same vs the Same - Contd.

132 John Wilshite vs James Fair - Contd.

133 George Robertson vs Wm. Griffin - Contd.

116 134 Benj. Odom vs James Fair - Admr. of Benj. Bird. Former judgment confirmed Land not Liable to execution by consent of parties

135 Nathaniel Walker vs Burr Harrison - Contd.

136 William Taylor vs James Fair - Continued

138 Joseph Dick vs Thomas /TPL/ Galphin. Dismissed at the Plaintiff's Costs.

139 Joseph Dick vs Thomas /TPL/ Galphin. Dismissed at Plaintiffs Costs.

140 Ardis & Bowers vs Newman & Holmes. Judgmt. Confessed for Ł 60 Ster & with interest from or on Oct. 1787, Staying Execution 6 weeks.

142 Moses Johnson vs John Redd & Job Redd. Verdict for five pounds eight Shillings and nine pence & Costs.

143 Absolom Causey vs John Fitts Dismissed at Plff's Costs except Deft's Attys fees.

144 Benj. Odom, Junr. Assignee of Jones vs Wm. Davis, Continued.

145 Wm. Davis vs John Wyld, Esq. Continued.

146 Sabert Odom vs Wm. Woodcock - Continued

149 Eleanor Welch vs Tooley French - Continued, under Arbitration with leave of Umpirage.

150 Thomas Crawford vs Wm. Carr. Settled at the Defendant's Cost except Plaintiff's Attorneys fees

153 Joseph Obannon vs Arthur Turner dismissed each party paying their own cost.

156 William Turner vs John Green referred to Walter Robertson & Joseph Harley with leave of Umpirage the award returned & judgment according to award.

157 John C. Smith vs Wm. Davis continued at the Plaintiff's cost.

116 158 Arthur Jenkins as gnee of C. Tilman vs Ezekiel Harding on Writ of Enquire. Judgment 19 ₤ 1 & Costs.

163 William Buford vs Frederick Brant repared to Isham Clayton & William Creech with leave of Umpirage.

164 William Buford vs Jacob Cope same order

166 William Hancock vs Christopher Hall Contd.

180 Chas. Wheeler vs Hezekiah Coleman - Contd. Attchmt.

183 Thos. Obannon vs Benj. Byrd - Contd Attachment.

170 Aron Smith vs John Weekly Judgment confessd, agreeable to note, subject to the instalment Law upon giving the legal security if required.

175 Sarah Davis, Benj. Odom, Sen. Ass & Batty. The Jury to wit Wm. Tuten, Foreman, Elisha Abston, Reub Roundtree, Henry Woods, Benj. Blunt, Benj. Blunt, Wm. Adams, Geo. Cope, Isham Jordan, George Crosley, Silas Rolls, Dal. Philpot
      1   2   3
      4   5   6   7
      8   9   10   11   12

We find for Plff 20/ & all Costs.

Jno. Mitchell appointed Constable in the Room of Joseph OBannon.

James Garner appointed Overseer /in/ the Room of Nathaniel Abney, Decd.

Joseph Brabham appointed Overseer / in the Room/ of Robt. Jordan, Dec'd.

Sarah Davis 9 Days/ Eliza Powell, Do 9 Powell Odom Plaintiff James Montgomery provd. Attendance 4 Days vs Bartlett Brown, Jun. vs Odom Plain & Liddia Collins 9 Days.

Thomas Obannon proved Attendance 4 Days Att Harrison vs Sunn & Copy.

Ordered the Minutes be read & the Court adjourned to the next Court in Course.
             John Wyld
             Thos. Knight
             Thos. Obannon

117 At a Court held for Winton County Monday the 4th Day of May, 1789 at the Plantation of James Mitchell on the Head of Cedar Branch.

           Present the Worshipfull
                        Richard Tradaway)
                        Thos. Knight   ) Esq.
                        Jesse Winburn   )

The Jury Box being produced a Girl in the Province of the Worshipful Court drew the following persons to Serve as Grand Jurors & Petitt Jurors for August Court, Viz.

Grand Jurors
John Cochran-Arthur Davis
Thos. Weathersby-Jno. Fitts
Wm. Creech-David Drennon
Isaac Boush-Jno. Green, blacksm
Saml. Way-Kenny Creech
Willm Cato-Willm Boyet
Moses Collins -Isham Clayton
Bartlett Brown-James Roberts
Alex Kennaday-Wm. Williams
George Robison, Sen.
Chas. Beck
Job Roundtree   21

Copy delivered High
Sheriff

Petit Jurors - James Brown
John Obannon - Joseph Redd
George Miller-John Miller
Garrat Buckaloo-James Joice
Rich. Creech-Nathen Powers
Jno. McCane-Danl. Philpot
Silas Rowls-Zach Griffin
Saml. Dennis-Burrell Parker
John Wyche - Isaac Deeson
James Davis - Willm Owens
Abra. Johnson-Chas. Nix
Josl. Bradham-Benj. Blunt
Fred Brant-Adam McNeeley
Absalom Best, Wm. Roberts
Wm. Tuten - Robert Adams
Joseph Vince - Danl. Odom
-31-

Order. That Hezekiah Davis, Joseph Lard & George Miller or any two of them Appraise the Estate of Jno. Mysser & make return.

Charles Stewart as Executor of Jno. Myssers Estate was Qualified by taking the Oath accordingly.

The Inventory & Appraisement of the Estate of Robt. Lee was returned & Ordered to be Recorded.

The acct. of Expences against the sd. Estate was produced in Court & allowed & ordered to be recorded ₺ 25 13-9

On the application of Zadock Woolley for Licence to keep Tavern Granted & Jesse Winburn Esq. became his Surity & Gave Bond accordingly.

118 Henry Wood acknowledged his Deed of Lease & Release to George Miller & Ordered to be recorded.

Tarlton Brown Esq. High Sheriff, Acknowledged his Deed to Jos. Obannon for 246 Acres & Ordered to be recorded.

Zadock Woolley is appointed Constable & took the Cash accordingly.

The Pettit Jury was called that were summoned for May Court & the following persons appeared.
    1   2   3   4   5
Edwd. Nix, John Cook, James Lee, Geo. Robison, Jacob Rivers
  6   7   8   9
Lionel Lee, Joseph Redd, George Kersh, Henry Creech,
  10   11   12   13
Richd. Vince, Wm. Ashley, Wm. Bryant, Robt. Lancaster,
  14   15   16   17
Jas. Matthews, Alex. Kenneday, Jno. Randall, Wm. Smith,
  18   19   21
Rich. Kirkland, Robt. Brown, Wm. Freeman.

Nathl. Walker as a Minister of the Gospell Excused.

Ordered that Joseph Harley & Thomas Shields be appointed to Examine, Settle & Make their report of the Acct of Willm

Browns/Expences as/Administrator of John Brown's Estate, against the said Estate -- Copy Dld.

A Lease & Release from Sampson Griffin & Mary his wife, to Mary Fryer for one hundred acres of Land being proved by the Oath of Jacob Foreman before Jesse Winburn, Esq. was produced in Court and ordered to be recorded.

A Deed of gift from Mary Fryer to John Fryer for sundry articles therein expressed was produced in Court and being acknowledged by the said Mary Fryer as her act. & deed Was ordered to be recorded.

The Last Will & Testament of William Everet was produced in Court and further proved in open Court, by the Oath of Jacob Brazel/and ordered to be recorded/Ordered that Commission issue directed to Isaac Bush, John Bush & Henry Dias, to appoint the estate on oaths and the appraisement so made to be by them returned to next Court.

The Settlement of John Brown's Estate was returned in Court and ordered to be recorded.

119   The Minutes of this day being read the Court adjourned till tomorrow, morning 9 O'Clock.   Richard Tradaway
Thos. Knight
Jesse Winbourn

The Worshipful Court met according to Adjournment on Tuesday the 5th Day of May 1789.

Present the Worshipful   Richard Tradaway)
Thomas Knight)
Jesse Winbourn) Esqrs.
Jno. C. Smith, Esq.)
John Wyld)

The List of the Petitt Jury that were discharged till 9 O the Clock this Morning being called, the following Persons appeared, Viz
    2   3   1   4
John Cook, James Lee, George Robison, Joseph Redd, Henry
    5   6   7   8
Creech, Richd. Vince, Willm Ashley, Willm Bryant, Willm.
    9   10   11
Smith, Richd. Kirkland, Robt. Brown & Willm Freeman

The State vs John Chavers on a Charge for Murder. Orderd that he be committed to Jail.

Ordered George Robison, Foreman.

John Mysers Bill of Sale being proved before Thos. Obannon, Esq. to Charles Stewart - Orderd to be recorded.

Solomon Owens acknowledged his Deed to George Kersh & ordered to be recorded.

The State   ) Indictment - The Jury being sworn to wit
     vs   ) John Cook, James Lee, Geo. Robertson,
Henry McMillan   ) Joseph Redd, Henry Creech, Richd. Vince,
                      William Ashley, Wm. Briant, Wm. Smith,
Richd. Kirkland, Robt Brown, Wm. Freeman
do say. We find the Defendant Guilty of Contempt.
                              Geo. Robertson, Foreman

Whereupon the Court considered that the said Henry McMillan pay a fine of one Shilling & Costs of Prosecution & be thereafter discharged.

120 Gill & others   ) Interpleader
         vs   ) Verdict February Seven against Defendant
     Thos. Shields   ) on which an appeal was prayed and the
                         proceedings not having been Carried up to
the last District Court and an Execution having in the interim been levied on the property of Defendant Ordered that the execution be suspended till the appeal be determined & that Thos. Shields, with Adam McNeeley & Jno. Pattison his Surities give Bond as the Law direct.

Ordered that a Road be opend from the Head fo the Horse Penn on the Road from Fort Moore to Rousers Ford to the Upper Three Runs from thence, the nearest & best way, to intersect the Charleston Road & that James Jackson be Overseer from / the Horse Penn to the Three Runs & John Cochran, Overseer from the Three Runs to Willm Ashleys & Wm. Ashley, Overseer from his house/ to intersect the Road to Charles Town   all the hands below/ Timms Branch & on the Branch & all the hands in Pindar Town & all below/ Tinkers Creek/ for two miles to Work on the Same & all the Hands on the lower Sides of Tinkers Creek except James Roberts, to Work on the Same Road

Davis vs Wyld. We find agreeable to our Opinion for each party to pay his own Cost & the suit to be dismist.

Willm. Brown, Garnishee Green vs Turner being sworn declares that he has no effects that he knows of the Property of the sd. Wm. Turner

Sarah Cathorn being Sworn declares that She has Ten shillings & four Pence in her Hands the Property of Wm. Turner to be paid in Home Spunn Cloth at 3/4 P Yard

The Minutes being read the Court adjourned till tomorrow Morning 9 of the Clock.
                              Richard Tradaway
                              Jesse Winborne
                              Thomas Knight

21 The Worshipful Court met according to Adjourment one
    Wednesday the 6th May 1789.
            Present the Worshipful Richard Tradaway)
                                    John Wyld   )
                                    Jesse Winbourn) Esqrs.
                                    Wm. Robison   )
                                    Jno. C. Smith   )

Ordered that John Young as Orphan be bound to Elijah Peters a Wheel Wright & Turner to be learnt his Trade &/ to be/

educated & Schooled 2 Years & treated as other Apprentices according to Custom & Law

15 Benj. Harris vs Jno. Wyld Judgmt confessd P Note Staying Execution 3 Months with Costs.

Leack Brooker vs Jos. Brooker.

40 The Jury being Sworn, Viz George Robison, Foreman.[1] Jno. Cook[2], James Lee[3], Rowland Williams[4], Henry Creech[5], Rich. Vince[6], William Bryant[8], Richd. Vince, Willim. Smith[9], Robt. Brown[10], Willm. Freeman[11], Rich Kirkland

We of the Jury do find for the Defend. Clear of all Costs Geo. Robison, Foreman.

Ordered that be a Rule of the Pleadings in this Court that where the Defendant produces no Evidence, the Deft. Attorney has the liberty of Concluding.

Sarah Southwell Executrix of Edwd Southwells Last Will & Testament, Came into Court & made Oath that the Last Will of Testament of Edward Southwell now produced in the Last Will & Testament of Edw Southwell Dec. was Ordered to be recorded & took the Oath of an Executrix accordingly.

Ordered that Reuben Golikely, James Myrick & Thoms Morris be appointed Appraisers of the said Estate & make their Report to next Court.

James Murphy, E. Gillett, Jos. Miller, Danl. Philpot, acknowledged their Bonds for the Administration of Jno. Newmans Estate.

On the Petition of the Inhabitants of this County complaining of the Main Road of this County bein impassable by reason of the over flowing of the Mill Dam of Doctor Crocker at Murcoucks branch/ Tis Ordered that the said old Main Road be opened & made passable by drawing off the Water, Or to make & keep in good repair a sufficient Bridge/below his mill/ at the Expence of the said Crocker or the future Proprietors of the said Mill & the above order/ to/ be imediatled put in Execution for the relief of the Petitions, &C

122 Ordered that the Sheriff take Doc. John Crocker into Custody for an Insult & Contempt of the Court.

Ordered that the Court be adjourned for one Hour.

The Court met again according to adjournment.

Ordered James C. Murphy appointed Administrator of all & Singular the Goods & Chattels, Rights & Credits of John Newman Deceased, in Stead of Stephen Smith, who is Dead, and others who have resigned.

Ordered that all the papers and documents in the hands of the dormer Administrator, be delivered to the present Administrator James C. Murphy, who has this Day given Bond & Security for the faithful discharge of his Duty as Administrator

    Copy delivered & Bond Taken.

Doc. John Crocker was ordered to be brought into Court to make his defence for Insulting & for Contempt of the Court, who made suitable confession & was dischargd out of Custody without costs.   Verdict for Plaintiff

87 Adam McNeeley vs Henry Cannon, for Ł 10 & Costs.
                      Geo. Robison, Forem.

91 Saml Earl vs Danl Shaw - Discontinued as Pf Cost.

97 Leah Brooker vs Jos. Brooker - Discontinued Plff Cost.

    Ordered that Joseph Miller, on returning a Certificate of the Citation of Thos. Castelows Estate, have Letters of Administration granted vs John Collins & John Wyche be Securitys and give Bond in Ł2000

100 Jno. Green vs Rich. Creech, a Jury /prayed by/ the Deft which was had accordingly at his Cost, verdict for the Plaintiff Ł & Costs.

The Minutes being read the Court was adjourned to tomorrow Morning 9 of the Clock.
                      Jno. C. Smith
                      Richard Tradaway
                      John Wyld

123 The Court met according to Adjournment on Thursday the 7th day of May, 1789.

    Present the Worshipful
                      Richard Tradaway)
                      John Wyld   )
                      Willm Buford   ) Esqrs.
                      Jno. C. Smith   )

The Jury being called the following persons Appeard viz
   1   2   3   4
George Robison, John Cooke, Richd. James Lee, Henry Creech
   5   6   7   8   9
Wm. Bryant, Wm. Bryant, Wm. Smith, Richd Vince, Wm. Freeman
  10   11   12
Robt. Brown, Wm. Ashley, Adam McNeeley

107 Jno. Davis vs Rich. Creech - Contd under Art & order renewed.

100 Elijah & Elisha Gillett vs Wm. Davis - Contd. Same order

116 John Mallett & Wife vs George Dykes - Discontd.

123 Jno. Wickly vs Wm. Ashley - Ord for Ashley renew the order for Art

128 Wm. Davis vs Wm. Christie - Contd. by Consent

130 David Chester vs James Fair - Contd.

131 The Same vs The Same - Same Order

132 John Wiltshire vs Jas. Fair. We of the Jury do find for the Plaintiff ₤ 50 /Geo Robison, Foreman/ Ordered for the property to be sold & Money returned to the next Court-Contd.

135 Nathl. Walker vs Burr Harrison - Contd. at Plaintiffs Cost.

136 Wm. Taylor vs Jas. Fair   Contd.

144 Benj. Odom vs Wm. Davis Verdict accordg to Note & Int./Installment/ G. Robison F__

145 Wm. Davis vs John Wyld, Esq. Verdict each man to pay his own Cost. George Robison __ Foreman __ Dismist.

George Crosslie & James Rousham proved a Deed of L. & Release from Charity Reed to Moses Plummer. Ordered to be recorded

Thomas P. Carnes, Attorney at Law, vs) A motion was Elijah Gillett, late High Sheriff   ) made by the Plaintiff in this Cause for a judgment against the Defendant for the sum of either pounds eleven Shillings and ine pence Sterling agreeable to the County Court Law on which judgment was given for the sum aforesaid & Cost against the Defendant, Subject to the following order.
Ordered that John P. Smith and John Wyld esquires be appointed Commissioners to examine all the accounts between the /late/High Sheriff the present defendant/& the Officers of the Court/ on or before the fifteenth day of June next and that the adjudication and determination of the said examiners be returned to the Clerk's office under their hands & seals.

133 Geo. Robison vs Wm. Griffin. Judgmt obtained for ₤ 6 & Cost at August Court ordered to be Dismist at Defendts Cost. Issue Execution.
146
124 Sabert Odom vs Wm. Woodcock Verdict for Plaintiff for ₤ 20 with Cost of Suit. Geo. Robison, Foreman.

149 Eleanor Welch vs Laurana French - Contd by Consent.

157 Jno. C. Smith, Esq. vs Wm. Davis referred to Jno. Lightfoot, Jno. Parkinson & Wm. Dunbarr, Esq. to be returned next Court.

163 Wm. Buford, Esq. vs Fred Brant. Award/returned/that the Deft pay all Costs.

164 The Same vs Jacob Cope The same Award

166 Wm. Hancock vs Chris Hall - Dismist at Plaintiff's Cost

57 Peter Carnes vs Peter Banner - Judgmt accord to Note.

Jno. Wyche Garnishee. Thos Morris vs Edwd Myles says he owes between fifteen & Twenty Pounds to Edwd Myles.

Wm. Hill Garnishee. Jno. Green vs Wm. Turner, being sworn says he owes in goods to the value of Five pounds nineteen Shills & the goods are ready.

Arthur Turner/Garnishee/ Jas. Montgomery vs Arthur Turner & Thos. Obannon - says he owes between Eight & Ten Pounds.

By the consent of Charles I. Brown & John Green it is directed that the Jury procede to try the right and title of a certain negro woman called Eady and her child Brutus and if the negroes be found to be the property of the said Brown, it is agreed that the said Green shall deliver up the negroes, and pay such damges as the Jury shall say the said Brown shall be entitled to for the time the said Green has had them in his possession.

177 Willm. Wilkanson vs Willm Newman Dismist at Plffffs Cost

180 Chas Wheeler vs Hezek Coleman - Contd. Property returned Sold for ₺7-9-1 Dismist

183 Thos. Obannon vs Byrd - Contd.

2 Ebenezer Platt vs Danl. Shaw - Dismist at Plaintiffs Cost

8 Bartlett Brown, Jun. vs Willm Minor - Verdict for the Plaintiff ₺ 42-10-0 & Cost George Robison, Foreman. On Motion of the Deft Attorney for a new Trial - Granted.

Ordered that the Treasurer pay Chas. Wheeler his Acct. for the State vs Jno. Chavers One pound Twelve & eight Pence.

10 Michl. Odom & Wife vs Moses Diesto & Absalom Causey. Abated.

12 Robt. Montgomery vs Jno. Wickly - Discontinued at Plaintiff's Cost - Renewed. NB to summons Evidences to the Bond.

13 Thos. Golphin & G vs Benj. Odom, Exec. - Contd.

14 Andrew Rogers vs Jno. Craddock - Dismist at Defts. Cost.

21 George Miller vs Lott Lowe - Dismisd at Defts Costs.

26 Henry Hampton vs Henry Best - Contd under Arbitration.

28 Jno. Collins vs Jno. Adam Neisler - Judgmt P. Notes accord. to Installmt.

125 The Minutes being read the Court was adjourned till tomorrow 9 of the Clock
       John Wyld
       Richd. Tradaway
       Jno. C. Smith

The Court met according to adjournment on Friday, the 18th

Day of May, 1789.   Richd. Tradaway)
Present the Worshipful   Jno. C. Smith   ) Esqrs.
                           Jno. Wyld   )

Jacob Harley Esq. produced in open Court
his Commission as Coroner &
Proposed aaron Smith, Esq. William Pulley Security were
proved of & was qualified accordingly
**Note above stricken

Joseph Harley, Esq. appointed Coroner for this County produced his Commission in Open Court Signed by his Excellency the Governor of this State and offered Aaron Smith and Elijah Gillett, Esquires as his Security, who were approved of by the Court. Ordered that they together with the Coroner give the Bond and security required by Law, for fifteen hundred pounds Sterling, for the due performance of his duty, and/that the Coroner qualify as the Law directs, which was done accordingly.

The Jury being Called and Appeared except Rich. Vince who was fined fifteen Shillings for neglect of Duty.
         1   2   3   4
George Robison, John Cook, James Lee, Henry Creech, Wm.
   5   6   7   8   9
Bryant, Wm. Smith, Sabert Oodom, Wm. Freeman, Danl. Odom
   10   11   12
Wm. Ashley, Adam McNeely, John Collins - Jurors

24 Wm. Wilkinson vs Wm. Newman - Dismist - Plffs Cost

27 Jacob Swicord vs Jno. Wickly Contd at Defendt Cost & ruled to Trial next Court.

30 John Obannon vs Jno. Tronmonger - Contd.

31 Jno Obannon vs Adam McNeeley - Dismist at Plaintiffs Cost

32 Peter DeRoussee vs Jno. Wych. Judgmnt confessd under Installment.

33 Thos. Pulley vs Henry Creech - Dismist Deft Cost a Juror withdrawn.

34 Jno. Grymes vs Wm. Newman - Judgment Bond Ł 17-0-0 & Costs

35 Jno. Randall vs Redd & Goss - Dismist at Plffs Cost

Appearance Docket called for the last Time.

The Jury was Discharged and thanked for their Diligence.

126 37 Wm. Minor vs Wm. Brown - Contd at Pv Cost with Liberty of Jas. Browns' deposition being taken before a Justice & read as Evidence given legal Notice.

38 Thoms. Lamar vs Jno Randal - Abated

42 Chas. Jones Brown vs Jno. Green - Contd. to O. V. to apppoint G. Walker, Atty

Bartlett Brown, Jun. vs Wm. Minor - DePo to Georgia to Examine Geo. Spencer, Justice Schiver, Maj. Sheek, for Deft giving legal notice of Time & Place.

43 State vs Jno Wickly - Contd.

44 Jno. Grimes vs David Gavin - Dismist, renew vs Wm. Newman

45 James Rainey vs Jno. Wickly, Contd.

46 Wm. Willis vs Danl. Shaw - Contd.

47 Alex. Newman vs Samson Griffin - Judgmt by Default Contd.

48 Wm. Williamson vs John Bates - Contd.

49 George Davis vs Benj. Odom - Contd.

50 James Montgomery vs Arthur Turner & Thos. Obannon - Contd.

51 John Wych vs Wm. Robertson & Lark Robertson - Contd.

52 Laurana French vs Thomas Night - Contd.

53 Isham Clayton vs Henry Woods - Contd.

54 David Campbell vs John Wyche - Contd.

55 Peter Carnes vs John Cone - Contd.

56 Peter Carnes vs Robt. Nixon Settled at Deft's /Costs/

57 Peter Carnes vs Peter Banner - judgmt according to Note.

58 Mary Rivers vs Elizth. Gillett - Contd.

59 Winniford Arnand - Contd - vs Joseph Brooker.

60 John Fitts vs Charles Garburrow - Judgmt by Default - Contd.

61 Mary Blunt vs Sabert Odom - Contd.

62 Wm. Downs vs Elijah Gillett - Judgmt confessd for Debt & Cost Installment.

63 Richd. Jackson vs John Welsh - judgmt by default

69 John Croker vs Nath. Twining Attachmt. The Attachment Bond appearing to be Illegal Orderd to be Dismist

70 Samuel Jones vs John Randal - Contd.

71 Robt. S. Miners vs William Ashley - Judgmt by Default.

Ordered that Richd Tradaway be allowed 4 Days attendance Jno. Randall vs Jno. Redd & Elijah Tradaway be allowed 4 Days attendance in the same on the Acct of the Defendt. Order delivered being proved legally.

Isaach Bush, Jno Bush & Ezeh Williams /appointed/Appraisers of Thos. Castelow Estate.

72 Robt. A Mayes vs Pricilla McClennon & Robt. Mayes - judgment by default.

73 Jno. Goss vs Thomas Procter discontinued.

74 Thos. Dobbins vs Muccleroyth - Contd.

75 The Same vs Att Thos. Nixon - Contd.

Jno Wyld vs Wm. Gilbert, Order for the Attached Property to be Sold

Ordered that John Bates pay Jas. Montgomery 5 Days attendance advs Willm Williamson at 2/6 P Day.

The Minutes being Read the Court then adjourned until the Court in Course.
       Richard Tradaway
       Jno. C. Smith
       John Wyld.

127 At a Court held for Winton County at the Court House on Cedar Branch on Monday the 3rd Day of August, 1789, Present the Worshipfull
      Richard Tradaway)
      Jesse Winburn)
      Thomas Obannon)
      Daniel Green) Esqrs.
      Willm. Sisson)
      John Wyld   )

The Jury Box being produced a Boy of about 12 Years of Age drew the following persons to Serve as Pettit Jurors for Novem. Court. George Kersh, Benj. Crocket, John Griffin, Isham Jourdan, Daniel Howell, James Jackson, John Williams, Richard Blaoch, John Snealing, William Davis, Micajah Matthews, Jacob Harley, Joseph Turner, Arthur Jenkins, James Brown, James Simms, Michael Swicord, Sampson Griffin, Willm. Adams, Alex. Newman, C. Ned.

The List of Grand Jurors Sum to appear this Court.
  1   2   3   4
Arthur Davis, Thos. Weathersby, Jno. Fitts, Wm. Creech,
  5   6   7   8
David Drennon, Geo. Robison, John Green, Saml. Way, Wm.
  9   10   11   12
Boyet, Moses Collins, Isham Clayton, Bartlett Brown, Alex
  13   14
Kennaday, Job Roundtree, George Robison, Forem./James Roberts

The Grand Jury being Sworn were discharged till toMorrow 9 O the Clock.

Thomas Wyld offered the Worshipful Court, the Use of his House to hold Court in until they could conveniently build one & the Offer was accepted.

A Proclamation Signed by his Excellency Charles Pinkney

esqr. Governor of this State Commanding all executive and Judicial Officers to take an Oath prescribed by the Congress of the United States to an Act of that body passed in Congress on the first day of June 1789, was produced in Court when Richard Tradaway, Jesse Winburn, Thomas Obannon, Daniel Green, William Sisson & John Wyld/ esquires, Magistrates.

Thomas Wyld, Deputy Clerk, Thomas P. Carnes, Esq. County Attorney, Peter Carnes, George Walker & Robt. Stark, practicing Attornies in the Court, Tarlton Brown, Esq. high Sheriff & John Bates, Deputy Sheriff in open Court took the oath pointed out in the above mentioned Act of Congress

The Pettit Jury being Sworn, Viz - John Obannon [1] Geo. Miller [2], James Joice [3], Richd. Creech [4], Danl Philpot [5], Burrell Parker [6], Jno. Wyche [7], Joseph Brabham [8], Benj. Blunt [9], Fred Brant [10], Absolom Best [11], Wm. Roberts [12], Robert Adams [13], Jos. Vince [14], Danl. Odom [15], Silas Rawls [16].

Orderd they be discharged till to Morrow Morning 9 O the Clock.

Orderd that Rich Vince Excuse be admitted his Fine be remitted

The Inventory & Appraisement of the Estate of Willm. Everet being returned was orderd to be recorded.

128   The Citation of Patience Anthony being Returned - Orderd that Letters of Administration be Granted and that John Wyche & Thomas Obannon give Bond & Security in Ł 500 John Wyche, Isaac Bush & John Bush, Appraisers.

The acct. of the Sale of the Estate of Isaac Odom, Dec'd./OC/& of Debts paid by the Adm. was returned & order to be recorded.

The Last Will of Wm. Hicks was provd by the Oaths of John Snead & Anthony Leach two of the Witnesses & orderd to be Recorded & that Letters Testament & probat be granted to Wilmot Hicks & Armstead Hicks & that John Snead, Jacob Adams & Shadrack Adkins be appointed Appraisers

Chas. Stewart acknowledged his Deed of L & Release to Joseph Lard and orderd to be recorded Qualified.

John Bush & Jno Miller returnd Citation on Edmd Bentleys Estate.
Orderd that Letters of Adminis. be granted & that he Give Bond & Security.
Isaac Boush & Jno. Wyche Bond for Ł500 & that Henry Deas, Isaac Bush & John Wyche be appointed Appraisers Qualified.

On the Motion of P. Carnes Attorney for the Deft. Orderd that Leave be given till the next Court for legal

proofs /to/ be made to establish the Titles of the Land.
    O. that Eliza Chirman has Liberty to keep Tavern on giving Bond & Security according to Law for one Year.
    The Orders being read the Court was adjourned till to Morrow Morning 9 of the Clock.
                                    Richard Tradaway
                                    Wm. Sisson
                                    Jesse Winborne

The Worshipful Court met according to adjournment on Tuesday the 4th Day of August 1789.

	Danl. Green)
	Richd. Tradaway)
Present the Worshipfull	Jesse Winbourn)
	Wm. Sisson)
	John Wyld)
	Thos. Obannon)
	Wm. Dunbar)

    The last Will & Testament of Thos. Philpot was provd. by the Oath of Wm. Willm Vince one of the Witnesses, who also Swore that he saw Thos. Galphin & Thomas Newman Sign the Same as Witnesses & Orderd to be recorded. John McLehany was Qualified by taking the Oath as an Executor.
    Orders that Letters Testamentary Want. of Appraismt be Granted to the said Executors.
    Orderd that Alex Newman, Isaac Bush & Henry Cocker be appointed Appraisers
    Willm. Cochran acknowledged his deed to Moses Richison Ordered to be rec.
    Orderd that Thos. Weathersby be appointed Overseer in the Room of Elkanah Green.
    Ordered that James Roberts be appointed Overseer in the Room of Chas. Wheeler.

129   Ordered that a Road be opened from the Court House at the head of Cedar branch to Morris Ford from thence to intersect the nearest & best way to the Charles Town road & that Thos. Morris be Overseer from the Court House to Morris's Ford & Sabard Odom from the Ford to the sd Charles Town road in the room of Joseph Collins and that the adjacent hands work on the said road.

    Ordered that in all Causes, New Subpoenas be issued to each succeed/ing/Court.

    Ordered that James Mitchells Licence to keep Tavern be renewed.

No. 8 Bartlett Brown Junr. vs Willm. Minor. The Jury being Sworn Viz
      1   2   3   4
John Obannon, James Joice, Richd. Creech, Danl. Philpot,
      5   6   7   8
John Wyche, Joseph Brabham, Benj. Blunt, Fred Brant,
      9   10   11   12
Wm. Roberts, Robt. Adams, Joseph Vince, Burrell Parker.

    The Jury being Sworn do Say. We do find for the Defendant that he has paid the Plank & the Plaintiff should pay all Costs, John Wyche, Foreman.

Willm. Boyet made oath that he saw Edmd. Bentley Sign, Seal & deliver a Bill of Sale for a Negro Wench/to Wm. Green/ & also that he saw Josias Boyett Sign the same as a Witness with him Self & Ordered to be recorded.

The State vs Thos. Grayham, Abner Glover & Peter Graham. Orderd that a Bench Warnt. be imediately issued to apprehend the /Defendt &/ bring the   to Justice.

Willm. Dunbar, Esq. Acknowledged his Deed to Jacob Blount O. to be record.

Daniel Philpot allowed 6 Days Brown vs Minor be Defendt.

David Shelley allowed 2 Days Attendance for Deft.

Jos. Tuten allowed 2 Days Attendance for Deft.

The Court was Adjourned for an Hour

The Court met according to Adjournment.

Arthur Davis being sick was discharged from Serving as a Grand Juryman.

Isaac Sterling acknowledged his Deed of Gift to Rebecca Davis O. to be record.

The State vs Simon Yonn & Lettice Chavers for Bastardy. The Deft. Sim. Yonn came into Court & Confesd to the Fact, whereon the Court found them ℔ 5 each Procl. money. Yonn undertook to pay the whole & give Security for the Maintenance of the Child whereupon Simon Yonn, Willm Yonn & Wm. Morris acknowledged themselves bound in the Sum of Twenty Five pounds each for the Maintenance of the sd. Child, bond given.

Orderd that Citation be granted to Rich. King on the Estate of Milley King.

Simon Yon paid his Fine & fees Ordered that the Sheriff deliver the Horse of Wm. Minor which was executed at the Suit of Bartlett Brown and that the said execution be set aside.

John Wyld Esq. acknowledged a Deed of Conveyance to Wm. Thompson Ordered to be recorded.

The Orders being read the Court adjourned until tomorrow nine o"clock.
                        John Wyld
                        Wm. Sisson
                        Jesse Winborn

130 The Worshipful Court met according to adjournment Wednesday 5th Aug. 1789.
    Present the Worshipful   Richard Tradaway
                             John Wyld
                             Willm Sisson   Thos. Obannon
                             Willm Dunbar   Jno C. Smith
                             Danl. Green
                             Jesse Winborn   Esqrs.

John Mitchell acknowledged his Deed of Gift for Two Acres of Land for the Public Buildings to be erected on O. to be recorded.

Thomas Wyld acknowledged his Deed of Gift for one Acre of Land for the Public Buildings to be erected on Ordered to be recorded.

Jenkins & Buford vs Obannon - Dismist at Defends Cost. 82

John Davis vs Richd. Creech - reference Continued. 107

113 Elijah & Eliza Gillett vs Wm. Davis. The Jury being Sworn to Wit, John Obannon.

Joseph Vince, James Joice, Richd. Creech, Danl. Philpot, Burrell Parker, John Wyche, Jos. Brabham, Benj. Blunt, Fred Brant, Wm. Roberts, Robt. Adams, do say. We of the Jury do find for the Plaintiff Ł 18-4-8 with Cost of Suit/ under Instalment/ John Wyche, Foreman.

The Grand Jury recd the thanks of the Court for their Diligence & were Discharged.

Jno/Dunbar/Caraway Smith - Magistrates & Aaron Smith Clerk of the Court, took the Oaths according to the Act of Congress.

135 Nathl. Walker vs Burr Harrison Attachmt. Dismist the Bond not being lodged in Office.

123 John Wickly vs Wm. Ashley - Contd. Order for reference renewed.

128 Wm. Davis vs Wm. Christie   Nonsuit

130 David Chester vs Jas. Fair Dismist at Defend Costs.

131 David Chester vs Jas. Fair Dismist at Defendts Costs.

132 John Wiltshie vs Jas. Fair - Settled & Dismist

149 Eleanor Welch vs Laurana French. Dismist at Plaintiffs Cost

136 Wm. Taylor vs Jas. Fair. Judgment for Debts & Cost

157 Jno. C. Smith vs Wm. Davis Contd. under Arbitration

183 Thoms. Obannon vs Benj. Byrd Ł 2-19-0 & Costs. Judgmt with Interest.

The Court adjourned for one Hour

The Court met according to Adjournment when the Minutes being Read the Court was adjourned till to Morrow Morning 9 o' the Clock.
      John Wyld
      John C. Smith
      Wm. Sisson

The Worshipful Court met according to Adjournment Thursday 6th Aug. 1789.

Present the Worshipful   John C. Smith   )
                         John Wyld   )
                         Willm Sisson   )
                         Thomas. Obannon)

Ordered that /on/ the Road leading from Cambridge to Charles Town, That John Snead be appointed Overseer from the District Post to the Rocky Spring; that all the Male Inhabitants from the District Line to South Edisto including Benj. Kirkland, thence down the river to the Rocky Springs Work on the same. That Armstead Hicks be Overseer from the Rocky Springs to Hoomes Camp. That all the Male Inhabitants from the Rocky Springs down Edisto to Hoomes Camp do work on the same under Armstead Hicks.

13 Golphin &C vs Benj. Odom, Jun. Contd.

30 Jno. Obannon vs Jno. Tronmonger - Contd.

26 Henry Hampton vs Henry Best - Contd.

27 Swicord vs Christie - Attacht. Levied in the Hands of John Wickly who has given a replevin Bond he claiming the Property as Administrator of Josiah Murdock Decd. Ordered that the right of Property in the Negroes be tried by the Jury - Executions by the Attorney for Christie 1st-That no Replevin bond appears in the Clerks Office 2d. No replevin lies in this Case The Court Overrruled these objections, it appearing by the Oath of Colo. Wm. Davis that such Bond was given to the Sheriff, to which he was security & Ordered that the Parties go to Trial on the General issues. The Jury being Sworn to wit, Joseph Harley, Rich. Creech, James Joice, Daniel Philpot, Burrel Parker, John Wyche, Jas. Brabham, Benj. Blunt, Fred Brank, Absalom Best, Wm. Roberts, Danl. Odom, do say We find for the Defendant Christie, the Negroes/mentioned in the Declaration to be his property & the Plaintiff to pay costs of Suit. John Wyche, Foreman.

37 Willm. Minor vs Willm. Brown - Judgt for One Pound five Shillings & Two Pence & Costs.

Andrew Nimmons took the Oath of Under Sheriff & also the Oath according to Congress.

Ordered the Estrays to be Sold to Morrow 4 O'Clock.

The Order being read, The Court was adjourned till to Morrow morning 9 0 the Clock.
                         Wm. Sisson
                         John Wyld
                         Thos. Obannon

132 The Worshipful Court met according to adjournment Friday the 7th August 1789.
    Presdent the Worshipful   John Wyld   )
                              Willm Sisson   )
                              Thos. Obannon   ) Esqrs.
                              Willm. Robison   )

Willm. Robison, Esqr. a Magist took the Oath required by Act of Congress.

42 Charles J. Brown vs John Green. The Jury being Sworn to Wit, Richd. Creech, James Joice, Burrel Parker, John Wyche, James Brabham, Benj. Blunt, Fredk. Brank, Wm. Roberts, Danl. Odom, James Geddins, Willm. Wickly, George Collins, Do Say: We find for the Plaintiff Chas. Brown, that the Defendant John Green shall return the negroes with three pounds damage & Cost of Suit. John Wyche, Foreman.

The State vs Robt Mays. Indict for Assault Jos. Harley vs Jno. Fitts Came into Court & acknowledged themselves Security in the Sums of ₤ 25 each for the Appearance Jas. Gregs & Jas. Montgomery to appear at next Court to give Evidence in behalf of the state vs Robt. Mays on the above Indictmnt.

The State vs Thos. Knight, Esq. Jos. Harley came into Court & acknowledged himself security in the above sum for the appearance Isham Clayton as Witness, in behalf of the State on the above Indictmt Ord. Capias issue against the Avoce Defts.

The State vs Thos. Graham Abner & Peter Graham, Judgmt. Jos. Harley the Same for Ishal Clayton as a Witness for the State A Bench Warrt vs Defendt.

The State vs John Dixon, Indictmt. Asst & Batty. Richd. Jackson Security for Thos. Dobbins appearance as a Witness on the Indictment, on the Like penalty of ₤ 25

Lurana French vs Thos. Knight, Esq. Judgmnt ₤ 10 & Cost 52

James /Rainey/ vs John Wickly - Judgmet by Default.   45

47 Alex Newman vs Sampson Griffin - Dismist at Defendats Cost.

48 William Wilkinson vs Jno. Bates - Nonsuit

49 Geo. Davis vs Benj. Odom, Sen. Judgmnt each man pay his own Cost. Jno Wyche, Foreman

Ordered. Reuben Golikely Attendance 11 Days. Brown vs Green
    James Harley   Do - 10 Days   Ditto
    Jas. Geddins, Do - 5 Days   Ditto
    Danl. Odom,   Do - 9 Days - Chrisrie vs Wikley
    Geo. Collins Do - 5 Days - Brown vs Green

53 Isham Clayton vs Henry Wood - Contd.

54 Duncan Campbell vs Jno. Wyche - Contd.

55 Peter Carnes vs Jno. Cone Dismist Defts Cost Judgmnt. ₤ 1-1-19 the ballance due

62 Mary Rivers vs Elijah Gillett Judgmt Confesd 3 Months

46 William Wilson vs Danl Shaw - Contd

The State vs John Bates Indict for Trespass Wm. Robison, Esq. enterd himself Security for his Appearance next Court.

Ned Shipes & Teagle Myles Witnesses for the State & Wm. Myles, their Security.

The Presentment of the Grand Jury were Recd. Ordered to be filed & taken up next Court, the Orders to be issued & filled up by the Clerk, necessary to the next Court.

133 Ordered that/ all the Causes now on the issue & / the Appearance Docket be continued over & Stand as at issue next Court. The Minutes being Read the Court was adjourned to the next Court in Course.
        John Wyld
        Thos. Obannon
        Wm. Sisson

Appearance Docket entered agreeable to the above Order.

76   John C. Smith Esq. vs Nathl. Twining - Contd.

77   Thos. Morris vs Edwd Myles - Contd.

2   Ebenez. S. Platt vs Danl. Shaw - N E to be returned

5   James Robertson vs Jno. Watson - Contd.

11   Saml. Willison vs James Frank - Judgmt Confsd with Interest, Staying Execution 3 Months.

12   Robt. Montgomery vs John Wickly - Contd.

44   Jno. Grimes vs Wm. Newman - NE Dismiss

78   Willm Hardin vs Allen Williams; Exor - Contd.

79   James Jackson, Admr. vs Thos. Philpot - Abates by Death renew against the Ext. Thos. Philpot.

30   Idem vs Idem - Abates by Death renew vs the Exct.

81   Thos. Wyld vs Elijah Gillett, The Defendant making suitable acknowledgements to the satisfaction of the Plaintiff, agreed that the suit be dismist at Defendant Cost.

82   Beaufort & Jenkins vs Thos. Obannon, Esq. Dismist at Defendants Cost.

83   Tarlton Brown, Esq. vs Wm. Newman. Dismist by return NE

84   Id vs Chas. Yarbrough - Dismist by return NE

85   Id - vs Robt. McLewrath - Dismist.

87   Benj. Odom, Jun. vs Jno. C. Smith, Contd.

88   Judith Corbat vs Thos. Moore - Contd.

89   Richd. Vince vs Willm Sisson - Contd.

90 Lark Robison vs Wyche & Tanner - Contd.

91 James Brabham vs James Simms - Contd.

92 Robt. Stark vs James Fransh - Contd. by Const.

93 John Parkinson vs Geo. Robison - Contd.

94 Id vs Alex. Newman Crackr Neck - Contd.

95 John Fields vs Anth Bourdeaux - Contd.

96 Nathl. Walker vs Absolom Tyler - Dismist by consent at equal Cost.

97 Fred Sunn vs Edwd. Myles - Contd.

98 Wm. Little vs Jno. & Mary Davis - NE - to be renewed by order Wm. Green

99 John Mooney vs Jonathan Clark - Dismist being Settled.

100 Joseph Duncan vs Edwd Myles. Dismist at Defendts Cost.

101 Willm Shields vs Purl Johnson - Contd.

102 Solom Owens vs Benj. Allen, Contd.

103 Simeon Taylor vs Thoms. Shields - Contd. by Consent.

104 Joseph Solomon vs David Shipes - Contd.

105 Id. vs Arthur Jenkins - Contd.

106 Malachy Powell vs Thoms. Burton NE to be renewed.

107 John Parkinson vs George Crosley - Dismist at Defendants Cost.

134 John C. Smith vs John Crecher Came too late to be renewed

109 Barbara Grimer vs John Clayton - Contd.

110 Willm Myles vs The Execu/of/ James D Roache - Contd.

111 James Cook vs Andw. Walker - Contd.

112 John Wyld Appett. advs Nichs. Nobles Respond. an Appeal from a Justice - Contd.

113 Benj. Odom, Appellt. advs Jno. Randal Respondt. Appeal Id. Judgmt reversed.

Issue Docket enterd agreable to the above Order

50 James Montgomery vs Arthur Turner & Thos. Obannon - Cont

51 John Wyche vs Willm Robison, Esq. Contd.

64 Winif. Arnand vs Jos. Brooker - Contd.

65 John Fitts vs Chas. Yarbrough - Contd.

66 Marg. Blount vs Sabart Odom - Contd.

68 Richd. Jackson vs John Welch Dismist at Plaintiffs Costs

70 Saml Jones vs John Randall - Contd.

71 Roberts & Mayers vs Willm Ashley - Contd.

72 Roberts & Mayers vs Priscilla Mclinton & Robt. Maise, Contd.

74 Thoms. Dobbins vs Robt. McLewrath - Contd.

75 Thos. Dobbins vs Jno. Nixon - Contd.

The Presentments of the Grant Jury

We, the Grand Jurors for the County of Winton do/represent/ as a Grievance that the Road from the Run Bridge to Capt. John Fitts, by order of this Court. & to intersect the Charleston Road to Woolmers old Place in Beaufort District, we presume is much out of repair & as this Worshipful Court, was pleas'd to order a new Road to laid out by Wm. Weekley, Joseph Brooker & Solomon Owens from the Lower Runs Bridge to Woolmers Place, & to be viewed by Willm Roberts, Rich. Creech and Arthur Jenkins to view the said Road on Oath, in order to determine for the greatest convenience which was neglected, We request that order to be renewed and inforced.
Geo. Robison, Foreman.

We also /re/presnet as a grate grievance to the Publick, that the Main Road from augusta to Matthews Bluff on Savannah River is unpassable at Doctor John Crockers Mill, by reason of his raising the Water at his Mill Dam.
Geo. Robison, Foreman

We, as Grand Jurors for the County of Winton do unanimously say and agree that the Road leading down Savannah River to Matthews Bluff/where/ the said Road Intersects the Mill Pond is rendered unpassable to the great prejudice of the public who shall at a certain distance above the flowing of the said Mill Dam mark & lay off, out of the old Road, one other Road to intersect the old road below, and that the said markt out Road to be cut and cleard out by and at the Expence of the said John Crocker imediately for the benefit of the Publick.
Geo. Robison, Foreman

135 John Wyld, Elijah Gillett, Absalom Best & John Weckly or any three of them, are appointed to lay out & mark off the said Road, the nearest, best & most convenient Way & see that the same is cleard imediately, for the relief of the Petitioners & the Publick.

We also represent that the Road Orderd by this Worshipful Court from the Widow Williams Ford on great Saltketcher to intersect the little Saltketcher at the old Savannah Ford is much out of repair for want of Overseers.
George Robison, Foreman

Agreeable to the former Order the Court was adjourned to the next Court in Course.

The Court met according to adjournment on Monday the 2nd
Day of November 1789.

Present the worshipful
William Sisson   )
Daniel Green   )
Thomas Night &   )   Esquires
Jesse Winbourn   )

The Jury box was produced and the following persons
drawn to serve on the Public jury at the next Court.

1	Joseph Obannon	11	Blanchard Cowlins
2	John Byles	12	Elijah Alsten
3	Robt. Bradley	13	Robert Jordan
4	Robt. Adams	14	Adam Lark
5	George Coopee	15	Thomas Owings
6	Jacob River	16	Newton Dunn
7	Joseph Geeter	17	Ephraim Herington
8	Zacariah Williams	18	Charles Boyles
9	Jacob Roundtree	19	Joseph Red
10	William Vince	20	John Randal
24	Thos. Shields	21	Levi Johnson
25	William Jones	22	Bartholomew Johnson
26	Mathew Cole	23	John Newman - So
27	John Mires		
28	Saml Sims		
29	Rowley Williams		
30	Anthony Leach		

The following persons were drawn for a Grand Jury to
serve at the next Court.

1	John Bush	11	Joshua Smith
2	Peter DeRousee	12	David Jackson
3	Thos. Morris	13	William Bryant
4	James Geddins	14	John Herington
5	Robt. Lancaster	15	Benjmain Corbett
6	Wm. Price	16	Henry Roberson
7	Joseph Duncan	17	Jacob Adams
8	Parbuck MeElmurry	18	John Tarber
9	Parlevint Johnson	19	Edwd Weeks
10	John Joice	20	David Shipes

136 The Pettit Jury who were called to serve at this Court
being called the following persons appeared.

GeorgeKersh 1, Isham Jordan 2, James Jackson 3, Jno.
Williams 4, Richd. Boyles 5, John Snelling 6, Wm. Davis 7,
Micajah Matthews 8, Arthur Jenkins 9, James Simms 10,
Michl. Swicord 11, Sampson Griffin 12.

                            Arthur Jenkins, Foreman

30. John Obannon vs)
           vs   ) Dismist at Defts Costs
     John Ironmonger)

Charles Stewart Acct. (as Exor of John Myers) for Expences
for the said Estate was allowed & Ordered to be recorded.

Thos. Knight, Esq. Took the Oath appointed by Congress in open Court.

Chris. Hicks Inventory and appraisement of Estate ord to be recorded.

Lark Robison   )
   vs   ) Michael Swicord Security for
John Wyche J. Tanner)   Cost Contd.

William Hardin   ) Security for cost being demanded because
   vs   ) the Plaintiff resides out of the State.
Allen Williams   ) J. P. Mitchell acknowledged himself Sec. for Costs. - Contd.

    A writing was produced in Court and proved by the Oath of Robt. Adams & Job Darrington to be the Last Will of John Turner, Decd. Ordered to be recorded.

    Ordered that Letters Testamentary be granted/ on the same/ to Robt Adams/ & that Henry Corcher and Amos Way, Jno Darrington be appraisers.

Chas. Stewart acknowledged his Deed to Jno. Stewart O to be Recorded.

Edmunt Bentleys Appraiser's produced the appraisement of his Estate ord. to /be recorded/ John Wyche and Isaac Bush who were appointed to adjust the accts. of Edmund Bentley with the orphans of Joseph Johnson report that the find the said Bentley indebted to the said Orphans the sum of fifty six pounds five shillings & three pence Orderd to be recorded

    The last Will and Testament of James Collins was proved in Court & proved by the oath of Danl. Odom, Junr. Danl. Odom, Geo. Collins, Benj. Odom & Jos. Duncan, or any three of them, appointed appraisers & ordered to be record

137 Levin Collins and James Collins, Exor of the Last Will and testament of James Collins took the oath of an Executor.

Order that Letters Testamentary Probatt & be Granted.

Inventory & Appriasement of Jno. Anthonny Estate was recd & O to be recorded.

William Boyet) Orderd that the Corn attachd be the Sheriff
   advs   ) and Constable be sold according to Law
Wm. Williams)

The Minutes being read the Court was adjourned till to Morrow Morning 9 of the Clock.
                Daniel Green
                Thos. Knight
                Wm. Sisson
                Jesse Winborne

The Court met according to adjournment on Tuesday the third Day of November 1789.

Present the Worshipfull   Willm Robison)
                         Wm. Sisson   )
                         Danl. Green   ) Esqrs.
                         Jesse Winbourn)
                         Thos. Knight)

2 Ebenez S. Platt vs Danl. Shaw - Ruled for Security Nonsuit

79 Jos. Jackson vs Thos. Philpot, Exor. Contd.

80 Same vs Same same order

98 William Little vs John & Mary Davis non est dismst

106 Malcha Powell vs Thos Burton none est dismit

108 John C. Smith vs John Crocker Contd.

114 Allen Williams vs John Green/referd to William Robertson & John Pacely Contd.

115 Same vs Same. William Hardin none est renewd

116 Kennedy vs King, settled each part to pay their own costs.

117 John Wych, Assee vs Boush & Miller Contd.

118 Nehemiah Powers vs Rawls & Clayton dismist at deft cost

119 Fredk. Sunn vs Edwd Miller Contd.

120 Solo Owins vs Benj. Allen dismist at Plffs costs.

121 Geo. Wiggins vs Sarah Young dismist at Plffs Costs.

122 The State vs Graham Glover Issue an Alias Capias

123 The Same vs Robt Mays. Settled at Deft costs Vide 5 Nov.

124 Idem vs John Nixon - Contd.

125 Same vs Thos. Knight - Contd.

126 Same vs John Bates, Jun. Indict Vide 5th Nov.

127 Walker Robertson vs James Davis, Junr. at Plffs Costs.

138 128 Hugh Gibbony vs Isham Clayto dismst at Defts Costs.

129 Edmd Miles vs Danl. Odom dismissed at Plffs Costs.

130 Robt. Stark, Junr. vs Step Collins, Contd.

131 John Randal vs Red & Goss - Contd.

132 James C. Murphy vs Alex. Newman. Contd.

133 Eneas McLeod vs Wm. Christie - Contd.

134 Henry Levingston vs Wm. Irvin dismist at defendants cost.

135 Danl. Bough vs Exor. of Hankerson - Contd.

136 Fara Merret vs Bera Williams - Contd.

137 Martin Shepherd vs John Green - Contd. Jno Fitts Sec for John Green.

138 Owen Jones vs John Green - Contd.

139 Job Jourdan vs William Thomas non est dismst

140 Exor of Step Smith vs Danl Green - Contd.

141 James Doane vs Jonathan Clark - Contd Ordrd that the Property attchd be dlivered up.

142 Aaron Smith vs William Sturgis)   R. McElrath, Bail.
143 John Weekly vs William Sturgis)   Contd none est dismist.
non est dismist

144 Bartlett Brown vs Elijah Gillett. Judgt. Exec. ord. by T.P.C The plaintiff not appearing on Sc Fa

145 State vs Jesse Kerney - Contd.

146 Robt. Stark vs John Walker Contd.

147 Same vs Wm. Sisson Esq. Contd.

148 Matthew Talbot vs William Davis none suit

149 Frederick Sunn vs Eliza Redding N E to be renewed.

152 John Tolson Lowe vs Leonard Marbury Judg. by default On a Writ of Enquiry. The jury to wit, George Kersh, Isham Jordan, Jas. Jackson, Jno. Williams, Rich. Blalock, John Snelling, William Davis, Micajah Matthews, Arthur Jenkins, James Sims, Michael Swicherd, Sampson Griffin, being elected tried & sworn upon their oaths returned a verdict for the Plaintiff one hundred twenty five pounds one shilling & four pence, /with interest from May 1786/ Arthur Jenkins, Foreman.

150 John Kersh vs Shields Brooker - Contd.

151 Aaron Smith vs William Sturgis dismist at Plff's costs.

153 Peter Carnes vs Jasper Wert Judgmt by Default

154 Same vs Same Tover judgment by default

155 Same vs Same Trover Judgment by Default

156 Same vs Same Trov. Judgment by default

157 Same vs Same   Judgment by default Case

158 Same vs Same - Debt Judgment by default - Contd.

159 Danl Shaw - appelant
         vs   ) Judgment reversed
     James Pendergrass, Respt.

97

Thomas Newman was appointed Guardian to Jno. Newman, an infant above the age of fourteen years. Alexander Newman enters himself security in the sum of five hundred pounds for the faithful and legal conduct of the Guardian. Prdrd that the said Guardian take the property of his ward where he can find it so it be done peacibly & legally.

Gideon Jones, Appellant) on an appeal from the Decree of
vs) Willm Sisson, Esq. Judgmt con-
John Wilkson, Respondant) firmed

Richd Vince, /Plff
vs
Wm. Sisson / Judgment/ for Ten pounds /& Costs/ Staying

139 Execution 2 Months & a half

 92 Robt. Stark vs James French contd.
 95 John S. Fields vs Anthony Bardox. Pet & Sums Judgmt for Six Pounds & Nine Pence

 153 Peter Carnes) Att default, on a Writ of Enquiry
   vs) the same Jury as before being sworn
  Jasper Wert) return a verdict to wit, we find for
        the plaintiff ninety seven pounds
three shillings and seven pence for the within bond & interest Judgment accordingly.
        Arthur Jenkins, Foreman

 154 Same) Trover default. On a Writ of Enquiry the same
   vs) Jury as before being sworn return a verdict/
  Same) We find for the plaintiff the sum of fifty
      pounds/ for a negro Judy/ Judgment accordingly.
Arthur Jenkins, Foreman

 155 Same) Trov default. Writ of Enquiry the same jury
   vs) as before being sworn. We find for the
  Same) Plaintiff theirty five pounds for a negro
     wench Nelly.
        Arthur Jenkins, Foreman

 156 Same) Trov. Judgmt default on a Writ on Enquiry the
   vs) same jury being sworn as before return a
  Same) Verdict to wit, We find for the Plff. twenty
     pounds for the Boy Andrew. Arthur Jenkins,
      Foreman - Judgmt.

 157 Same) Case Judgment by default On a writ of Enquiry
   vs) The Same jury as before being sworn return a
  Same) Verdict to wit. We find for the Plaintiff the
sum of forty six pounds for the hire of the negroes
        Arthur Jenkins, Foreman
Judgment accordingly.

No. 91 James Brabham vs Jos. Simms, Judgment 55/& Cost.

140 152 John T. Lowe) Attachment
    vs) Peter Carnes, Esq. Summoned as Garnishee
  Leonard Marbury came into Court and made oath that he
        was indebted to the Defendant in the
sum of forth shillings & upwards on an unsettled account.
Ordered that the said sum of forty shillings be

condemned in Peter Carne's /hands/ for the use of the Plaintiff and any other sum that may appear due to said Marbury by said Carnes on Settlement provided execution is not otherwise Satisfied
Court then adjourned till tomorrow Morning 9 O'Clock.
Wm. Robison
Wm. Sisson
Thos. Knight.

The Court met according /to/ adjournment on Wednesday the 4th Day of November 1789.

Present Wm. Sisson   )
         Danl. Green   )
         Jesse Winbourn) Esquires
         Thos. Knight   )

Samuel Willson) Judgt Confessed for Six Pounds eighteen
     vs   ) shillings & six pence with interest from
James French   ) the first October 1787. The advantage
of the instrument Law being waved by the defendant Staying Execution two months, this Judgment being in full of one obtained last Term.

141 William Woodcock, Nich Nobles, James Montgomery, Charles Wheeler & Zadock Woolley, Constables, came into Court & took the Oath according to the appointment of Congress.

151 John Wyche vs Willm Robison, Esqr. Case & the jury to try the issue, Viz George Kersh, Isham Jordan, James Jackson, John Williams, Richd. Blalock, John Snelling, Micajah Matthews, Arthur Jenkins, James Sims, Stephen Collins, Sampson Griffin, /Jno Fields/ being elected, tried and sworn, upon their Oaths, return a verdict for the plaintiff Forty Pounds & Costs of Suit Judgment accordingly.
                              Arthur Jenkins, Foreman

109 Barbary Crimer) Judgment by default a Writ of Enquiry
       vs   ) The Same jury as before Say we find
    John Clayton   ) for the Plaintiff twenty four pounds
                      with interest from May 1780 to May
1789 & costs of Suit.   Ad. Jenkins, Foreman
Ordered that Ephream Puckett be appointed Overseer on the Longcain Road from Kellys Cowpen to the white ponds in the room of William Miles.

151 John Wyche vs William Robison, Esq. Case the Defendant prayed an appeal which is allowed he giving Security as the Law directs - Joseph Harley & John Bates, Sen. came into Court & acknowledged themselves bound in the sum of eighty pounds for the prosecution of the sd. Appeal with effects by the said William Robertson

John Fields vs Anthony Burdoux new Trial granted on paying witnesses wages and all other Cost Except Attorneys fees.

76 John C. Smith vs Nathaniel Twining Attachmt. Continued by Defendant's Costs.

Bartlett Brown proved 2 Days attendance in the Cause of Fields vs Burdeaux.

111 James Cook   ) Judgment by default on a Writ of Enquiry.
      vs   ) The Same Jury as beofre say we find for
And. Walker   ) the Plaintiff Forty Pounds and cost of
                   suit.

The Court then adjourned till tomorrow morning 9 O'Clock
                    John Wyld
                    Daniel Green
                    Jesse Winborne

The Court met according to Adjournment on Thursday the 5th
Day of November 1789.
Present   Wm. Buford   )
                    Daniel Green)
                    Thos. Knight) Esquires
                    John Wyld   )

Thos. Morris vs Edward Myles Att. Dismissed at the
Plaintiff's Costs   77

142 State vs John Bates, Jun./Trespass/Ruled to trial by the
Court on motion to Quash the Inditiment the Court are of
the opinion that the Inditiment be quashed   126

71 William Davis vs Benjamin Brown Atth Levied on Lands
supposed to be the property of Benjamin Brown, the sail of
said Land was prolonged until Bartlett Brown, Junr. and
James Brown who claimed title should make their right appear.
The titles being produced ordered that the said Land be not
subject to the said Execution and that the said William
Davis pay the Costs of this Collateral issue.

78 William Hardin vs Allen Williams Executor of Richard
Williams on Motion of the defendant by his Council Ordered
that on Dedimus issued to James Brownson Benjamin Lanier and
____ Wiley to take the deposition of Dorcas Gindratt in the
State of Georgia to be sworn on her Voir dier forbid by the
Plaintiff.

21 Alen William vs William Hardin ordered that a Dedimus
issue to the same Justices as take the deposition of the
said Dorcas Gindratt in the same manner.

111 James Cook vs Andrew Walker Edw Carrey who was summonsed as Garnishees appeared and made oath that he was
indebted to the said Walker in the sum of twenty nine pounds
nine and four pence same by virtue of a judgment obtained
by the said Walker against the said Curry in the Maclinburg
County in the State of North Carolina, Ordered that the said
sum be condemed in hands of Garnishee for the use of the
plaintiff

123 The State vs Robt. Mays settled at the Defendants Cost
except two dollars which are to be pay'd /by/James Gregg.

95 John Fields, Junr. vs Anthony Burdeau, John Fitts
acknowledged himself Bail for the said Burdeau

32 John Wyld, Esq.) Trover Verdict for Plaintiff in May
      vs   ) Term 1755 for twenty seven pounds ten
William Davis   ) shillings On Motion of the Attorney

for the plaintiff Resolved by the Court that the Defendant in this Case is not entitled to the benefit of the Instalment Law.

Willm Robinson, Esq. came into Court and Resigned his Commission as a Magistrate.

143 John Wyld, Esq. Appealent) on an Appeal from William
     vs   ) Buford, Esq. Decree. the
     Nich. Nobles, Respondant) Judgment confirmed.
     under the installment Law)

95 John Fields,   ) Ordered that a Dedimus issue to
    vs   ) James Benthean & Benjamin Legear,
    Anthony Bindox   ) Esqr. in Charleston to examine
                        Hugh Holland for the Defendant.

95 John Fields   ) Ordered that a Dedimus issue to Thos.
    vs   ) Hall and John Troop, Esqrs. in
    Anthony Burdox   ) Charleston to Examiner John Fields,
                        Senr. & Wilson Brown. Tried in
    behalf of the Plainff.

Jacob Burton came into Court & Proved his Attendance for three Days /as a witness/ in the suit of Wm. Davis vs Bartlett Brown, Jun.

Ordered that the County Treasurer Pay three Shillings to Wm. Woodcock which he payed for an Estray he took up to Danl. Green, Esq.

The Court adjourned till the next Court in order & all Causes to be continued in Course
                              Jno. C. Smith, J. P.
                              Daniel Green, J. P.
                              John Wyld, J. P.

   Issue Docket continued agreable to the above Order

   no. 5 James Robertson vs Jno. Watson - Contd.
   12 Robt. Montgomery vs John Wickly - Contd.
   87 Benj. Odom, Jun. vs John C. Smith, Esq. Contd.
   88 Judith Corbat - Thos. Moore - Contd.
   90 Lark Robison vs Jno. Wyches & Noah Tanner - Contd.
   93 Jno Parkinson vs Geo. Robison - Contd.
   94 John Parkinson vs Alex. Newman - Contd.
   97 Fred Sunn vs Edwd Myles - Att Contd.
   101 Willm Shields vs Purl Johnson - Contd.
   103 Simeon Taylor vs Thos. Shields - Contd.
   104 Joseph Solomon vs David Shipes - Contd.
   105 - id .... vs Arthur Jenkins - Contd.

144 105 Willm Myles vs Exec. James DeRoache - Contd.
     107 John Davis vs Willm Creech - Contd.
     123 John Wickly vs Willm Ashley - Contd.
     57   John C. Smith, Esq. vs Willm Davis - Contd.
     13   Golphin Dunbar vs Benj. Odom, Michl Odom Contd.
     26   Henry Hampton vs Henry Best - Contd.
     40   William Willis vs Danl. Shaw - Contd.
     50   James Montgomery vs Twiner & Obannon - Contd.
     54   Duncan Campbell vs Jno. Wyche - Contd.
     64   Winifred Arnand vs Jos. Brooker - Contd.

65	John Fitts vs Charles Yarbrough - Contd.	
66	Mary Blount vs Sabart Odom - Contd.	
70	Saml Jones vs John Randall - Contd.	
71	Roberts & Mayers vs Willm Ashley - Contd.	
72	id _____ vs McLinton & Maise - Contd.	
74	Thoms. Dobbins vs Robt. McLewrath - Contd.	
75	id _____ vs John Nixon - Contd.	

Lower Three Runs October 20th. 1789

We the Subscribers in Obedience to the Worshipful Court of Wintons Orders, have met & Viewed the Ground where we was directed to mark out a New Road, to Cross the Head of Doctor John Crockers Mill Creek above his Mill Pond, & do find it will be attended with Ten Times the Expence, as would make a Bridge and Causeway across the Creek below the Mill; the the New Road must be cut through a heavy Timberd Land, at least Six Miles, passing over several Boggy Branches.

        John Wickly
        John Wyld

Returned into Office)
Feby 1st. 1790)

X The Account of the Riot on the next page was read by E. Bellinger, Jr. on 26 March 1845 in his argument for J. G. Brown & others vs The State for a Riot in pulling down the House of Kersh in July 1844 as contrasted with this Riot. Verdict "Not Guilty" Judge Frost
For State J. D. Edwards
For Defendant A. Patterson, A. P. Aldrich, W. E. Martin & E. Bellinger, Jr.

145 At a Court in Course held for Winton County on Monday the first Day of February 1790.

When William Dunbar, Richard Tradaway, Danl. Green & William Buford Esq. appeared at the Court House in order to Sit in the Court House & proceed to do their Duties; But where prevented & threatned by a Riotous Mob, Headed by a certain John Wickly, & aided & encouraged by Col. Willm Davis, John Redd & others who delcared there should be no more County Courts & John Wickly tore down from the Court House all the Sheriff's Advertisements for Sales as Levied for Executions & the said Wickly declared openly that there should be no more Sales of Property in this County, & they also took a Riotous Possession of the Court House, tore down the Barr & The Justices & Juryments benches, took the Clerks Table, opend the Drawer & threw out in the Rain, the Record Book, the Appearance Docket & issue Docket prepared for Court, with the Bonds. Declarations &C/ & the Table/ & about the Break of Day on Tuesday Morning Set the House on Fire, willfully designedly & by a preconsulted agreement, & they stayed on Tuesday as they publicly declared to prevent any of the Justices from Sitting, in consequence of which there was no Court.

Therefore all Causes on the Docket are of Course Continued until the next Court according to Law.
  Certified by
         Thos. Wyld, DC WC
   ___ X _____

NB
That amongst the Advertisements tore down,)
there was property of the above said)
John Wickly, Willm Dunbar & John Redd,)
to be Sold that Court, taken by)
Virtue of Executions Levied)
    Certified by
        Thoms. Wyld, DC WC

Information is also made, that John Davis, Charles J. Brown, Willm Sturgis, Danl. Green, Esq. were aiding, assiting & encouraging the above said Mob. Which Information,/& the above Facts/ can be proved by the following Witnesses John Hammond of Edgefield County, Nathan Johnson of Lincoln, John Mitchell, Clevears D. Wyld, Jonathan Seely, Jacob Davis, Tarlton Brown, Peter Carnes, George Walker, Wm. Dunbar Esq. & Rich. Tradeaway, Esqr. ___ & Wm. Beauford, Esq. Wm. Fitts & Jno. Fitts.

146 Blank

147 At a Court in Course held at the Court House on Cedar Branch on Monday the third Day of May 1790.

    Present the Worshipful
                        John C. Smith   )
                        Richd. Tradeaway) Esquires
                        Thomas Knight   )

John Wyche, Elijah Gillett, Walker Robertson, and William Scarborough Esquires were appointed Justices for the County of Winton, and the said John Wyche and Elijah Gillett received/ the Oaths of Office, and took their seats accordingly.

The Oaths of Office were also administered to Walker Robertson, Esquire, who took his seat accordingly. Present John Wyche, Walker Robertson & Elijah Gillett, Esquire.

    The Jury box being produced the following persons were drawn to serve on the Petty Jury at the next Court. Abraham Deason, Moses Plummer, Thos. Enox, Zadock Woolley, Drewry Lain, Willm Walker, Rheubin Mixon, Absolom Tylor, Benjamin Odom, Ricd. Jackson, William Goode, Benjamin Buxton, James Kirkland, Arthur Fruger, Isaac Tool, John Cave, William Mooney, Jesse Rogers, George Robinson, Jun. Willm. Mason, Jacob Koope, Willm Weekley, Thos. Matthews, Garderner Davis, Wilson Cook, Francis Basset, Rawlin Roberts, Linoel Lee, Nathaniel Sanders, Joshua Williams.

Thomas Knight, Esquire, came into Court and resigned his Office as Justice of the Peace for the County of Winton.

148 A Deed from Charles Stewart to John Martin Strozier, was duly acknowledged in Court and ordered to be recorded.

The Minutes being Read the Court then adjourned until tomorrow morning nine o'clock.

        Jno. Car Smith   Walter Robinson   E. Gillett)
        Richd Tradeaway John Wyche   ) Esqrs.

At a Court Continued by adjournment to Tuesday the 4th Day of May 1790.

Present the Worshipful Justices
      Richd. Tradeaway)
      Walter Robinson)
      John Wyche) Esquires
      Danl Green   )
      Jesse Winbourn)
      Wm. Buford   )
Elijah Gillett & Thomas Obannon

Orderd That the order for a Road from Fort Moore Bluff to Rousees Ford to intersect the Charleston Road be revoked.

Orderd that the Rates of Liquor be Confirmed

Richard Creech, Administrator of Owen Williams decd. against John Cradock & Aaron Boyston Admrs. of Moses Boynenton, dec'd. On motion of Wm. Walker Atty for the Plaintiff orderd that the Constable be directed to sell the lands of the Defendant (as no other property can be found) to satisfy the judgment given by the Justice in the said Cause, provided the said judgment does not excede the sum of five pounds.
  Orderd that a Road be laid out from Demerys Ferry to the Pine Logg on the South Fork of Edisto & That Wm. Green be Overseer from Demerys Ferry to the 3 Runs - Godfrey Lee from thence to the Pine Log.

  Orderd that a Genl Scire Facias be issued against all the Defaulters of the Grand & Petit Jurors to this Court no Fees to be charged by the Clerk or Sheriff.
Issued 10th May 1790.

149 Thom Wyld making Oath that a Deed from James Fair to Isaac Tool being proved was ordered to be recorded, but was lost by a violent Gust or mislaid, Orderd that the Plott Grant & receint from Jos. Fair to the sd. Isaac Tool be recorded.

2 Thos. P. Carnes Asignee vs George Golphin on a Writ of Enquiry being duly sworn Viz
  1   2   3   4
William Key, James French, Elij Abston, Wm. Davis,
  5   6   7   8
James Jackson, Michl French, Jno Bush, Benajah Williams,
  9   10   11
Bartlett Brown, Sen., Bartlett Brown, Jun., Danl. Shingleton
 12
Jno Williams, _____ James Jackson, Foreman.

We of the Jury do find for the Plaintiff the sum of fifty pounds, with lawful interest & cost of Suit. James Jackson, Foreman.

Thomas P. Carnes, Esq. County Attorney, appeared in Court and returned his grateful acknowledgements for the attention & respect he has received from this Court while acint in a Publick capacity & begged leave to resign his said Office.

Ordered that his resignation be accepted & that the particular thanks of the Court be presented to Mr. Carnes for his great attention & fidelity in the Execution of the said Office.

Mr. George Walker was appointed by the unanimous consent of the Justices to the Office of County Atty who accepted the same.

On Motion of Mr. William Buford, To have the benefits of an Act of General Assembly (Entitled Act to Authorize Mathias Leverman to erect Bridges over the Salt Ketchers River at or near Williams' Ford and to vest a toll to be collected at the said Bridges in the said Mathias Leverman for a term therein mentioned) vested in him the said William Buford and it appearing to the satisfaction of the Court that the said Mathias Liverman has transfered all his benefit from the said Act to him the said William. It is ordered that the said Buford do procede to build & keep in repair the said Bridges, upon his giving Bond and Security to keep the same in good repair, and that the said Buford be allowed to receive as a toll and after the rates following (to wit)

for a man & Horse.	0.4d
For a single horse, or foot man	2
For a waggon team 2/	2.0
For a Cart & Horse 1/	1.0
For a Chair & Horse 1/	1.0
Nett Catta pr head	1
Sheep. Goats or Hogs pr head 1/2	1/2

Joseph Harley came into court and resigned his office as Coroner for the County of Winton, whereupon the Court appointed John Crocker, Esqr. to the said office in stead of the sd. Harley.

150   5   James Robertson vs Jno. Watson - Nonsuit

A letter from his Excellency the Governor address to the Court of Winton County was read in open Court & Orderd to be filed in Office.

Orderd that Wm. Wilson be appointed Overseer of the Road in the Room of Leven Collins.

12   Robt. Montgomery vs John Wickly - Judgmt by Default on a Writ of Enquiry. We of the Jury do find for the Plaintiff one hundred Pounds with Lawful interest & Cost of Suit.
Jas. Jackson, Foreman.

78   Wm. Harding vs Allen Williams - Contd.

87   Benj. Odom Jun. vs Jno. C. Smith - Contd.

Bill of Sale from Owen Odom & Jno. Stewart to Walter Robertson Ordered to be recorded.

A Bill of Sale from Saml Perry to Wm. Brown Ordered to be recorded.

Ordered that Jos. Miller & Jno. Bush sell the Estate of Edmd. Bentley, Decd.

88   Judith Corbatt vs Thos. Moore Dismist at Plaintiff's Costs.

Sarah Griffin appeared in Court on a Charge of Bastardy & made Oath that Bartholomew Laurence was the Father of her Child whereupon the Court ordered that the sd. Sarah be find five pounds Prol money to be paid within nine months & Walter Robertson & Jesse Winbourn, Esq became Security for the Same.

92   Robt Stark vs James French - Nonsuit.

Ordered that Ann Johnson, the widow of Jno. McKnight Johnson, be granted Letters of Administration & that Wm. Robison & Wm. Cato be her Securities & that Edwd Wimberly, Michl. Swicord & Jacob Swicord be appointed Appraisers to the Estate of Jno. McKnight Johnson accordingly.

93   John Parkinson vs Geo. Robinson - Contd by Consent.

94   The Same vs Alexander Newman - Contd by Consent.

Ordered that Joseph Vince be granted Letters of Administration/ on the Estate of Absolom Roushar & that Andrew Nimmons & Leven Collins be his Security.

Orderd that /an/ Inventory & Appraisement of the Estate of James Collins being prouced in Court be recorded.

104   Hos. Solomon vs David Shipes - Nonsuit.

Edward Wimberly as the Executor of Stephen Smith, Judgment Confessed according to Note with Stay of Execution until November Court.

The Court then adjourned untill tomorrow morning nine o'clock.

          E. Gillett
          Thos. Obannon
          Jno. Car Smith

151   March 14th, 1790.
  Gentlemen,

In Consequence of an Information from the deputy Clerk of Winton County of a riot & opposition to the setting of the Court in that County which information has been laid before the Council, I am by their advice to inform you that you are requested to lay before the Executive a circumstantial account of the nature & the extent of the opposition & the names of the Persons against whom there are well founded proofs of their having been principals or accomplices - That where such proofs can be obtained, you will without delay in pursuance of your Powers as Justices, issue Warrants against the parties for the purpose of bringing them to trial at the next Court that shall be held for the District of Orangeburg. The information which is to be submitted to the executive ought to be from the majority of the Justices of the County.

                    I am Gentlemen
                    with respect
                    Your most obedient Servant,

                    Charles Pinckney.
To
   The Justices of the Court for Winton County.

   A True Copy.   Thoms. Wyld, DC WC

At a Court in course held for Winton County on Monday the
2nd Day of August 1790.

Present the Worshipful   William Beauford)
                          Thomas OBannon   )
                          John Wyche   ) Esqrs.
                          Danl. Green   )
                          Walter Robison   )

The Sale of Thomas Castillos Estate being returned / by
Jos. Miller, Admr/ O. to be recorded.

The Sale of Edmd Bentleys Estate being returned O. to be
recorded.

The Jury Box being produced the following Persons were drew
by a Child in open Court to serve as Petitt Jurors for Nov.
Court Richd. Vince 1, Peter Banner 2, Joseph Lancaster 3,
Wm. Hitchcock 4, Leven Collins 5, Jacob Swicord 6, James
Lee 7, Wm. Freeman 8, David Reeves 9, Charles Richmond 10,
Nathan Cocker 11, Jon. Gregory 12, Wm. Carr 13, James
Walker 14, Jno Dunn 15, Joseph Brooker 16, George Corssly
17, Rich. Kirkland 18, Joshua Smith 10, Henry McMillan 20,
James Morris, Jun. 21, Charles Brown 22, Alex Newman Cr
Neck 23, John Drummond 24, Geo. Kirkland 25, Solomon Owens
26, Saml. Dennis 27, Simon Bryan 28, Danl. Crocket 29,
Joseph Youngblood 30.

Thomas Newman was appointed Constable & took the Oaths of
Qual.

James Thurston was appointed Constable & took the Oath of
Qual.

Priscilla Myles haveing returned a Citation Orderd that
Letters of Administration be Granted her on the Estate of
Edwd Myles on her giving Bond & Secruity with Benj. Odom
Jun.

Orderd that Jesse Lancaster, Robt. Lancaster & Leven Collins
be appointed Appraisers of the sd estate & Priscilla Myles
was qualified accordingly.

The Grand Jury being Summoned on a Scire Facias the following Persons when called appeared Jno Bush 1, Peter
DeRoushee 2, /Wm. Bryant/3, Robt. Lancaster 4, Wm. Price
5, Jos. Duncan 6, John Joice 7, Joshua Smith 8, David
Jackson 9, John Harington 10, Benj. Corbett 11, Edwd Nicks
12, David Shipes 13, Jos. Duncan appointed Foreman.

Ann Brook having returned a Citation of the Estate of Thoms. Brook Decd. - Ordered that Letters of Administration be granted her on Giving Bond & Willm Vince & Elijah Wardend her Securitys in a Bond of one Thousand Pounds O. Thos Golphin, Wm. Thomas, & Alex. Newman appointed appraisers & was Qualified.

Orderd that John Wickly be appointed Overseer of the Road in the room of John Harington.

John Bush was appointed Constable & took the Oaths of Qualificat

The Petit Jury that were Cited to appear by Sci Fa having appeared were orderd to be dismist.

153 Orderd that the Children of Eliza Wallen /be/ bound out by Willm Dunbarr, Esq. to such persons as he shall approve off

The appraisement of the Estate of John McKnight Johnson, Decd. being returned was orderd to be recorded.

The Court adjourned till 4 of the Clock.

The Court met according to Adjournment.

The State vs Lewis Frazer. Archd Frazer & Randal Lucas for Stealing a two Year old Steer the Property of Wm. Newton. A True Bill. Jos Duncan, Foreman.

Ordered that their Recognizance stand over & be ruled to Trial to Morrow. Nathl. Saunders Security.

Information being lodged agst James Mash William Boyet and Josiah Boyet for killing one estray Steer, knowing it to be an estray it is ordered that they be bound in the penalty of fifty pounds cash to appear tomorrow morning & answer such information. Whereupon the said James, William & Josiah severally acknowledged themselves to owe to the Justices of Winton County the sum of fifty pounds each to be levied on their several and respective Lands and tenements good & chattels, Upon condition that they shall be and appear tomorrow morning & answer the information aforesaid, abide the sentence of the Court & not depart without leave.

Amos Way, Robt Ashley & Benajah Williamson came into Court and severally acknowledged to owe to the County the sum of fifty pounds each, upon condition that they appear tomorrow and give informasion agst the aforesaid Jas. Mash, Wm. Boyet, and Josiah Boyet for killing a stray Steer, knowing it to be an estray, and not depart the Court without leave. Jas. Kirkland was discharged upon payment of Costs.

James Davis was appointed Constalbe & took the Oaths of Qualificat.

The Petit Jury being called they following Persons appeared. Thos. Enocks 1, Drury Lane 2, Reuben Nixon 3, Absm Tyler 4, Benj. Odom 5, Richd. Jackson 6, Wm. Googe 7, Benj. Buxton 8, Jas. Kirkland 9, Jno. Cave 10, Wm. Weekly 11, Wilson Cook 12

Gardner Davis/ Nath. Saunders/

The Petit Jury were discharged till tomorrow morning 9 of the Clock.

The Minutes being read the Court was adjourned till to Morrow 9 of the Clock.   John Wyche
Thos. Obannon
Walter Parkinson

154 The Court met according to adjournment Tuesday, the 3rd Day of August 1790.

Present the Worshipful   Willm Dunbar   )
                         John C. Smith   )
                         Elijah Gillett)
                         Thomas Obannon)
                         John Wyche   )   Esqrs.
                         William Buford)
                         Walter Robison)
                         Danl. Green   )

Orderd that the Clerk issue Sci Fa against all Persons that have taken up Estrays & Entered on the Toll Book to appear at the next Court with the Estrays or render acct. of & by whom Claimd.

An information being exhibited against Jas. Mash, William Boyet and Josiah Boyet for not advertising an Estray Steer, and for killing the same, knowing it to be an Estray, it is order that the said William Boyet, James Mash and Josiah Boyett do pay the sum of five pounds as a finee, with forty five shillings to be paid to Amos Way who was the owner of the said Steer with stay of Execution until next Court - with Cost to be paid to be paid before they are discharged

Ordered that the County Treasurer be directed to pay the Sheriff Tarlton Brown the sum of Seven pounds ten shillings out of any Money in the County Treasury being the sum allowed by Law for his Extra services & also the Clerk of Court Five pounds for his Extra Service.

O. that Isaac Tool be appointed Overseer of the Road in the room of Jesse Rogers who is removed.

O. that John Randall be appointed Overseer of the Road from the head of the three Runs to the upper end of the County Line as the former Commissioners laid it off.

Orderd that Jno C. Smith, Wm. Buford & Elijah Gillett Esq. or any two of them do Visit & Examine the Clerks Office & the State of the Treasury & Acco of Moneys recd for Estrays & make their reports to the next Court.

O. that all Overseers of the Roads in this County shall produce a Certificate from some Justice nearest the said Road/ that it/ is in good Repairs before they are released from their foremer Appointment & that the Sheriff give publick /notice/ of this order throughout the County & /that all Overseers do/ make their return to the next Court, or be fined Ł 3, according to Law.

155 Presentments of the Grand Jury, Viz
We present Mary Morris for Bastardy Information being made by William Smith.

We present the Overseer of the Road from the Court House to Morris' Ford.

We present the Overseer of the Road from Kellys Cowpen to the Cross Roads.

We present the Overseer of the Road from Maj. Bufords Toll Bridge to platts Mill also from the sd. Toll Bridge to the old Savannah Ford on the Little Saltketcher.

We present the Overseer of the Road from Toby's Creek to Benj Odoms on Turkey Creek across the Saltketchers.
Joseph Duncan, Foreman.

Ordered that the Clerk of the Court have the Liberty of the Est end of the Prison, to keep his Office, till an Office is built for that Purpose.

The State vs Lewis Frazer - Arch Frazer & Randall Lucus for Cow stealing. The Jury to Wit - Thos. Enocks, Drury Lane, Reuben Nixon, Absolom Tyler, Benj. Odom, Jun., Richd. Jackson, Benj. Buxton, Jas. Jackson, Jno. Cave, George Robison, Jun., William Weekly, Rowland Roberts, being duly sworn impanneld do Say that Lewis Frazier/Archibald/Frazer Guilty of Cow Stealing.
James Jackson, Foreman.

State vs Benj. Corbett Indictmt. Ass & Battery. A True Bill Witness Geo. David - Contd. under Traverse with recognisance for appearance to appear at next Court. Wm. Smith & Wm. Goode acknowledged themselves bound in the sum of £ fifty to appear at next Court & not depart wihout leave of the Court.

Wm. Frazer being brought unto Court as an Evidence it appeard that he made information on Oath against James Kirkland /&/ there appeard /to/ the Number of to /or/ more respectable /Evidences/ quite contrary to his deport & his behavour before the Court appearing so flagrant & insulting to this Court, it is orderd that he never more be admited as an Evidence in this Court & that the Sheriff take him into Custody & put him in the Stocks as a Publick Example for 2 Hours.

Orderd that Rev. Nathl Walker, Joseph Turner & /John Ashley/ be appointed Commissioners to View the Roads leading from Sykes Creek to the Head of the three Runs & report the most convenient Road to the next Court.

The Court adjourned till 4 of the Clock.

The Court met according to adjournment.

156 Lewis Frazer and Archibald Frazer being found guilty of Cow Steadling Order that they pay the sum of ten pounds Sterling each or receive thirty nine lashes on their bear backs each. The Court allowd them one hour to pay the fine which not being discharged they each received the punishment

of thirty nine lashings on their bear backs at the public whipping post.

Ordered that Wm. Frazer be committed to prison untill he gives Bond & two Sufficient Securities in ₤ 100 himself & his Securities in each ₤ 50 for his good behaviour for twelve months when Thos. Morris & Nathl. Saunders agreed to become his Securitys - & were approved.

The Petit Jury were discharged till tomorrow morning 9 of the Clock The Grand Jury recd the thanks of the Court & were discharged.

Jno Joice being Summonds as a Garnishee Jacob Griner vs Wm. & Bartlett Brown being Sworn Says that he has no Property. His hands belonging to Wm. & Bart. Brown now had he any at the time of serving the attachment; and said that he had given his Bond to Bartlett Brown for two Negroes and had taken his receipt against the sd Bond, and that the said Brown had given him his Bond to make titles to two tracts of Land & he had given the sd. Brown a receipt against his Bond, this he did to oblige Brown and in order to prevent Brown's Land being Sold for his debts and this was done at the request of the said Bartlet Brown Dismist Plf Cost.

The Court orderd, that from the Perusal of several Depositions against Jos. Williams now lodged in the Clerks Office, it plainly appeared to this Court, that he is Guilty of Wilful & Corrupt Perjury & O. never to be admitted as a Witness in this Court & O. to be recorded.

The Minutes being read the Court was adjourned till to morrow Morning 9 of the Clock.
      Wm. Dunbar
      E. Gillett
      Robinson
      John Wyche

157 The Court met according to adjournment on Wednesday the 4th Day of August 1790.
    Present the Worshipful John C. Smith)
             William Dunbarr)
             Walter Robison)
             Jno. Wyche   )
             Thoms. Obannon)
             Elijah Gillett)
             Willm Beauford)

On the application of John Bates Jun. to keep a Tavern at his House- Granted on his giving Bond & security according to Law.

On the application of John Mitchell to keep Tavern at his House Granted on his giving Bond & security according to Law.

Ordered that the Justices appointed to Visit the Clerks Office & Treasury Do lay off the Three Acres of Land given to the Publick to erect Publick Buildings & fix a place whereon to erect the Court House.

107 Jno. Davis vs Richd Creech   Dismist at Mutual Cost

114 Allen Williams vs Jno. Green Judgmt for ₤ 1 & Costs.

117 Jno Wyche vs Bush & Miller Judgmt ₤ 7 -1 -10 & Cost.

130 Robt Stark vs Stephen Collins - Dismist & Plaintiff's Cost.

66 Mary Blount vs Sabart Odom - Judgmt for 50/ & Costs Staying Execution for 3 months.

74 Thos. Dobbins vs Robt. McLewrath - Judgmt ₤ 6 -6-0 & Costs.

95 Jno. Fields vs Anthl. Bourdeau - Judgmt ₤ 7-10-11 & Cost.

10 Willm Brown vs Joseph Garnett - Dismist at Plaintiff's Costs.

11 Willm Brown vs Jos. Garnett - Dismist at Plaintiff's Costs.

14 Thos. Burton vs Jno Wyld - Judgmt P Note Int & Costs.

28 Robt. Write vs George Golphin - Withdrawn by Consent at Michl. Swicord Costs except the Lawyers fees.

39 Charles Goodwin vs Danl. Shaw - Judgmt for ₤ Note & Cost.

41 Hezek Roberts vs Benj. Odom, Jun. Dismist at Plaintiffs Cost.

43 Idem . . . . vs Wm. Kee - Dismist at Plaintiffs Cost.

48 Willm Scarbrough vs Henry Cocker - Dismist at Plaintiffs Cost

55 John Dave vs Robt. McLewrath - Judgmt Staying Ex 3 Months Note & Int & Cost.

58 Elijah Gillett, Esq. vs Joseph Garnett - Dismist at Deft Cost.

65 John Fitts vs Chas. Yarbrough/John Wickly Security/ ₤ 8-0-0 Cost.   Jas Jackson, Foreman.

33 Elijah Gillett, Esq. Thoms. Harley - Judgment on Writ of Enquiry. We find for the Plaintiff ₤ 50 & Costs.

51 Thom. Wyld vs Adam McNeeley - Judgmt ₤ 3 & Costs Stay Exe. 3 Months. James Simms his Security to pay the Costs in 2 months & the Debt.

158 Orderd the Treasurer pay Jno Dave one Daollar for Constables Staves

52 Rachael McGregory vs Chas. Stuart - Nonsuit.

57   Saml. Way vs Willm Shields - Contd.

110 Willm Myles vs Exec. DeRoache Dismist Thos. Obannon
     to pay Costs.

124 State   vs Jno. Nichson - Contd.

125 State   vs Thos. Knight Contd in the former Recognizance

46   State   vs John Barfield Judgmt for 10₺ paid by /5/
     installments & Costs.

On application of Walker Robison to keep Tavern at his House granted on his giving Bond & security according to Law.

On the Complaint of Antho Bourdeaux requiring Jno. Bates, Sen. Jno Bates, Jun. & Wm. Gest be bound to their good behavour for one Year when Wm. Vince & Tarlton Brown became there Security /the Principal in 50 ₺ & Security in 25 ₺ each/

On the Complaint of Jno. Bates, Sen. Jno Bates, Jun., & Wm. Guest requiring Anthn Bourdeaux to be bound to his good behavour for one Years when Robt. McLewrath & Jno. Fitts became his Security & they to give their Bonds in Office Principal in ₺ 50 & Security in 25 ₺ each.

Ordered that Wm. Kee pay James Jackson for 3 Days Attendance Robert vs Kee/ for Deft/

James Doane vs /Jonathan/Clark - Attachment for debt, It appearing by the Oath of the Plaintiff that the note given by Wm. Clarke to the said Doan was lost or mislaid so that it could not be found and the said Jonathan Clark acknowledging that he gave such a Note bearing date about June or July in the year 1788 which note he said amounted principal & interest to about fifty seven pounds two shillings & three pence. The sd. Clark therefore confessd Judgment for the same with say of Execution six months.

The Jury Jas. Jackson, Foreman, Thos. Enocks, Drury Lane, Reuben Nixon, Absm Tylor, Richd. Jackson, Benj. Buckston, Jas. Kirkland, Jno. Dave, Geo. Robison, Rowland Roberts for this Court.

The Court adjourned for one Hour

& the Court met according to Adjournment.

Ordered that the Sheriff take a Sufficient Posse Commn to take the body of James Mitchell to bring him before the Court to answer the Misdemeanor for taking a Horse Executed /by the Sheriff John Bates/ by order of Court out of his Custody.

James Mitchell appeard & on his making suitable acknowledgements to the satisfaction of the Court - Orderd to be discharged out of Custody.

87   Benj. Odom, Jun. vs Jno. C. Smith/ the same Jury as before/ The Jury do find for the Defendant Judgmt accordingly Jas. Jackson, Foreman

Ordered that Colo Wm. Davis, Jno Broxton & George Broxton be find twenty Shillings each for a Riott in face of the Court & to be kept in Custody till the Money is paid & that John Davis be find Twenty shillings for an Insult & Contempt of the Court & to be in Custody till the Money paid & that he pay Ten Shillings for two Oaths swore in the Court.

114 Jno Beauford & Robt. McLewrath agrees to enter themselves Securities for the Debt & Costs of Allen Williams vs John Green agreeable to Installments & Costs & they oblige themselves to pay the two Instalments due with cost or deliver the property (to wit) a horse now under Execution at the next Court.

                          Jno Buford
                          Richd. McLewrath.

64 Winiford Arnard) Case the Defendant being three times
            vs   ) solemnly called and not appearing
    Joseph Brooker) order that Judgmt of Nonsuit be
                          entered up which is accordingly
done Dismist at Plaintiffs Cost.

The Minutes being read the Court adjourned until tomorrow morning nine o'clock.

23 Wm. Minor   ) Dismist at the Defendants Cost
       vs   )
    John McElhany)   E. Gillett
                            Wm. Dunbar
                            John Wyche

160 The Court met according to adjournment on Thursday the 5th day of August, 1790.

    Present the Worshipful   John C. Smith)
                                      Elijah Gillett)
                                      John Wyche   ) Esqrs.
                                      Wm. Beauford)
                                      Thos. Obannon)
                                      Wm. Dunbar   )

78 Wm. Harding vs Allen Williams, Settled by mutual consent by Arbitrators.

93 Jno. Parkinson vs Geo. Robison - Dismist at Defts Cost

94 Idem   vs Alex Newman - Dismist at Defts Cost.

123 Jno Wickly vs Wm. Ashley - Contd under Reference

The parties that wer fined yesterday for the Riott on coming into Court & making Suitable acknowledgements there fines were remitted on paying Cost.

13 Golphin & Dunbar vs Benj. Odom, Admr. Michl. Odom Estate - Contd.

26 Henry Hampton vs Henry Best - Judgmt by Default.

46 Wm. Willis vs Danl Shaw - Contd.

	50	James Montgomery vs Turner & Obannon - Contd.
	54	Installments Staying Execut till 10th January 1791.
	70	Saml. Jones vs Jno. Randal - Contd.
	71	Roberts & Myers vs Wm. Ashley - Dismist at Plaintiff Cost
	72	Idem . . . . vs Mclinton & Mayes /Nonsuit/ at Plffs Cost.
	75	Thos. Dobbins vs Jno. Nickson - Dismist Plffs Cost.
	79	James Jackson vs Jno. Mcleheney - Contd.
	80	Idem ____ vs Idem ____ Contd.
	108	Jno C. Smith vs Jno. Crocker - Judgment by Default-Contd.
	111	Allen Williams vs Wm. Harding - Dismist at Mutual Cost
	131	Jno. Randall vs Redd & Goss - Contd.
	132	Jas. C. Murphy vs Alex Newman - Dismist Plff Cost.
	133	Eneas Mcleod vs Wm. Christie - Judgt by Default
	135	Danl Bough vs Hoomes & Hankinson - Nonsuit
	136	Phar Merritt vs Beray Williamson - Nonsuit
	45	Thos. Beckham be allowed 6 days attendance & comeing Miles Twice at the suit of Randal vs Redd for Randall.
	137	Martin Shepherd vs Jno. Green abates by Death of Plaintiff
	138	Owen Jones vs Jno. Green - Contd.
	140	Jno. Parkinson vs Danl Green - Contd.
	146	Robt. Stark vs Jno. Watson - Nonsuit.
	147	Iden ___ vs Wm. Sisson - Contd.
	158	Peter Carnes vs Jasper Wert - Contd.
161	44	Hez. Roberts vs Zodack Woolley - Contd.
	37	Mary Mitchell vs Robt. Mclewrath - Contd.
	4	Danl. Bourdeaux vs Willm Robison - Contd.
	7	Robt. Mclewrath vs Jas. Mitchell - Dismist at Plain Cost
	12	Jno. Peoples vs Tarlton Brown - Contd.
	15	Elijah Padget vs Geo. Golphin - Nonsuit

20 Thos. Garnett vs Jas. McKoy - Contd.

21 Idem   vs George Golphin - Contd.

23 Wm. Minor vs Jno. Mcleheney - Dismist at Deft Cost.

24 Idem   vs Theo. Baxter - Contd.

25 Bennit vs Wm. Brown - Dismist Plaintiff Cost.

26 Jos. Garnett vs Wm. Brown - Contd.

30 Thos. Jones vs Geo & Jno. Golphin - Contd.

31 Jno. Crocker vs Nathl. Twining - Nonsuit.

32 C. D. Wyld vs Wm. Davis - Contd.

34 Chas. Palmer vs Elij. Gillett - Dismist at Defendts Cost.

45 Ruth Townsend vs Jno. Parkinson -Contd.

47 Queney Anthony vs Wm. Boyett - referd.

53 Geo. Robison vs Jno. Parkinson Judg Confsd 15-15-0 Stay Exec 6 Months.

   Thoms. Morris acknowledged his Bill of Sale for a Negroe to Thos. Enocks ___) to be Recorded

49 Wm. Scarbrough vs /Wm. Davis/ Contd.

50 Idem ___ vs Sampson Griffin - Judgment Staying Exec. till January the 3rd. 1791.

54 Jno. Cave vs Robt. Mclewrath - Contd.

59 Robt. Browne vs Benj. Odom Sen. Judgt Ł 4-17-1 & Cost

35 Willm Little vs Jno. & Mary David Contd.

13 Golphin & Dunbarr vs Benj. Odom, Jun. - Contd.

   Appearance Docket calld the Last Time.

60 The State vs Grand & Pet Jurors - Discharged

61 Alex. Skirving vs Geo. Golphin - Dismist

62 Idem   vs Idem - Dismist

63 Jno. Wiltshire vs Wm. Robison Judgmt by Default / Judgt P. Note & Cost Ł 11-12-10/ on Writ of Enq/ James Jackson, Foreman.

64 Jas. Solomon vs David Shipes - Contd.

65 Wm. Minor vs Jno. Shelley - Judgmt Confst Ł 10 Judgt Stay Ex 1st Nov.

66 Idem   vs Sampson Griffen   Judgt Confd ₺ 17-1-1
    Ju Ex Stay Ex. 1st Jany.

67 Idem   vs Henry Crocker - Contd.

68 Joseph Vince vs Jonath Gregory Judgt by Default

69 Elijah Gillett vs Laurana French. We of the Jury
    find for Pff ₺ s & Cost.

70 The State vs Lewis Frazier & Randal Lucas. Wm. Frazer
    & Lewis Frazer Guilty of Cow Stealing - Randal Lucas
    Acquitted.

71 Willm Vince vs Wm. Christie - Judgmt by Default on a
    Writ of Inquiry. We find for the Plaintiff the Sum of
    ₺ 39 -1-3 & Cost, orderd that the property attached be
    sold to satisfy the Judgment & Cost.

162 Orderd that Wm. Dunbar Esq. be appointed to lett out to the
    lowest bidder, The Repairs to be made to the Bridge over
    the three runs near Joseph Harley's, the money to be paid
    at the next Court on producing Wm. Dunbarr Esq. Certificate,
    of the work being done according to agreement ___ as the
    said Bridge is allowd by the Court to be paid by the Publick
    being to large a charge for the Private Neighbours.

72 Richd. Creech vs James Simms - We find for Plaintiff
    one hundred pounds & Cost & Ordered the property attacht be
    sold to pay Debts & Costs ___. Jas. Jackson, foreman.

73 Fred Womack vs Sus Hankinson & Wm. Hoomes, Dismist Pff
    Cost rec/5/

74 Wm. Trover vs Susanna Hankinson &C Judg. for 6-13-7
    & Cost and Install

75 Robt Smith vs Jno Bush & Jos. Miller - Contd.

76 Isaac McPherson vs Elijah Gillett Judgmt confest P.
    Bond & Cost

77 Fred. Sunn vs Robt Mclewrath - Came to late

78 The State vs Jos. Kirkland - No Bill O. D to be dismist
    on paying fees.

79 Mary Palmer vs Luke Long - to be renewed.

80 Willm Sturgess vs Henry Hughes   Judgt by Default - Contd.

81 Jacob Griner vs Wm. & Bartl Brown - Dismist

82 Adam Priester vs James Simms - Settled by Consent each
    party paying their own Cost - Dismist.

83 Jas. Way vs Robt. Cook - Dismist.

Sarah Fitts allowed 7 Days Atrendance Arnond vs Brooker for
Deft.

Chas. Biles allowed 4 Days Attendante Gillett vs French - Plaintiff

Elias Jenkins - 4 Days Attendance Do Plaintiff.

Tarlton Brown 7 Days - Fields vs Bourdeaux - Plff

Parker Savage 9 Days Do   Do _____ Plff

Jno. Gallaher - 4 Days Minor vs Sampson Griffin for Plff

Jno. Mitchell Wyld vs McNeely for Plaintiff.

The Court adjourned for one Hour.

The Court met after adjournment.

163 Order that John C. Smith, Elijah Gillett, & Wm. Buford do examine the Clerk's Office and report the Condition thereof, the Examination to take place on the last Saturday in August Instant And that the High Sheriff do settle the account with the Clerk for all fees due from the Sheriff for accounts delivered by the said Clerk before the said Commissioners & returned in Clks Office.

Nich. Nobles allowed 12 Days Attendance Stark vs Collins for Plaint.

Elijah Gillett Esq. allowed 12 Days attendance Stark vs Collins for Plaint.

Saml. Bennet allowed 4 Days Attendance Creech vs Simms - Plaintiff.

James Thurston allowed 4 Days Attendance   Do.

Thos. Knight allowed 1 Day ___ ___ Do Do ___

James Thurston allowed 2 Days - Simms advs Priester for Simms

84 Priscilla Odom vs Malachy Powell - Dismist at Plaintiff Cost

Orderd that all the Persons delinquents on the Petty Jury be sumd by Sci Fa to next Court.

On application of James Myrcik to keep Tavern at his House granted on giving Bond & Security according to Law.

On application of Jno. Fitts to keep Tavern at his House granted on giving bond & Security according to Law.

The Minutes being read the Court was adjourned to the next Court in Course.

       Jno. Car Smith
       E. Gillett   Esqrs.
       W. Buford

164 Blank.

165 At a Court in Course held for Winton County at the Court House on Monday the first day of November 1790.
Present the Worshipful   John C. Smith   )
                          Richd. Tradeaway   )
                          Jesse Winburn   )
                          Jno. Wyche, Esq.   ) Esqrs.
                          Wm. Buford   )
                          Thos. Obannon   )
                          Walter Robison   )

The Jury Box being produced the following persons were drawn to Serve as Grand Jurymen next Court.

Jno. Miller 1, Jos. Redd 2, Gardner Davis 3, Edwd Nix 4, Garrat Buckaloo 5, Jno. Herrington 6, Geo. Robinson 7, Blanchard Collden 8, Jno Fitts 9, Jno. Williams 10, Moses Collins 11, Micajah Matthews 12, Thos. Wethersby 13, Robt. Adams 14, Wm. Thompson 15, Rowland Roberts 16, Chas. Boils 17, Jacob Adams 18, Henry Creech 19, David Shipes 20, Jno. Myers 21.

Pettit Jury Chas. Beck 1, Elijah Abslom 2, Purlevant Johnson 3, Simon Bryant 4, Wm. Jones 5, Thos. Morris 6, Richd. Blalock 7, Adam Lard 8, Robt. Bradley 9, Joshua Williams 10, Lionel Lee 11, Thos. Enicks 12, James Jackson 13, Jos. Duncan 14, John Griffen 15, Saml Simms 16, Wilson Cook 17, Isham Jourdan 18, Ephraim Herrington 19, Nehem Powers 20, Jno. Platts 21, Jos. Brooker 22, Wm. Freeman 23, Drury Lane 24, Wm. Hall 25, Barthl. Roberts 26, Benj. Crocket 27, Richd. Kirkland 28, Saml Dennis 29, Michl. Swicord 30 -- 31

Orderd Thos. Weekley be appointed Guardian for Jno Wickley & Wm. Weekly & that he give Bond & Security in the Clerk's Office with Willm Bluford & Wm. Carr his Securitys in the sum of Three thousand pounds.

Jesse Winbourne made oath that he saw David Edwards Sign Seal & publish his last Will & /Testament/ also saw Jesse Rogers & Charles Cardin Sign the same as Witnesses & Orderd to be recorded.

Citation on the Estate of James Bonds returned into Court & order for letters of Admr be granted & Isham Clayton & Wm. Williams be her Security in three hundred Pounds bond to be given in Office Isham Clayton, Geo. Kirkland, Nathan Grimes.

Jos. Turner & David Edwards, Jun. took the Oaths of Qualification /as Executors/ & Jesse Winbourn & Zadock Wooley/ & Jesse Rogers/ were appointed Appriasers of David Edwards Estate.

112 Thos. Gordon as John Wyche, Debt judgment confessed for the amount of the Bond with stay of Execution six months subject to the Instalment Law of the said Wyche produces satisfactory /proof/ to next May Court that the said debt is within that Act and subject to all legal discounts which the said Wyche may produce.

130 Danl. Shaw Appelant vs Robt. Ashley, Respondnt appeal

from John Wyche Esq. from a Judgment for 5 ℔ Orderd that
this Judgment be confirmed with double Cost.

166 88 Barbara Grimes vs Priscilla Odom. Mr. Peter Carnes
Counsel for the defent moved to set aside this Writ alled-
ging a varience between the Original Writ and the copy and
it appearing that the error in the proceedings was a mere
crerical [sic] mistake or inattention and not the effect
or design or ill judgment Orderd that the Action procede and
that the parties amend without Cost.

The Deft requiring Security for Costs - Wm. Vince became
security.

The Petit Jury being called the following Persons appear
Richd. Vince, Leven Collins, 2 Nathan Cocker, James Morris
Jun. 4, Geo. Kirkland 5, Wm. Freeman 6, Chas. Richmond 7,
Jos. Brooker 8, Richd. Kirkland 9, Chas. Brown 10, Jno
Drummond 11, Jno. Youngblood 12,

90 State vs Benj. Corbett/a the Jury return the party
guilty/ & orderd by the Court to be fined Twenty two Shil-
lings/ & Six Pences / & Cost & kept in custody till the
Cash are paid NB 20/ pd in part of Fine.

The Petit Jury discharge till to Morrow nine of the Clock.

131 The State vs Jerad Walker Assee John Ashley the prosecutor in the case and further recognized when Richard
Tredawaw agreed to be bound with him the sum of fifty pounds
to be levied on their respective goods and chattels Lands
and tenements to be void upon condition that the said
John Ashley shall appear at the next Court to prosecute a
Bill of Indictment against the said Walker for an Assault.

John M. Strozer and John Cook witness in the same case and
Joseph Turner agreed /to/ be jointly bound with them/
to the State/ in the sum of twenty pounds each to be res-
pectively levied on their Lands and tenements goods and
Chattels upon the Condition that the said John Martin
Strozer and John Cook shall appear at the next Court to give
testimony on the part of the State in a Bill of Indictment
to be exhibited against Israel Walker and not depart without
leave.

The Court then proceeded to the Choice of a Sheriff the
ballots being counted ie appeared that Richard Creech and
James Works had four votes each. The election was deferred
until tomorrow ten o'clock.

125 The State aginast Benjamin Corbit Cow Stealing the
defendant appeared and was ordered to /be/ further
recognized when Richard Creech and William Williams
acknowledged themselves indebted jointly with him to the
County in the sum of fifty pounds each to be levied on
their respective goods and chattels Land and tenements upon
Condition that the said Benj. Corbit shall appear at the
next Court to answer a Bill of Indictment for cow stealing
and not depart without leave.

167 Gibbion Jones who was cited to appear and shew cause why
he had not delivered an Estray in his Custody and it

appearing /that/ the said Estray had been proved away from said Jones /ordered/ that he be discharged.

The Minutes being read the Court adjourned until tomorrow morning nine o'clock.

       W. Buford
       Jesse Winborne
       Walter Robinson

At a Court held for Winton County on Tuesday the 2d Nov. 1790. Present the Worshipful

William Buford	)
Jno. Carraway Smith	)
Alex Newman Or. Heck	
Richd. Tradeaway	)
Jesse Winburn	) Esquires
Danl. Green	)
Walter Robison	)
Thos. Obannon	)
John Wyche	)

Jas Roberts Overseer from the three Runs to the White Ponds produced a Certificate from Rich Tradaway, Esq.

Thos. Weathersby returnd a Certificate from Ditto & Elkanah Green appointed in her Room.

Jos. Harley produced a Certificate from Thos. Obannon Esq. & James Geddins appointed in his Room.

Mary Duesto was Qualified & Took the Oaths accordingly & Letters of Admr. & Orderd.

Jno. Bates, Jun. acknowledged his Deed to Jno. Green O. to be recorded.

 Ordered that Nathan Grimes be appointed overseer of a road from Bluford Bridge to intersect the road at the old Savannah ford on the Little Saltcatcher in the room of Moses Disto deceased.

125 The State vs Thos. Knight, Esq. Ind. Plea Not Guilty. Motion to Quash Indictment overruled by the Court
The defendant in this case being brought to the bar and asked if he was prepared for trial answered in the affirmative
Whereupon came a jury, to-wit, Richard Vince, Leven Collins, Nathan Croker, James Walker, George Kirkland, William Freeman, Charles Richmond, Joseph Brooker, Richard Kirkland, Charles Brooker, John Drummond & Joseph Youngblood who being empannelled sworn and charged do Say we find the defendant guilty Richd. Kirkland, foreman & Orderd to be fine 2/6 & Costs.

The State	)	Scire Facias
vs	)	Orderd that the defendant
Lazarus Wooley	)	be discharged without cost

168 129 William Dunbar) Attachment. Alexander Newman being
    vs   ) Summoned as Garnishee came into
  Timothy Barnard) Court and made oath that he was

justly indebted to the said Barnard by note of hand the sum of twenty five pounds with some Interest.

John Parkinson and William Vince esquires Executors of the Last Will and testament of Stephen Smith, deceased returned an Acct. current of the said estates from the death of Stephen Smith to this date, disbursements and receipts, which, after being sworn to was ordered to be received & filed.

132 State vs Celia Marsh & Nancy Berry) Recognized to appear at the next when William Robertson and Nathnl Sanders jointly with the defendants acknowledged to owe to the County of Winton the sum of twenty five pounds each to be Levied on their respective goods and chattels Lands and Tenements provided the defendants Do not appear at the next Court to be held for this County, to answer an Indictment to be preferred against the said Celia Marsh and Nancy Berry for an Assault.

Alexander Newman Esquire appeared in open Court and qualified as a justice of the peace by taking the oath of office & the one to support the Constitution of the United States

Zadock Wooley produced a Certificate from Jesse Winburn that his Road was Suft.

Isaac Tool produced a Certificate from Ditto.

Wm. Weekly produced a Certificate from Wm. Buford, Esq.

Benj. Kirkland affirmed the Estray taken up by him Died pd.

Zadock Wooley produced a Certificate of the Estray he took up pd.

Littlebury Nicks produced a Certificate for the Estray taken up by him - pd.

James French produced a Certificate from Wm. Sisson, Esq. for the Estray taken up.

The Court then proceeded to the Choice of a Sheriff when Richard Creech Esq. was appointed to that office.

169 Ordered that the several persons who have alledged that they have the Estrays were proved from them by sufficient affidavits, ordered that they be severally discharged upon pay the Sheriff fees by next Court.

Ruth Townsend vs Jno. Parkinson Exc. Step. Smith Dismist at Plaintiffs Cost.

John Fields vs Anthony Burdeux) On Motion to set aside the Execution, Ordered that the Execution be suspended until next Court.

Ordered that this court be adjourned until tomorrow 9 o'Clock.

W. Buford
Walter Robinson

The Court met agreable to Adjournal on Wednesday the 3
November 1790
Present the Worshipful Court   Jno. C. Smith   )
                               Danl. Green   )
                               Richd. Tradeaway) Esqrs
                               Walter Robison)
                               Thos. Obannon)

105 James Jackson, Admor.)
     of George Fallas,   ) The Plaintiff's Council in this
             vs   ) Case made a Motion that the
     John Parkinson, Exor.) names of the other Executors
     Stephen Smith   ) be inserted in this process
                            by the Court the motion was
overruled and the Suit dismist at the Plaintiffs costs

107 John Collins   )
             vs   ) Dismised at Plaintiff's Costs on
     John Parkinson, Exor of) the same principle as the above
     Stephen Smith   ) action

     No. 85 Jno. Bates vs Adam McNeeley - Dismist

121 George Houston
             vs
     William Vince, Exor. of Stephen Smith, /on Motion/ to
     amend the writ and insert the names of the other Executors
     Orderd they be amended upon paymt of Cost which

170 which was accordingly done.

     122 Same)
              vs) Same Vrdct.
          Same)

     123 Same)
              vs) Same Order
          Same)

     124 Same)
              vs) Same Order
          Same)

     87 Robt. Bradley vs Chas. Matheney - Dismist by Consent.

     88 Barbary Griner vs Priscilla Odom Court writ amended
         Wm. Vince, Security for Costs.

     89 Henry Long vs Barthl. Craddock - Dismist

     90 The State vs Benj. Corbett - Guilty fined 22/6 & Costs

     91 Mary Palmer vs Luke Long - dism.

     94 Thos. Golphin vs Hez. Roberts - Non Est dismist

     95 Idem vs John Wood - Stopd by Order of Wm. Dunbar -
         dismist

     96 Idem vs Joh. Miller advs Geo. Newman Do agreeable to
         Note

97 John Bush vs Hankinson Exor. Judg confest Staying Exc. 6 months under Instalmt

98 Idem vs Ditto - Judgt confest Staying Exec 6 Months Do

99 Idem vs Ditto - Judgt Staying Exec Ds under Ins/alment/

100 State vs Wooley &C Released on paying the Sheriff 2/6

101 State vs Wreeley - Dismist

105 Jas. Jackson vs Jno Parkinson - To be renewed

106 Patience Bowers vs Sally Hoomes /did not/ dismist & Settled Plffs Cost

107 Jno Collins vs Jno. Parkinson & Wm. Vince to be renewed

108 Wm. Davis vs Wm. Sarbrough - Contd by Consent

110 Jno C. Smith vs Elijah Gillett. Service acknowledged Judgmt confessed.

112 Thos. Gordon vs Jno Wyche Judgmt confesed for amt. of Bond subject to Instalmt if the said Wyche produces sufficient proofs & lawful accts to stay Exec 6 months.

115 The State Qui Fam vs Jno Fitts - Dismist

116 Idem __ vs Jas. Myrick - Dismist

120 Jno Parkinson vs Wm. Vince Es &C Dismist at Plaintiffs cost

171 57 Way vs Wm. Shields - Dismist

124 State vs Nickson - Dismist

126 Henry Hamton)
         vs   ) Settled.
    Henry Best   )

46 Wm. Willis   )
         vs   ) Refd to John Wych - his award to be
    Danl. Shaw   ) final.

70 Saml Jones) Judgmt confess agreeable to Note Stay
         vs   ) Exon six months to be discharged with
    John Randal) property valued by three men to be chosen
                   by the Sheriff and Thos. Redd security
for the payment.

79 Jas. Jackson, Admr.) Judgmt/agreeable to note/with
         vs   ) stay three months. Subject to
    Jno McElhany   ) Instalment

80 Same) Judmt agreeable to note stay of Execution
    vs   ) 3 months subject to Instalment.
    Same)

131 John Randal   ) Debt. judgment confessed for the
        vs   ) amount of Note and interest with stay
    John Red & Goss) of Execution six months.

It appearing to the Court that a Red ashed Sowe 2 Years Old marked a cross in each Ear a Split in one Ear and nick in the under side of the other in possession of Walter Robtson, Esq. as an Estray, Ordered that the said Sow be apprised by two persons and the amount of the appraisement be deposted in the Clks office after paying the legal fees.

35 William Little   ) A jury being sworn to wit Rich
        vs   ) Kirkland and others return a verdict
    John & Mary Davis) We find for the

172 Plaintiff/amount of the note with Interest and Cost and Judgment accordingly. Cid. Kirkland, foreman

Orderd that the Sheriff give notice that all Persons bring the Estrays to be Sold to Morrow at 3 of the Clock & the Sheriff proceed accordingly.

50 Jas. Montgomery   ) The same jury as before returned/
        vs   ) a verdict/ we find for the Plain-
    Turner & Obannon) tiff the amount of the Note with
                       Cost of Suit
                       Richard Kirkland, foreman, and
judgment accordingly under Instalment.

125 State vs Corbett - Continued.

Jno Parkinson Provd his Attendance 20 Days Golphin vs Odom for Deft

108 Jno. C. Smith vs Jno. Crocker Judgmt by Default on a Writ of Enquiry We of the jury do find for the plaintiff thirty nine pounds eleven shillings & four pence with costs of suit. Richd. Kirkland, foreman.

Elijah Hubbard provd his Attendance 18 Days Winstd Arnaud vs Jo. Brocker for the plaintiff orderd to be allowed the same.

82 The State   ) On Motion - Orderd that this recog-
        vs   ) nizance be Continued until next Court
   Nathl. Dyal, William) and that they the securities produce
   Willson, Benja. Odom) their principal by next Court.

124 The State   ) Ind. Asst. & Batty. on Motion, Ordered
        vs   ) that Robt. McLewrath Security for the
    John Nixon   ) appearance of the Defendant, and the Pro-
                      secutor not appearing, be discharged from
his recognizance on payment of Costs.

Ordered that a Sci Fa issue against Thomas Dobbins and his Securities to shew cause at the next Court why the principal did not appear according to the tenor of their recognizance and why their recognizance be not forfeited.

173 Higdon Spilliards proved seven days atten in the Cause of William Little vs John and Mary Davis at 60 miles

distance issued for 3 days by order of G Walker.

The Minutes being read the Court adjourned until tomorrow mroning eight o'clock.
        Jno. Car Smith, J.P.
        Daniel Green, J.P.
        W. Buford, J.P.

174 At a Court held in Course for Winton County this 7th Feby 1791
Present Richard Tradaway, Jesse Winburn & Walter Robertson, Esqrs.

The Jury Box being produced the following persons were drawn to serve as Pettit Jurors /to May Term/ John Cockerham 2 Robt Lankerster 3 Richd Vince 4 Lewis Johnston 5 Jacob Harlam 6 John Randal 7 Abraham Deeson 8 James Brown 9 Willm Mason 10 Reubin Nixon 11 Anthony Leach 12 James Morris 13 Joshua Smith 14 Rheubin Golikely 15 Willm Mounts 16 Leven Collins 17 Jacob Rivers 18 Willm Williams 19 Willm Roberts 20 Ezekiel Williams 21 Willm Price 22 Peter Banner 23 Joseph Bradham 24 Isaac Deeson 25 John Green 26 Willm Owens 27 John Joice 28 Willm Addams 29 George Robinson 30 Bartlett Brown

A motion being made for the appointment of a Deputy Clerk Mr. George Latham was unanimously appointed to that office and ordered to be qualified accordingly.

O. that Jacob Swicord /Last/ Will and Testament be recd & Recorded it being proved by the Oath of Thomas Frederick in open Court.

Willm Robinsons last Will & Testament being produced to the Court order to be recorded it being provd by the Oaths of Michael Swicord & Willm Harden & thereupon Ordered to be Recorded.

Michael Swicord, Gurge Swicord and Mayes Hutn came into Court and was qualified Executors to the last Will & Testament of Jacob.

175 Swicord deceased and Ordered that Joseph Vince, George Robertson & Thomas Frederick be appointed Appraisers to the Estate of Jacob Swicord, decd.

Allen Robison came into Court and was qualified as Executor to the Estate of William Robison decd. Ordered that John /Bates, Sen./ Michael Swicord and /Andrew Nimmons/ be appointed appraisers to the Estate of William Robison, decd.

John Mitchell came into Court and made oath that he saw Sarah Southwell sign the Will produced to Coart as her last Will & Testament whereupon it is as Ordered to be Recorded.

Ordered that the High Sheriff be paid Seven Pounds, Ten Shillings for his Extra Services for the year 1790. Orderd that the Clerk of Winton County be paid Five pounds for his Extra Services for the year 1790.

Elizabeth Best came into Court and made Oath that she saw Absolom Best sign the /Will/ produced to Court as his last Will and Testament, whereupon it was ordered to be recorded.

Richard Kirkland and Bartlett Brown came into Court and were qualified as Executors to the Estate of Absolom Best, decd.

Ordered that George Robison, Jr. be appointed Guardian to George Robison a Minor, Son of William Robison, Decd.

The Minutes being read the County adjourned till tomorrow Ten O'Clock.
        Richd. Tradaway
        Jesse Winborne
        Walter Robinson

The Court met according to Adjournment the 8th. February 1791. Present Rich. Tradaway, Walter Robinson & Jesse Winburn, Esqrs.
Ordered that Absalom Causey, James McKay, and Jacob Buckston, be appointed appriasers to the Estate of Absolom Best, decd.

The Minutes being read the Court adjourned till Court in Course.
        Richard Tradaway
        Walter Robison
        Jesse Winborne

176

177

178

INDEX

Date	Page		Date	Page
17th Oct. 1786	1 (Begins)		6 August 1788	91
18 " "	2		7 " "	93
19 " "	5		3 November "	97
16 Jan. 1787	7		4 " "	98
18 " "	17		5 " "	100
17 April "	21		6 " "	102
18 " "	21		2 February 1789	106
19 " "	23		3 " "	107
20 " "	28		4 " "	109
18 July "	30 41		5 " "	111
19 " "	43		6 " "	113
16 Oct. "	54		4 May 1789	117
17 " "	56		5 " "	119
18 " "	63		6 " "	121
15 Jany 1788	67		7 " "	123
16 " "	68		8 " "	125
17 " "	70		3 August 1789	127
18 " "	72		4 " "	128
5 May "	77		5 " "	130
6 " "	79		6 " "	131
7 " "	82		7 " "	132
8 " "	84		2 November "	135
4 August "	89		3 " "	137
5 " "	89		4 " "	140

5	November 1789	Page	141
1	Feby 1790	"	145
3	May "	"	147
4	" "	"	148
2	August 1790	"	152
3	" "	"	154
4	" "	"	157
5	" "	"	160
1	November "	"	165
2	" "	"	167
3	" "	"	169
8	February 1791 (Ends)	"	175

179 Blank

180 Thomas Wyld.

    Thomas Williams

    James Mercer, Esquire,
       Richmond,
          Virginia.

BARNWELL (WINTON) COUNTY WILL BOOK 1

Page 1: South Carolina, Winton County: Frederick Frances of the
county aforesaid, planter, for Ł 110 pd by Joseph Vince
of same, negro felloe named Simon, negro wench named Venos, negro
boy Joe...10 Jan 1787. Fed. Francis, Wit: Stephen Smith, _____
Vince. Rec. 12 April 1787.

Page 2: South Carolina, Winton County: William Robison of county
aforesaid, for Ł 32 s 10 pd. by Mary Mitchell, of same,
a Negro woman slave named Sylvia...9 April 1787, Wm Robison.
Wit: Rd Vince, Lark Robison. Ack. by William Robison, 18 April
1787. Rec. 1 June 1787.

Pp 3-4: South Carolina, County of Winton: Will of Martin Kimberhide of the Destrict of Orangeburgh....unto Ruben Brunton,
one Cow and Calf and a two year old heifer, likewise unto Margaret Brunton, two Horses and my stock of hogs and all the house-
hodl furniture and working Tools...the ramindr. of all my cattle
to Jacob Brunton and all my right and possession of Land...if it
please god to take either of my children before coming of age the
above right and property to fall into Marget Bruntons hands...
Arthur Jinkins Exr...6 June 1787 Martin Kimberhid (Ma) Wit:
Wm Buford, Wm Roberts (X), W. Creech (W). Wm Miner.
Prov. by Wm Creech (W), before Wm Buford, JP, 14 June 1787.
Rec. 8 Aug 1787.

Page 4: William Buford of Winton County for Ł 50 pd. by John
Buford of the State of Georgia and Burk County, planter, negro
slave named Bob with one Chesnut couloured (sic) mare and a gray
horse (Brands given)...__ July 178_. Wm Buford. Rec. 10 Sept
1787. Wit: (named torn off).

Page 5: Robert Lee of Orangeburg District, South Carolina, planter, for Ł 68 sterling pd. by Jno Wood of same dist.,
planter, negro wench named Hagar 14 years of age, and child
Abraham about 6 months old...12 May 1784. Robert Lee, Wit:
Jno B. G. Wallen, Elkana Green. Rec. 17 Sept 1787.

Pp. 5-6: S. C. Winton County: Owen Odom of County aforesaid, for
Ł 125 sterling pd by Levin Collins, one negrow Woman
Saffo, negro boy named Jerry...Owen Odom (O), 17 Jan 1787., Wit:
Sally Odom, Uriah Odom (H O). Rec. 17 Sept 1787.

Pp. 6-7: William Brown & James Brown of Orangeburgh District
bound to Alexander Newman of same, in the sum of Ł 1000
sterling money, 23 May 1786, to make title to a tract of land
on Swaycord mill Creek, 290 A by 1 Feb 1790...Wm Brown (Seal),
Jams. Brown (Seal), Wit: Ths. Carson, Wm Minor.

Page 7: Alexr Newman for Ł 200 sterling transferred above bond
to Wm Scaborigh and Wm Cooke of Charleston, Merchants,
for 220 A on Swaycords mill Creek, 26 Mar 1787. Alexr Newman, Wit:
Jno Mitchel. Rec. 17 Sept 1787.

Page 8: Robert Cord of State of S. C., planter, for natural love
and affection to Buford Weekley of same state, the whole
stock of neat cattle and one small bay mare branded 97, but in
case the said Buford Weekly should dye without Issue of his Body,
to Joseph Weekly, son of Wm Weekly...16 June 1787...Robt Cord (R)
Wit: Wm Buford, Wm Roberts. Rec. 17 Sept 1787.

Pp. 9-10: Wm Weekley of the State of S. C., Planter, for love and
affection to George Weekley of same, 100 A in Orangeburgh District adj. Joseph Brooker, and sd. George Weekley, & also
a Negro man slave named Butler, 13 June 1787...William Weekley
(Seal0, Wit: W. Buford, William Roberts (X). Prov. by William
Weekely. Rec. 1 Oct 1787.

Pp. 11-17: A List of Taxeable Persons in Winton County deliverd
by Elijah Gillett Esqr. Sheriff into the Clerks Office.

John Parkerson
John Bates
Sarah Dabney
Rudford Cannon
Pugh Cannon
Peter Banner
Henry Cannon
Frances Bassett
John Airs
Arthur Davis
Nathaniel Sanders
Lewis Clark
Isham Clayton
William Mason
William Ashley
James Matthews
William Adams
Samuel way
John Cave
Micajah Matthews
Fause
William Carr
James Bradlam
Robert McLewrath
Frederick Brant
George Walker Senr
Robert Lancaster
James Walker
David Jackson
Thomas Daughton
John Ashley
Randolph Adams
John Randolph

\-\-\-am Edenfield
\-\-\-hard Creech
\-\-\-rge Kersh
\-\-hn Kersh
\-\-\-n Creech
\-\-mes Neal
\-\-\-ah Deweese
\-\-rthur Jenkins
\-\-\-n Leroche
\-\-\-nis Belcher
\-\-hn Herrington
\-\-hn Deen
\-\-\-avid Reeves
\-\-adrach Reed
\-\-ias Gess
\-\-\-rles Bekc
\-\-\-\-ander Kennaday
Evans

Lewis Clark Jun
William Frazer
Lewis Frazer
John Tarber
Elisha Abeton
Jonathan Clark
William Causey
William Davis
James Arnold
James Jackson
Richard Jackson
Drury Lane
John Platt
Jacob Harler
Thomas Matthews
Robert Adams
William Catre
Robert Bradley
William Matthews
Absalom Cawsey
Robert Hankinson
Joseph Bradlam
Elijah Wasden
Alexander McMillen
Charles Carden
Nathaniel Walker
Joseph Lancaster
Ruebin Harrison
William Daniel
John McCain
Jacob Adams
Richard Blalock

David Canfield
James Lee
Lionel Lee
Richard Creetch
William Creech
Henry Creech
Absalom Best
Duke Leester
William Freeman
Verdamon Clemons
John Snelin
Willis Read
Hardy Reed
Thomas Enock
John Nelson
William Weekley
Alexander Newman
Reuben Newman

---omas Sheilds
--obert Shields
    steele
--aac Deeson
--ement Clements
-braham Peacock
-benjamin Eaves
-awrence Teaster
--ohn Creek
--mes Wells
--hn Elkins

Susannah Budd
William Tuten
Joseph Humphreys
William Hughs
John Grubbs
Arthur Turner
John Mulkey
Shadrach Quinly
Benjamin Blunt
John Drummond
Jacob Buxton
Matthew Murphy
Joseph Turner
John Hutchenson

William Bryan
Michael Swycord
John Wyld
John Byles

---lomon Owen
--roh Boyenton
Thomas Owen
--arles Blomett
--omas Long
John Collins
Charles Boyles
-alekiah Powell
-ames Joice
Benjamin Corbett
Moses Odom
Joseph Morris
Joseph Collins
-ames Roberts
Bartholomew Roberts
-annan Gore
-homas Powell
--orge Crosley
--liam Brooker
--exander Wood
--hro Wood
-homas Obannan
Daniel Crockett
--cob Roundtree
-oseph Brooker
--mes Moody
--rk Robinson
--rlevant Johnson
---- Morris Junr
James Brown

William Newman
John Newman
    Jeter
Abraham Deeson
Abnor Deen
Frederick Lee
Joseph Red
Lewis Peacock
Anthony Leach
Samuel Denne

Thomas Tuten
Moses Plummer
Archibald Fruger
William Buford
Lovett Bunch
Nudon Buxton
Samuel Buxton
John Dunn
Jacob Surrincy
Benjamin Buxton
William Dunbar
Isaac Buch
James Truck
John Eubanks

Simon Bryan
John Myers
Charles Byles
Absolom Tylor

William Moore
Jeribah Boyenton
Blancahrd Coleing
Sarah Southwell
Levi Long
Moses Collins
James Montgomry
William Roberts
James Morris
Thomas Morris
George Collins
James Collins
Tarlton Brown
William Goode
George Robinson
Nolly Gore
Uriah Odom
Nicholas Nobles
Rueben Roundtree
Matthew Cone
George Coupee
Bartlet Brown
William Robertson
John McKnight Johnson
Rowland Roberts
Nathan Cooker
John Cockran
Thomas Cox
Joseph Corbett
    Jordan

-sham Jordan
-ilas Rolls
-saac Tool
William Jones
--ven Collins
--adoch Wooley
--hn Cook
--bert Brown
---aham Johnston

Richard Vince
Reuben Likeley
Stephen Smith
Willis Grimes
Edward Nix
Robert Nix
James Kirkland
Thomas Wiggins
Joseph Vince
John Nimons
William Price
Thomas Philpott
John White
Thomas Knight Esqr
Charles Richmond
Zachariah Griffen
Reuben Mixon
Jacob Rivers
George Nix
John Wickly
Joshua Smith
Moses Disto
James Simms
    Richardson
Jacob Swicord
David Mills
William Miles
John Rivers Junr
David Shipes
David Gipson
Jonathan Grigorey
Ezekiel Williams

Daniel Odom
Jacob Powell
Daniel Howell

George Robertson
Nehemiah Powers
David Tool
Henry Wood
Joseph Youngblood
Abraham Cook
Abdell Stot
Edward Morris
Jesse Rogers

John Williams
Richard Kirkland
George Miller
Cornelious Tinsley
Charles Nix
George Kirkland
William Vince
John Michell
William Dikes
Daniel Price
Rawley Williams
Shadrach Quinley
Jacob Swicord
Nathan Stinson
William Griffin
Daniel Philpott
William Hidgcock
Andrew Nimmons
James Gideons
Joshua Williams
William Smith
Samson Griffen
William Williams
Nehemiah Powers (stricken)
Michael Swicord
Edward Miles
John Rivers
John Elkins (stricken)
William Griffin
Benjamin Kirkland
Jesse Winbourn
John Fittzs

(Pages 18-19 must be read directly across and correspond to the next two pages)

132

A List of Sundry Fines due to Winton County

Date		Persons Names	The Cause of the Fine
1788			
Janua	18	Robert Shields	For misdemeanour & Assault & C
	18	Willm Weekley	For Tavern Licence
	18	James Myrick	For Tavern Licence
	18	John Gill	For Tavern Licence
Feby	6	John Fitts	For Tavern Licence
	10	Solomon Owen	For Tavern Licence
Oct 18 1787		Ann Collins with Charles Wheeler Security for Bastardy	

1787
July 18 John Ward fined by Order of Court 20/
         & the Sheriff ordered immediately to Levy the Same
     N. B. to inquire of the H: Sheriff

1788
May   7   Walter Robinson   For Tavern Licence New Act
        31   Christopher Hall   For Tavern Licence New Act
July   13   Joseph Duncan   For Tavern Licence   Ditto
             Mary Southwell & Fras Bassett Security Indemnification
             Eliza. Myrick & James Myrick Security   Ditto
             Willm Southwell & Francis Bassett   Ditto
Augst   5   David Mills for a Stray Horse No. 1 P Bond & Security
         6   John Wickly   one Ditto   2 P Bond
         6   Frederick Sunn   one Ditto   3 P Ditto
         6   Thos P Carnes   one Ditto   4 P Ditto
         6   James Kirkland   one Ditto   5 P Ditto
         6   Burrel Parker   one Ditto   7 P Ditto
         6   Francis Bassett one Ditto   10 P Ditto
         6   William Woodcock one Do   11 P Ditto
         6   Thomas Wyld   one Do   13 P Ditto
         6   Willm Buford   one Do   15 P Ditto
Nov   8   Willm Newman   E Gillett Sec   12   Elijah Gillett Sec
         5   James Babcock   14   Lark Robison Sec
         5   James Mitchell   23   Jno Mitchell Sec
1789
Jany   1   John Crocker   For Tavern Licence for 1789
  ?   5   John Mixon   Do   1789

to be paid to Aaron Smith Esqr   The Treasurer

The Fine			When Received & paid to the Treasurer
£	S	D	
7	10	0	By Fine Remitted by order of Court Novr 4 1788
3			August 16th By Cash
3			May the 18th 1788 By Cash recd
3			By Aaron Smith
3			August the 8th 1788 By Cash recd
3			August the 8th 1788 By Cash recd
5			Proclamation, payble in 9 Months)
			Remitted by Order of August Court 1788)

1	10		By Cash Novemr 5th 1789
1	10		By Cash Augst 8th 1788
1	10		By Cash Pd A Smith
50			Penalty For maintaing a Bastard
150			Penalty For Maintaining a Bastard
50			Penalty For Maintaining a Bastard
1	5	0	Payable in three Montsh By Cash Novr 7th 1788
3			Ditto By Cash April 25th 1789
1	18		Ditto By Cash pd Thomas Wooton
3	8		Ditto By Cash Novr 7th 1788
3	7		Ditto By Thos Obannon pd Thos Wooton
2			Ditto By Cash Novr 7th 1788
1	10		Ditto By Aaron Smith
3	11		Ditto By Cash February the 5th 1789
6	2		Ditto By Cash Novr 7th 1788
4			Ditto By Cash February 13th 1789
1	16		Ditto By A Smith
2	5		Ditto By A Smith
4	1		Ditto By A Smith
1	10		Ditto By A Smith
1	10	0	Ditto By A Smith

			(L	S)
1788		Page 20:		
May 8	To Cash of James Myrick for Ordinary Licence		3	
Aug 8	To Cash of John Fitts for Ditto		3	
8	To Cash of Solomon Owen for Ditto		3	
16	To Cash of William Weekley for Ditto		3	
	To Cash of Christopher Hall for Ditto		1	10
Nov 1	To Cash recd of Docr. Sunn for an Estray No 3		1	18
7	To Cash recd of David Mills for Do	1	1	5
	To Ditto Thos Peters Carnes for Do	4	4	8
	To Ditto Burrell Parker for Do	7	2	
1789	To Ditto Thomas Wyld for Do	13	6	2
Feby 5	To Ditto Willm Woodcock for Do	11	3	11
13	To Ditto Willm Buford Esqr for Do	15	4	
	To Ditto Thos Obannon Esqr accot. Jas Kirkland			
		5	3	7
April 25	To Ditto of John Wickly for Do	2		
	To John Gill Ord. Licence		3	
	To Joseph Duncan Ditto		1	10
	To Frans. Bassett & Wm Buford Estray No. 10		1	10
	To Wm Newman & E. Gillett Do 12		1	16
	To James Babcock & Lark Robison Do 14		2	5
	To James Mitchell & John Mitchell Do 23		4	1
	To Walter Robison Ordinary Licence		1	10
	To Docr John Crocker for Licence for 1789		1	10
	To John Mixon for Ordinary Licence 1789		1	10
			L61	13

(The following entries are marked through.)

1789				
April 25	To the Ballance as P Contra		3	9
May 6	To James Myrick Licence renewd		1	10
	To Zadoc Woolly Ditto		1	10
	To William Weckley Ditto		1	10
	To John Fitts Ditto		1	10
	To John Gill Ditto		1	10

Page 21:				
	Cash received as Treasurer			
1788				
Sep 4	By Cash paid Thos Wooton in part for building the Prison	13		
	By Cash paid Ditto P Christopher Hall	1	3	
Nov 1	By Order Court to pay Willm Vince Clerk for 1787	5		
3	By Order of Court to pay Elijah Gillett Esqr High Sheriff his Sallary for the Year 1787	7	10	
	By Order of Court to Pay Elijah Gillett High Sheriff his Sallary for the Year 1788	7	10	
5	By Order of Court to Pay A Smith Esqr Clerk his Fees for Tolling & Certificates of Estrays out of the Sales of the Estrays @ 3/6 each Sold to this Term 13	2	5	6
	By an Order to pay Thoms. Wooton for surplus Work done to the Jail not mentioned in the agreement	1	1	10½
6	By Order of Court to pay A Smith Esqr his Salary as Clerk for Extra Services for the Year 1788	5		
	By Cash pd Thos Wooton the Ballance of 25.15.0 the Price the Prison & Stocks were lett at	9	14	
	By Cash pd Thos Wooton by Order of Court for Work done more then the agreement	chargd as above		

1789			55	2	4½
Aprl 25	By Commission of ₺ 61 13 0 a 5 P C		3	1	7½
			58	4	
	By Ballance due to the Treasury		3	9	
		₺	61	13	

1789				
May 6	By Cash pd. Chas Wheeler p order of Court	1	12	8
	By pd for a Table John Cave		12	6
	By pd. for a Jury Box		2	6
	By pd. Jno (Thos?) Nash for 1 pr Hand Casfs(?)		4	8
	Carrd. to Folio (22)			

[entire above entry stricken]

Page 22:

1789	Dr Aaron Smith Esqr. Treasurer				
April					
25	To Ballance brot. over as P Settlement		3	9	
May 7	To Cash of Willm. Weekley Tavern Tax		1	10	
	To Cash of Capt. John Fitss Do		1	10	
	To Cash of James Myrick Do		1	10	
	To Wm Smith for an Estray No. 20		1	7	
	To Absalom Causey Estray No 27		4	5	6
	To Moses Johnson 2 Estrays No 21 & 29		5	1	
8	To Zadoc Wooley Tavern Tax		1	10	
	To Henry McMillian a Fine			1	
Aug 5	To Simon Yowns & Lettice Chavers a fine for)				
	Bastardy & c. ₺ 10 Proclamation money)	5	16	8	
1790					
May 6	To James Mitchell Tavern Tax		1	10	
Aug 25	To John Gill Tavern Tax		1	10	
			29	2	
	To John Kirkland an Estra(sic) No 26		4	5	
			33	5	2

Page 23:

1789					
May	By Cash paid Charles Wheeler by Order Court	1	12	8	
	By paid John Cave for a table		12	6	
	By paid Jno Hill for a Jury Box		2	6	
	By paid Thos Nash for 1 pair Hand Cuffs		4	8	
nov 1790	By paid Wm Woodcock by order of Court		3	6	
Aug 5	By paid John Cave for 6 Constables staves		5		
	By order Court to pay Tarlton Brown High Sheriff)				
	for extra Services for the Year 1789)	7	10	-	
	By order Court to pay A Smith Esqr Clerk Do for				
	1789		5		
		15	10	10	
1791					
Febr.	By Order Court to pay Do Do for 1790	5	-	-	
	By Do to pay Tarlton Brown Sheriff for				
	Extra Services for the year 1790	7	10		
		28	-	10	
	By Commissions on ₺ 30 10 d 5 P Ct.	1	10		
		29	10	10	
	By Ballance due	3	14	4	
	₺	33	5	2	

Page 24:
                Robert Shields   Dr.
1788
Jan 18   To Fine for Misdemeanour & c by ord. of Court   7 10 -

1788   Dr. William Weekley

Jany 18   To Fee for Tavern Licence   3 0 0
          To Tavern Licence renewed   1 10
          To Tavern Licence renewed   1 10
                                                           ─────
                                                           £ 6

1788   Dr. James Myrick
Jany 18   To Fee for Tavern Licence   3 - -
1789
Jany 18   To Tavern Licence renewed   1 10
1790
Aug 5   To Tavern Licence renewed   1 10

1788   Dr. John Gill   Wm Weekley Secu.

Jany 18   To Fee for Tavern Licence   3 -
1789
Jany   To Licence Renewed   1 10

Page 25:

1788   Per Contra
Nov 4   By Fine Remitted by order of Court   7 10

1788   Contra
Aug 16   By Cash pd. Aaron Smith   3 - -
1790
May   By Cash pd. Thoms. Wyld   1 10
          Gon to Tom Bigba with all his family)
          By Ballance due   )   1 10
                                                           ─────
                                                           £ 6

1788   Contra
May 8   By Cash paid the Treasurer   3 - -
1789
May   By Cash pd. T. Wyld   1 10

                    Contra
1789   By A Smith   3
Apl 25   By T. Wyld   1 10

Page 26:

          John Fitts
1788
Feby 6   To Fee for Tavern Licence   3
1789   To Ditto   Renewed   1 10
Feby 5
1790   To Ditto Renewed   1 10
Aug 5

1788   Dr. Solomon Owen
Feby 10   To Fee for Tavern Licence   3

1790   Dr. John Barfield
Aug 5   To a fine of £ 10 to be paid by 5 Installmts.   10

	Dr. Ann Collins & Chas Wheeler Security	
	To Fine for Bastardy Ł 5 proc. Money	2 18 4
1790 May 3	Sarah Griffen for Bastardy	
	To a fine for Bastrady Ł 5 Procl. Money to be paid in 9 Months	2 18 4
1787 July 18	Dr. John Ward To a Fine by the Order of Court	1
1790 Aug 5	Dr. James Mash, Willm Boyet & Josias Boyet To a fine for killing a Stray Steer	5

Page 27:

1788 Aug 8	Contra By Cash at Court pd. the Treasurer	3
1789 May	By Cash pd. T. Wyld	1 10 -
1791 Jany	By Do. Do A. Smith	1 10 -
		6

Jesse Winburn & Walter Robinson Secuy.   Cr.

Page 28: 1788 May 7	Dr. Walter Robinson To Fee for Tavern Licence	1 10
1789 May	To Ditto Renewed	1 10
1790 Aug 5	To Ditto Renewed	1 10
1788 May 31	Dr. Christopher Hall To Fee for Tavern Licence	1 10
1788 May 8	Dr. Joseph Duncan To Fee for Tavern Licence	1 10

1788 Sep 4	Dr. Thomas Wooton Jno. C. Smith Esqr. Security	
	To Cash pd you P the Treasurer	13 - -
	To Cash recd of Christopher Hall	1 3
Nov 1	To Cash recd of Jno C. Smith accot. Docr. Fred. Sunn	1 18
3	To pd. Alexr Newman P Aaron Smith	1
	To pd. Alexr Newman the Ballance of your Accot.	1 2 6
	To John Fitts 4/6 Ditto for Willm Hough 1/2	5 8
	To Cash pd. Thos Wooton by Thos Obannon Esqr.	3 7
1789 Feby 4	To Cash pd. by Doc. John Crocker acct. Wm Buford	2 11 1
	To Cash pd. Sampson Hough	1 6 10
	To Cash of Aaron Smith for the Ballance 19/1½) to paid Jas. Collins 18/8 1 20d Nails 1/6)	2 2 9½
	To paid Sampson Houg for Making Prison Door 3/6	
	Ł	27 16 10½

Page 29:
[several lines containing no names omitted]

1788 Sep 4	Contra By Building a Prison & Stocks as P Bond	25 15 -
Nov 5	By Order of Court for Work done more then the agreemt.	2 1 10½
		27 16 10½

	N. B. Cr. by Aaron Smith for the Balla		19	1½
	By Jno C. Smith for Ballance		5	10½
			1 5	0
	Dr. to Pd. Jos. Brooker by ordr. Jno C. Smith		1 5	0

Page 30: David Mills & Willm Roberts Security

1788 Aug 7	To your Bond for an Estray No. 1	1 5	-
1788 Aug 7	Dr. John Wickly & Banja. Odom Junr. Security To your Bond for an Estray No 2	3	-
1788 Aug 7	Dr. Docr. Fredk. Sunn To your Bond for An Estray No. 3	1 18	
1789 April	Dr. To tavern Licence Fee	1 10	
1788 Aug 7	Dr. Thomas P. Carnes & Thos Wyld Security To your Bond for an Estray No. 4	4	8

Page 31: Per Contra

1788	By Cash of Willm Roberts	1	5
1789 Apr 25	By A Smith	3	- -
July 14	Pd. John Mitchell 20/3 pd. by Aaron Smith 15/ pd. Jno Mitchell 16.3 by B. Odom 5 2. 16. 6		
Nov 1 1788	By Jno C. Smith pd. Thomas Wooton fo 28	1	18
1790 Aug 25	By Tarlton Brown	1	10
1788 Nov 7	By Cash of Elijah Gillett fo 35	4	8

Page 32:

1788 Aug 7	Dr. James Kirkland & Thos Obannon Security To your Bond for an Estray No. 5	3 7	-
1788 Aug 7	Dr. Burrel Parker & Bartlet Brown Sen Security To your Bond for an Estray No. 7	2	- -
1788 Aug 7	Francis Basset & Willm Buford Security To your Bond for an Estray No. 10	1	10
1788 Aug 7	Thomas Wyld & Thomas P. Carnes Security Dr. To Bond for an Estray No. 13	6	2

Page 32: No names, only carry-overs

Page 37:   A List of Sundry Fees & Fines due to Winton County
1789
Jany. 18   Capt Willm Weekly   Tavern Licence Fee   Error
Feby 5   Capt John Fitts   Ditto   pd   1 10 -
Feby 5   Capt Willm Weekley   Ditto   pd   1 10
Feby 5   James Myrick   Ditto   pd   1 10
Feby 5   John Gills   Ditto   pd   1 10
Feby 5   Walter Robinson   Ditto   pd   1 10
            Willm Smiths Bond Wm Robinson Sec. Estray #20   1 7
            Absalom Cawsey, Wm Tuton Security Ditto No. 27   4 5 6
            Moses Johnson, John Read, Sec. Ditto 21 & 29   5 1 -
May 4   Zadock Wooley   Tavern Licence   1 10
    8   Richd Vince A Fine for neglect of Duty   15
    5   Henry McMillian a Fine for Contempt   1
Aug 5   Simm. Yowns & Lettice Chavers Fine Basty.ᴸ 10   5 16 8
    5   Eliza. Chismans   Tavern Licence Fee   1 10
1790   James Mitchell for Tavern Licence   1 10
Aug 4   John Bates   Tavern Tax fee   1 10
            James Mitchell   Tavern tax fee   1 10
            James Mash, Wm Boyet & Josias Boyet a Fine)
       killing an Estray Steer, knowing it to be an Estray)5
            John Barfield a Fine of ᴸ 10.10 to be paid by)
            5 Installmts. for Breach of an Ordinance of)
            Congress   )10
            John Fitts   Tavern tax fee   Error
            James Myrick   Tavern tax fee   1 10
            Capt Willm Weekley   Tavern tax fee   1 10
            Walter Robison Esqr   Tavern tax fee   1 10
May   Sarah Griffen for Bastardy fined ᴸ 5 Procl)
the 4th   Jesse Winburn & Walter Robinson Esqrs became) 2 18 4
            her security to pay the sum in 9 months   )
            Ann Collins for Bastardy fined ᴸ 5 Procl.)
            Charles Wheeler Security Octo. 16th 1787)   2 18 4
Aug 5   James Mash, Willm Boyet & Josias Boyet)
            a fine for killing an Estray Steer   )   Error
    25   To Willm Williams for an Estray No. 35   8 12
                                     gon to Georgia
            To Wm Buford for an Estray   33   1 12
                       Due the 11th September 1790   ᴸ   43 - 8

Page 34: Dr. William Buford & Fras. Bassett Security
1788
Aug 7   To Bond for an Estray   No. 15   4
1790
Aug 4   To Bond for an Estray No. 33   Richd Creech Sec.   1 12

1788   Dr. William Woodcock
Aug 6   To one Estray Mare   No. 11   3 11

1788   William Vince
Nov 5   To Cash P Receipt   5 -

1788   Dr. Elijah Gillett Esqr High Sheriff
Nov 5   To Thos P. Carnes   fo (30)   4 8
1789   To the Ballance carried to your Cash accot.,)
June 5   in the Fee Book fo (48)   ) 11 14 3
                                                            16 2 3

Page 35: [several lines showing only amts. carried over]

1789
Feby 2   By Cash recd of John Obannon accot. the Tax   1 2 3

Page 36:
1788   Dr. Aaron Smith Esqr.
Nov 7th To Thomas Wyld for Part of an Estray No. 13 fo (32)
                                                              5 -

1789   Dr. Charles Wheeler Constable
May 7   To Creditt in Your accot. Fee Book (fo. 38)   1 12 8

1789   Dr. Willm Newman & Elijah Gillett Esqr
Apr 25   To an Estray No. 12   1 16

1789   Dr.   Winton County
May 7   To pd. Chas Wheeler by order of Court   1 12 8
         To 1 Jury Box   2 6
         To Sampson for a Table of Jno Cave   12 6
         To To thos Nash for a pr. Hand cuffs   4 8

1788   Per Contra
Nov 7   By an Order of Court on the Treasurer for one
         Years Sallary as Clerk for Extra Services for
         1788   5

1789   By Order of Court to pay your Accot. for
May 7   the State vs John Chavers   1 12 8

1789   By Aaron Smith on accot. Elijah Gillett Esqr   1 16
Apr 25

Page 38: to be Paid to Aaron Smith Esqr: The Treasurer
1789
May 7	By Cash	Error
Augst	By Cash	1 10
May	By Cash	1 10
	By Cash	1 10
Augst	By Cahs	1 10
1790 Aug 25	By Cash	1 10
Augst	By Cash	1 7
May 9	By Cash in part 37/9 By Cahs for Ballance	4 5 6
June 30	By Thomas Wyld ded. Jno Bates to collect	5 1
Augst	By Cash	1 10
Augst	By Fine Remitted	15
	By Cash	1
	By Cash	5 16 8
May 1	By Cash	1 10

[End of Part I of this Volume
Pagination recommences in Part II]

Page 1: Jaremiah Joynar of Winton County, planter, for Ł 50 ster.
pd by Sarh Southwell, for a Negro boy named Solomon...4
May [1787-- year from WPA copy]. Jaremiah Joyner (J) (Seal), Wit:
Thomas Morris, Nathanel Sandres, Thos Obannon, Wm Robison, Moses
Duesto.
At a Court held for Winton County at a place known by the name of
the Big House on Tuesday the 16th Oct 1787, the above Bill of
Sale for a Negro Boy named Solomon from Jaremiah Joyner to Sarah
Southwell was Legally proved in open Cout by the oath of Tho
Morris & Nathaniel Sandres and Ordred to be recorded.
Examined & Recorded the 21st day of Decr 1787.
                                    Certified by A. Smith, C. W. C.

Pp. 2-3: William Christie of Berk (sic) County, Ga., for Ł 35 ster.
to John Collins of Winton Co., SC, a likely Negroe Fellow
named Quauco and one likely Negro Girl Named Priss, daughter to
the said fellow...1 Nov [1786--year from WPA copy and wit. names
from WPA copy] Wm Christie (Seal), Wit: Stephen Collins, Hezekiah
Nobles (X).
At a Court held for Winton County at a place call'd the Big House
on Tuesday the 16th October 1787 the preceding Bill of sale for
a Negro Fellow named Quauco and Negro Firl named Priss from William
Christie to John Collins was proved by the oath of Stephen Collins
and Ordered to lay over for furthur proof.
At a court held for the above sd. County at the Plantation of
James Mitchell on Tuesday the 15th January 1788 the preceding Bill
of Sale was proved by the oath of Hezekiah Nobles and ordered to
be Recorded.
Examined & recorded 12th February 1788.
The recorded Bills of Sale to this Place were sent to the
Secretarys Office Janr 1st 1788 by John C. Smith Esqr.

Pp. 3-4: Winton County, John Parkenson of Reachmount, State and
County aforesd., for and in Consideration of a Certain
Tract of Land 200 A in the State of Georgia on Lamberths big Creek
Vallued at Ł 175, have sold unto Marey McNeilley, Widdow, three
Negroes known by the names of Dublin, Cork & Bella with her future increase...24 July 1787...John Parkinson (Seal), Wit: Sarah
Plummer, MOses Plummer.
Proven at a court held at the Plantation of James Mitchell on Tuesday 15th Jan 1788, acknowledged by John Parkinson. Examined &
Recorded 13th Febry 1788.

Page 4: Will of Nathaniel Abney...to wife Lucy, all my Estate Real
and personal and at her death to be divided among all
my children...1 July 1787, Wife appointed Extx, Nathaniel Abney
(Seal). Wit: [from WPA copy] John Wyld, David Seely, Cleavers D.
Wyld, Thomas Wyld. Prov at a Court held for Winton County on
Tuesday 15 Jan 1788, by Thos. Wyld & Cleavers D. Wyld. Examined
and recorded 11 March 1788.

Page 5: Inventory and Appraisment of the Estate of Joseph
Natures Decd, as returnd by Joseph Vince, Willm Vince
and Jonathan Clarke, Appraisers, 22 Nov 1787. Total Ł 10 3. 8.
Sold at Publick Sale 8 Dec 1787, by Lark Robinson, D. S. W. C.
Examind and Recorded 12 March 1788.

Page 6: Inventory and Appraisment of the Estate of William Baxter
by Robert Lark, Henry Coker and Amos Way, appraisers,
as shown to them by Catherine Baxter, Admx., 12 Jan 1788.
Includes Negroes Dub, Doll, David, and other not named, Total
evaluation Ł 414 8 6, Examined and recorded 12 Mar 1788.

Page 7: Inventory and Appraisment of the Estate of Richard Creetch decd as returnd by John Williams, William Creech, and Reuben Golikely appraisers, as shewn to them Richard Creetch & Ann Creetch, admrs., 25 Aug 1787. Total Ł 240 2 5. Examined & Recorded 11 Mar 1788.

Pp. 8-10:Will of William Crossle of Winton County in Orangeburg District, to beloved Wife Rachael Crossle, 150 A on Ogeechey, part of 850 A & she is to have the cleared Land that is on it, also a negro girl Cornelia, etc. and at her death to descend to my two Sons I have by my wife Rachael, named John and Andrew Crossle...in case these two sons should dve without issue, to my sons George & Henry Crossle and to my daughter Mary Crossle... to son George Crossle, one negro fellow Ireland, 200 A of the 850 A tract colt branded G C and all my smiths tools, etc...to son Henry Crossly, 500 A of my land on Ogeechey; to my daughter Mary Crossle, Ł 18 lawful money, 25 Sept 1787...William Crossle (=) (Seal), Wit: John Parkinson, Moses Plummer, John Bennet. At a court held for Winton County on Fryday 18 Jan 1788 the above will was proved by John Parkinson and Moses Plummer. Examined & recorded 11 Mar 1788.
Codicil: my daughter Molly to have Ł 6 sterling from my wife... 2/3 of estate to George, Henry & Molly & the remaining third to my wife and my two children by her...1 Nov 1787. Wit: John Parkinson, James C. Murphey.

Page 10: Inventory and appraisment of the Estate of Martin Kimberhide decd., returnd by John Craddock, John William, and William Weekly being first sworn by Wm. Buford, JP as shewn them by Arthur Jenkins, Exor, 10 Oct 1787. Includes 100 acres of land, Total Ł 71 0 0. Examined and Recorded 11 March 1788.

Page 11: Articles of agreement made and done 24 Dec 1785 between Silas Halsey of New Jersey and Mrs. Sarah Wilson of South Carolina, for Ł 390 sterling, bond which sd. Halsey now holds against the estate of James Wilson decd., for Ł 400 Pa. money, dated 4 Sept 1762...Silas Halsey, Sarah Wilson, Wit: Hezek. Roberts, John Wickley. Prov. 29 Mar 1788 by oath of Capt. John Wickly, John C. Smith, JP. Examined & Recorded 7 Apr 1788.

Pp. 12-13: Reuben Newman and Alex. Newman of S. C., Orangeburgh District & Winton County, Gentlemen, for Ł 1000 ster. to Capt. John Wickley of same, 1468 A in Orangeburg District, on Murdaughs branch, waters of Savannah River, originally granted to sd. John Wickley, 14 June 1787. If the said Reuben and Alex. Newman do pay back Ł 1000 with interest by 1 Apr 1790 then the above bargain and sale to be void...Reuben Newman (Seal), Alexander Newman (Seal), Wit: Wm. Minor, Wm. Newman, Frederick King. Prov. before me by Will Newman, 31 Mar 1788, John C. Smith, JP.

Pp. 14-16: Will of John Wood of County of Winton, planter...to wife Mary, plantation where I now live, 200 A on Savannah River, with cattle, etc...to son John Wood, 100 A on Boggy Gutt after my wifes decease or marriage, the plantation where I now live, two Negroes Tom & the wench Agur, 65 A on upper side of Steele Creek, adj. land surveyed for John Collins, his three sisters Mary Wood, Lue Piney & Jane Wood...to my two grandsons Jesse & John Wood, son of my son Jethro Wood, all the cattle their Fath hath in his possession at the Time...to son Jethro Wood, one shilling sterling in lieu of all other legacies... Capt. John Collins and wife Exrs...1 Feb 1788...John Wood (Seal), Wit: Stephen Smith, Richard King, Mary Deese. Proved in open Court by Stephen Smith & Mary Deese, and ordered to be recorded

6 May 1788. Examined & recorded 30 May 1788.

Page 17: John Wickly of Winton County, appoint Elijah Gillett, Esq. of county aforesaid, my lawful attorney, to settle all accounts...3 July 1788...John Wickly (Seal), Wit: Thomas Wyld, A. Smith. Rec. 4 July 1788.

Page 18: James Collins of Winton County, for natural Love and good will to my wife Nancy Collins, do give 150 A which I lately purchased of Thomas Morris in Winton County, on E side Turkey Creek, waters of big Saltcatcher, adj. Thomas OBannon, James Morris, Nathaniel Saunders, and my other land, also Negro girl Violett...2 April 1798...James Collins (Seal), Wit: Wilson Cook Jun., Thomas Morris. Prov. by Wilson Cooke Jun., 9 June 1788. Examd. & Recorded 15 July 1788.

Page 19: Sarah Altman, widow, for love, good Will and affection to children Selah Padgett, Sarah & Liddea Pdget, James and Ervin and Henry Padgett & John Atlman, the trew (sic) heirs of my body, all my goods and chattels, one Negro man Joe, a Negro wench Rose, and two Negro children Patt and Silve, a boy named Jack, feather bedds, etc....22 Dec 1784...Sarah Altman (X) (Seal), Wit: William Blitchendon, Abraham Blitchendon (A), Lucretia Blitchendon (X). Prov. by William Blitchendon and Abraham Blitchendon, 13 Oct 1785, before James Fair, JP. Examin'd & Recorded 25 Aug 1788.

Page 20: Inventory & appraisment of the Estate of Nathan Williams as returned by Elijah Wasden, John Mooney & Willm Green sworn 7 Aug 1788. Total 8. 16. 4. Examd & Recorded 27 Aug 1788.

Page 21: James Collins of Winton County, for Love, good Will and affection to my Loveing son Daniel Collins of same, 150 A that the sd. James Collins bought of Thomas Morris, also to daughter Mary Collins of Winton County, a negro girl Violet, 5 Aug 1788. Wit: Joseph Collins, Thomas Morris. Prov. by Joseph Collins 5 Aug 1788 before Daniel Green, JP. Examind & recorded 10 Sept 1788.

Page 22: Gilshot Thomas of Winton County, for Ł 150 do sell one negro boy Bakus aged 16 or 17 years to Job Roundtree 24 June 1788...Gilshot Thomas (Seal), Wit: Thomas Filput, Rubin Roundtree (X). Prov. by Reuben Roundtree, 6 Aug 1788 before Daniel Green, JP. Examin'd & Recorded 10 Sept 1788. Copy sent to the Clerk of the Secretarys Office January 15, 1789.

Page 23: Inventory & Appraisment of the Estate of Nathaniel Abney, Decd., by Robert Garvin, James Garner, Robert Garvin Junr., appraisers. November 2, 1788. Includes one negro (not named), Total Ł 316. 17.3. Examin'd & recorded 6 Apr 1789.

Page 24: Mark Ratlif of the County of Colinton (sic) and Orangeburg District, authorise Isaac Odom of the County and Dist. aforesd., convey a parcel of cattle of thirty head, for ---- hundred and fifty pounds SC money, 4 Nov 1777. Mark Ratlif (Seal), Wit: Benjamin Byrd, Daniel Odom, William Eaves. Proved by Daniel Odom before Jesse Winburn, JP, 4 Nov 1788. Examind & Recorded 6 Apr 1789.

Page 25: Thoms. Morris for Ł 74 ster. pdy by John Platts, one Negro firl Dido, about 14 years old, 11 Aug 1788... Thomas Morris (Seal), Wit: Richard Creech, John Gill. Prov. by

Richard Creech, 5 Nov 1788 before W. Buford, JP. Examined & Recorded 8 Apr 1788.

Pp. 26-27: 20 Dec 1780, Mary Chapman, of Colleton County, to Elender Chapman and Frances Chapman, daughter and son of the sd. Mary Chapman, for natural Love and affection, cattle and horses (marks given)...Mary Chapman (X) (Seal), Wit: George Nix, John Shaw (X). Prov. by both wit. before Thos. Knight, JP, 5 July 1786. Examined & Recorded 8 May 1789.

Page 27: Will of John Mysser of Winton County...to my cousin Charles Stewart, 100 A on Rosemary Creek, Arthur Conney now live on, and the rest of my furniture, goods, etc., after payment of my debts...Charles Stewart, exr., 19 Sept 1788...John Mysser (l) (Seal), Wit: John Cook, Susannah Wood, Harmond Comings (l). Prov. by John Cook and Susannah Wood 30 Sept 1788 before Thomas Obannon, JP. Examined and recorded 9 Apr 1789.

Page 28: The Division of Willm Baxter Estate, 23 Jan 1788, by Willm Vince, Joseph Vince and John Collins...Catherine Baxter is to have Negroes Cuff and Pegg and Household Goods & Cattle; Theophilus Baxter is to have Doll, Cambridge, July & Lewis; Thomas Moore in behalf of Zachariah Griffen is to have Dublin & Dave. Wit: Amos Way.
We the Heirs of William Baxter do hereby acknowledge that We are perfectly sattisfied with the within Division...23 Jan 1788 Thomas Moore (X), Catherine Baxter (C), Theophilus Baxter (T). Examined and recorded 9 Apr 1789.

Page 28: The Estate of Andrew Tester (sic) to Jno Green, Admr. (list of expenses only). Rec. and Examind 9 Apr 1789.

Page 29: An Inventory & Appraisment of Andrew Feasters (Teasters?) Estate deceas'd, 1 Nov 1788.. Total ₤ 23 17 2, by William Edwards, Elknor Green, Henry Dias, appraisers. Examined and recorded 9 Apr 1789.

Page 30: Inventory of John Disharoon decd., 24 July 1788, Total ₤ 42 3 8. by John Parkinson, Stephen Smith, W. Vince, appraisers. Certified by W: Dunbar, Admr., Examind & recorded 9 Apr 1789.

Page 31: Inventory of Job Roundtree, decd., 24 July (year not given), to goods as shown by Reuben Roundtree, admr. Includes negroes (not named), by Stephen Smith, John Parkinson, John Collins, appraisers. Examined and recorded 10 Apr 1789.

Page 32: S. C. Winton County: John Myser hath bargained and sold to Charles Stewart of same, for ₤ 50, cattle (Marks given), 15 Sept 1788...John Mysser (Seal), Wit: John Cook, Susannah Wood. Proved by both wit. 30 Sept 1788 before Thos. Obannon, JP. Examin'd & Recorded 9 May 1789.

Page 33: A Bill of sale of four Negroes given from Henry Cannon to Solomon Owens & George Kersh, all of Winton County, for ₤ 100, negroes Rode her child China, a Girl Juday & Violet, 1 Jan 1789...Henry Cannon (Seal), Wit: D. Garvin, E. Gillett. Proved by Elijah Gillett before John Wyld, JP, 6 May 1789. Recorded 15 May 1789.

Page 34: An Inventory & Apraisment of the Estate of Robt Lee
Decd, April the 28th 1789. Includes negroes Ceasor,
Hannah, Jane, Minna, Buck, Violet, and James, 378 acres land, a
debt of ₺ 32 10 o North Carolina Money. Total ₺ 526 18 4.
John Hall, Charles Wheeler, Lazarus Wooley, appraisers. Examin'd
& Recorded 12th July 1789.

Page 35: Godfrey Lee's Acct for his Expences as Administrator of
the Estate of Robt Lee decd. Includes payment for
recording the Will in Johnson County, N Car. May 4th 1789.
Recorded July 13th 1789.

Page 36: Mary Fryer of County of Winton, Spinster, for love, good
will and affection to my son John Fryer of same, a Minor,
100 A in Winton County nearly adjoining a Pond called Peters Pond,
which was surveyed for Samp Griffin, 24 Aug 1784 and granted to
him 5th June 1786, and conveyed to Mary Fryer by Deeds of Lease &
Release, also 150 A in Winton County near to said Peters pond, part
of 300 A surveyed for Mary Fryer 1 July 1784, granted to her 5
July 1785...1 May 1789...Mary Fryer (X) (Seal), Wit: Elijah Tradaway, Jacob Foreman (X), Joseph Redd (J). Proved 4 May 1789 by
Mary Fryer. Rec. 14 July 1789.

Page 37: Will of Willm. Everett of County of Winton, 4 Sept 1788.
to my son John M. Everitt one negroe Boy by the name of Will,
after my wifes widowhood also 400 A the upper side of the Horse
Penn to be possest with at the age of 21 years...to my son Thoms.
Everitt one Negro Boy Amos, after my wifes Widowhood, also my
Plantation and land where I now live, after the death of my wife &
the Marriage of my daughters Vizt. Polly, Suckey, Nancy, Salley
& Tempe...to my son in law William Dyess, 100 A betwixt Chandlers
land & the upper Edge of the Little Gassey Pond & my Line near the
new Road...to my Loveing Wife Nancey Everitt, my Plantation &
Land thereto belonging, and the remainder of the estate except
what I have given to my sons to be divded between my Six Daughters
Elizabeth Dyess, Polly Everett, Suckey Everett, Nancy Everitt,
Sally Everitt, & Tempe Everitt, my son Willm Dyess, wife Nancy,
Exrs., William Everitt (Seal), Wit; Jacob Braziel, Jacob Knight,
Thoms Mark (X). Prov. 21 Feb by the oath of Thomas Dyess. Proven
4 May 1789 by oath of Jacob Braziel. Recorded 15 July 1789.

Page 38: Elijah Gillet of Winton County sell unto John Peoples
of same, planter, a certain number of cattle branded 37,
a black horse, household furniture, negro Daniel, negro wench
Srah, a boy Dick and boy Prince, 2 June 1789...Elijah Gillett
(Seal), Wit: Thomas Dobbins, Cinthia Wickly (Λ). Prov. by Thomas
Dobbins before Jno C. Smith, JP. Rec. 22 Aug 1789.

Pp. 39-40: Daniel Bourdeaux of Charleston, Esquire, by bond or
obligation bearing even Date with these presents stand
bound to Charles Prince of Charleston, Esquire, and Anna his wife,
Admx with the will annexed of Clement Lompriere of the state
aforesd, Esquire, decd, for ₺ 3360 sterling, for the payment of
₺ 1680 like money, negroes (named), 10 May 1787...Daniel Bourdeaux
(Seal), Wit: John J. Pringle. Prov. in Charleston District by
the Hon. John Julius Pringle, before PEter Freneau, 9 July 1787.
Rec. in Mortgage Book EEE, page 455 and Examined by Peter Freneau,
Secretary. Rec. 9 Sept 1789.

Page 41: State of North Carolina, Certified by Saml Johnson Gov. of NC, that Reuben Saunders whose Name is signed to these papers is Clerk of the Court of Pleas and Quarter Sessions for the County of Johnson, 30 Nov 1788.

Pp. 41-42: State of North Carolina. Will of Robert Lee of the State aforesd...to son Godfrey Lee, one Negro Woman Hannah and her two youngest children Jean and Page and all my Lands...to my grand daughter Sarah daughter to my son Lewis Lee negro Girl Jemimah; to my grandson Benjamin Odum Lee, one negro Named Bucks; the boy to be perfectly learnd to the Rule of three, the girl to read & write perfectly; to my daughter Sarah Peoples negro Seser and gril named Violett; to my daughter Winnefred Blackman, negro girl Hagar, and after her death to my granddaughter Zelpha Blackman; to wife Elizabeth one Grey Gilden, and feather bed & furniture; Henry Peoples, Godfrey Lee and George Ribosin, Exrs., 28 Oct 1782...Robert Lee (Seal), Wit: John Ballinger, Jesse Purvis, Phereby Collins (X). Proven in Winton County by certificate from the Clerk of Johnston County, NC, 4 Feb 1789. Rec. 22 Aug 1789. Proven in Johnston County, Nov Court 1788 by Willis Wigges.

Pp. 43-46: Will of Robert Hankinson of Winton County, farmer...
to wife Susanna Hankinson, four Negroes (named), I lend the plantation in Crackers Neck whereon I formerly lived joining to Island Creek to my Wife untill my son Richard Hankinson arrives at the age of 18 years, and then sd. Richard is to find for his Mother a deacent place as she shall chuse to live on, and to her five cows & calves, etc....estate to be equally divided among the children Richard, Sarah, Patsey & Mary Hankinson, and my wife shall keep all my children above mentioned untill they arrive to 18 years...to son Richard Hankinson, the old plantation in Crackers Neck & joining Island Creek & also 200 A known as Millers land and also lands formerly belonging to Samson Griffen, joining the sd. Millers land, and 100 A known as Fergusons land, and one tract of land bought from Tradewell adj. Millers land, and a tract bought from Brown & Foreman, adj. the above lands and six Negroes (named), etc.
to my daughter Sarah Hankinson, five Negroes (named); to Robt Hankinson; to daughter Pattey Hankins, five Negroes (named) and Blacksmith tools...to daughter Mary Hankinson, five Negroes (named), when she arrive at 18 years...
Executors to sell a Plantation known by the name of Foremans & purchased from John Milledge, also 100 A joining the upper side purchased from John Bush Sen, also a body of land on Town & Hollow Creek, it being part purchased and part Run by Pierce Butler of Charleston & Robert Hankinson, 100 A in the State of Georgia known by the name of Patridge Pon, near the Beaver Dams, also all the Lumber thay may be found upon hand after my Deceasd, also all the profits arising from the Mills till they are sold... the mills between Thos Filput and my Self should be rented out if not sold...to Richard Hankinson Sen my brother, the plantation whereon he now lives 100 A and six cows & calves, etc...William Holmes, Susanna Hankinson my wife, and Richard Hankinson my son Exrs...Robert Hankinson (Seal), Wit: John McElhenny Jun., Zachries Garner (X), J. Syms. Dated 5 July 1788. Prov. 3 Nov 1788 by James Syms. Recorded 25 Aug 1789.

Pp. 47-48: Inventory and Appraisment of the Estate of Robert Hankinson, decd., by Isac Boush, Noah Tanner & Henry Coker, appraisers 29 Nov 1788. Total ₤ 2177 19 2. Recorded 25 Aug 1789.

Pp. 49-50: Will of Stephen Smith of Good Hope, State of S. C., County of Winton...all the lands that I am at present possessed of in the State of South Carolina & Georgia, except the tract of Land I purchased from Alexn. Wood in this State and the Land I run joining it also one Tract opposite to it in Georgia, all the Lands that lyes convenient to my Saw Mill on Steel Creek to be sold by my Executor....
to my son Stephen Smith that Tract of Land I purchased from Alexr Wood with the Land I run joining it, also one track of land opposite to Woods Tract in the State of Georgia...my wife and children may live on my Plantation on Steel Creek and carry on the business of the Saw Mill untill the Children come of Age... to my wife Martha Smith, also to my dear Children Elinor Smith, Stephen Smith, Ann Smith & Henrietta Smith, the Plantation I now live on, on Steel Creek, also all my Negroes (not named)... my daughter Sarah Golphin to have Negroes (named) also one Horse & a Sute of Mourning...wife Martha Smith, John Parkinson, William Vince and Alexander Newman, exrs., 15 Oct 1788...Stephen Smith (Seal), Wit: John Collins, George Wiggins, Rachel Walker. Proved 3 Nov 1788 by John Collins and Rachel Walker. Rec. 26 Aug 1789.

Pp. 50-52: Inventory & Appraisment of the Estate of Stephen Smith decd, by John Collins, Robert Lark & Henry Cocker, 9 Dec 1788. Bonds and Notes of Hand due from John Casper Horreman, Willm, Briney, Jacob Price, Alexander Woods, Sarah Shepherd, Dal. Shaw, Danl. Green, Thoms. Golphin, David Zubly, John Anderson, Sampson Griffin, John C. Smith, Patrick Wallace, Henry Coker, Jonas Griffen, Benja. Knight, Needham Dees, Hezekiah Wade, Richard Capers, John Coley, John Gooden, David Shipes, Robert Lark, Godfrey Lee, Henry Somerall, Moses Odom, Willm Moor, James Harriss, John Newman, G. Leaver. Total ₤ 2777 2 5½. Certifyed 9 Dec 1788. Recorded 26 Aug 1789.

Page 53: An Inventory of the Goods and Chattles rights & credits of the late Decd. John Brown of all that comes within my knowledge viz.
Hamman Gallman Dr. to above Estate for a Horse the Decd left with me in his lifetime, which said Gallman Sold
Benja. Brown acknowledged that he recd from John Wyld Esqr. Sundries which was recd as the Decd John Browns goods
James Brown recd one Saddle
Robt Bradley acknowledged himself Indebted to the estate
Elizabeth Barker Dr. to an order on the Publick Treasurer for an Indent for one Beef one June 30th 1785
John Hicks Dr. to an order on the Publick Treasurer for an Indent for 1 Beef 16th October 1785
Richard Simmons Dr. to Note of Hand given 3 May 1784 payable the 15th June fifteen Guineas a bad Debt
My Self Dr. to a Pocket Book
Due from the Estate of Bartlet Brown decd. Total ₤ 114 11 3.
Returned by me William Brown Admr.
Recorded 28 Aug 1789.
A Bill of Appraisment of the goods & chattels of John Brown decd 17 Mar 1789 by Bartlet Brown, Absalom Causey, Benja. Blount, Rec. 28 Aug 1789.

Page 54: William Browne Administrator on the Estate of John Brown decd, His accot. for Expences on Accot. of the said Estate March Dr. 1785. Includes: Cash pd. Jos Garnett for a pr. of Saddle baggs, "My blacksmiths Tools you Sold to Robt Munson. Prov. 4 May 1789. Rec. 28 Aug 1789.

Page 55: Will of Edward Southwell of South Carolina, Orangeburg
District...to wife Sarah Southwell, all my Household
furniture, and after her decease to equally divide between my
three sons and my daughter Mary Southwell...sons Edward, John,
William...22 March 1775...Edward Southwell (✡) (seal), Wit:
John Clayton, Edward Southwell, Richard Jackson (P). Prov. by
John Clayton before Willm. Robison,JP 24 March 1778. Prov in
Winton County 6 May 1789. Rec. 29 Aug 1789.

Page 56: Inventory & Appraisement of the Estate of Edwd Southwell, decd, Total ₤ 92 13, Certified 13 June 1789, by
Reuben Golikely (R), Thomas Morris, James Myrick (I), Recorded
29 Aug 1789.

Page 56: Inventory & appraisment of the Estate of Willm Thomas,
13 June 1789 by Simon Bryan, Levi Long (X), William Bryan. Rec.
29 Aug 1789., James Thomas admr.

Page 57: South Carolina, Orangeburg District: James Jones of
Edisto, Charleston District, for ₤ 2000 sterling, pd. by
George Robison of Savanna River, Orangeburg District, 30 negroes
(named), 3 June 1786...James Jones, Wit: W Dunbar, Willm Stanley.
Prov. by Wm Dunbar, 4 Aug 1789, Wm Robison, JP. rec. 29 Aug 1789.

Page 58: Inventory & appraisment of the Estate of John Myser, decd.
Total ₤ 35 4 9, by Hezekiah Davis, Joseph Lard, George Miller,
20 July 1789, Thoms. Obannon, JP. Rec. 1 Sept 1789. Charles
Stewart, admr.

Page 58: Inventory & appraisment of the Estate of Thos. Castelow,
Total ₤ 435 13 8. Certified 31 July 1789, by Isaac
Bush, John Bush, Henry Dyess (HD); Joseph Miller, admr. Recorded
1 Sept 1789.

Page 59: Inventory and appraisment of the Estate of Willm Everet
Includes shoemakers tools & Leather, Taylors tools, and
three negroes (named), 30 July 1789 by Isaach Bush, John Bush,
Henry Dyas (HD), appraisers, Ann Everet, Wm Dyas, Exrs. Rec. 2
Sept 1789.

Page 59: The Estate of Isaac Odom decd to Daniel Odom admr.
Names mentioned Jethro Wood, Willm Robison, Eliza.
Shoemake, Willm Cato, Thomas Jones,Susanna Toney, Edwd Myles.
Rec. 3 Sept 1789. Recorded by order of Court on Monday 3 Aug
1789.

Page 60: Account of the Sale of the Estate of Isaac Odom sold
12 Nov 1784 by Danl Odom admr., Buyers: Nathl Walker
(bought negroes Adam and Brister), Danl Odom, Rachl. Odom.
Certified by James Fair, JP, Joseph Turner, Nathanael Walker.
Rec. 3 Sept 1789.

Pp. 61-62: South Carolina Winton County: Will of Thos. Filput,
planter...to wife Ann Filput, one negro wench Nell,
and three negro Boys Prince, Dick & Hard Times, and after her
death, to my son George Filput...to son Daniel Filput, negro
wench Tinah and Negroes Sambo and Ammoritta...to son Thoms.
Filput, negroes (named); to daughter Elizabeth Filput now McElhaney, five negroes (named); to wife Ann, tract of land on
the four Mile branch 100 A where I formerly had a Grist Mill
...to my grandson David Filput, son of my son Daniel Filput, a
tract of land my son Daniel now lives one 150 A...friend Alexander
Newman, Stephen Smith and John McElhenney, Exrs., 8 Aug 1787...

Thomas Filput (Seal), Wit: W. Vince, Thos Golphin, Thos. Newman.
Prov. 4 Aug 1789 by Willm Vince, rec. 5 Sept 1789.

Page 63: Will of Christopher Hicks of the County of Winton...to
my son Armstead Hicks the 150 A whereon I now live, provided nevertheless that my well beloved Wife Wilmoth hold possession of the same dureing her life time; I appoint them Exrs...to son Armstead a Waggon & gier thereunto belonging, I lend to my wife Negro George, after her death to be the Value thereof equally divided between my son Armstead & my two daughters Sarah & Prudence...7 Sept 1788...Christopher Hicks (H) (Seal), Wit: John Snead, Anthony Leach (X). Prov. by John Snead, 3 Aug 1789. Rec. 8 Sept 1789.

Page 64: Thomas Wyld of Winton County, for and in consideration of complying with a Law of this State, that the Justices of the several County Courts shall be impowerd to receive a Donation of two or more acres of Land whereon to erect a Court House & other Publick Buildings, I do hereby for that special Consideration, give to the Worshipful the Justices of the Court of Winton County for the Time being, one acre on which the Prison, Stocks, and Whipping post are now erected & joining to the said John Mitchells two Acres given by a Deed of Goft to this County, 3 Aug 1789...Thomas Wyld (Seal), Wit: Clevears D. Wyld. Acknowledged 3 Aug 1789. Rec. 10 Sept 1789.

Pp. 64-65: John Mitchell of Winton County, complying with a Law that the Justices of the County Courts shall be impowered to receive a Donation...two acres adj. my line, Willm Robisons line, just below the Prison...15 Mar 1789 Jno Mitchell (Seal), Wit: John Fitts, Thoms. Wyld. Prov. 3 Aug 1789. Rec. 10 Sept 1789.

Page 65: Isaac Sterling of Winton County, for love, good will, to Revecca Davis, daughter of Joseph Davis & Mary his wife, one black Horse about 6 years old branded SY, six cows, etc...4 Jan 1789...Isacc Sterling (I) (Seal), Wit: John Jemeyson, Peter Banner. Prov. 3 Aug 1789. Rec. 12 Sept 1789.

Page 66: South Carolina, Orangeburg District, Edmund Bentley of Dist. aforesd., for Ł 45 pd. by William Green of same, a negro Woman slave Fillis..11 Feb 1789 Edmund Bentley (M) Wit: Josias Boyett, Willm Boyett (W). Prov. 4 Aug by Willm Boyett. Rec. 14 Sept 1789.

Pp. 66-67: Winton County: James Simms for 40 likely young cows and calves, none to exceed the age of 7 years, to James Shingleton, mortgage for negroes Subinah, Mingo, Issac... 16 May 1789...James Simms (Seal), Wit: Samuel Bennet, Wm Buford. Prov. 5 Aug 1789 by Wm Buford before Thos Knight, JP. Rec. 20 Sept 1789. Copy sent from this Page to the Secretarys Office February 6, 1790 to Charleston. Copy sent Aprl 4, 1790 to Columbia.

Page 68: A True & Perfect Inventory & Appraisment of the Estate of Edmund Bentley, decd. Includes a note of hand on Levi Thrower, note of Jas. Castelow, not paid Edmd Bentley. Tutal Ł 103 1 10, 30 Oct 1789 by Isaac Bush, John Wyche, Elkanah Green (E). Rec. 7 Jan 1790.

Page 68: We the Subscribers being appoint by the Worshipful Court of Winton County to Examine the Accounts of Edmd. Bentley against the Orphans of Joseph Johnston, we have

Examined the Acct and find the said Bently to be Indebted to the said Orphans the sum of ₤ 56 s 5 d 3. Certified by us 29 Oct 1789
                                                      John Wyche
                                                      Isaac Bush.
Rec. 7 Jan 1790.

Page 69: A True and Perfect Inventory and Appraisment of the
    Estate of John Anthony decd. Includes: account proved against Willm Boyd, Acct provd against Thos Humphryes note dated Sept 1788 & the Note lost, Acct against Geo: Sadler due by note 1788, Accot against Hugh Stewart, Accounts against Drury Glover, Fras. Jenkins, David Bird, 29 Oct 1789, by Isaac Bush, John Wyche, John Bush, appraisers. Rec. 8 Jan 1790.

Page 70: Charles Stewarts Accot. for Expences as Executor of the
    Estate of John Myser decd. Names mentioned: Jas Kirkland, John Cook, Thos Obannon, James Walker, Wm Woodcock, Hezekiah Davis, Abraham Peacock, Arthur Conway, Joseph Williams. Total ₤ 17 13. 5. Prov. 2 Nov 1789. Rec. 8 Jan 1790.

Page 71: An Inventory & Apraisment of the Goods & Chattles of
    Christopher Hicks decd, 22 Aug 1789. Includes negro Boy George 9 years old. Total ₤ 147 15 6., by John Snead, Jacob Adams (I A), Shadrach Elkins (Y). Rec. 8 Jan 1790.

Page 72: The Inventory & Appraisment of the Estate of Thomas
    Filputs decd October the 9th 1789. Includes negroes (named), and debts due from John N Frey, Geo: B. Spencer, Henry Coker, Danl Filput, John McElhenney, Wm David, Sarah Wilson, Sarah Spears, Thos Filput Jun, Step: Smith, by A. Newman, Henry Coker (X), appraisers. Rec. 8 Jan 1790.

Page 73: South Carolina, Winton County: James Castiloe for ₤ 40
    pd by William Minor, negro fellow Moses, now in possession of Proc Baxter, 8 Oct 1788...James Castiloe (X) (Seal), Wit: John Gallaher, John Shillie (X). Prov. by John Galleher, 10 Nov 1789, before W. Dunbar, JP. Rec. 8 Jan 1790.

Pp. 74-75: 26 July 1789, Sampson Griffen of State of SC, planter,
    to Willm. Minor of same place, Deputy Surveyor, by bond dated 26 July 1789 stands bound to sd. Willm Minor in the penal sum of ₤ 34 s 14 d 3 sterling, there underwritten for the payment of ₤ 17 s 7 d 1 with Legal interest on 1 Apr 1790... negroe Woman Hannah & her Child Sal...Sampson Griffein (Seal), Wit: John Gallaher, Polly EVerett (X). Prov. by John Gallaher, 10 Nov 1789. Rec. 9 Jan 1790.

Page 76: 9 Sept 1788, John Turner's will...to my loveing daughter
    all household furniture (not named)...to sons James Turner and Willm Turner & Thom. Turner & Elizabeth Turner, all my lands, cattles, between my four sons and one daughter... Robert Adams (X) Executor, Job Darlington. Prov. by both wit. 2 Nov 1789. Rec. 9 Jan 1790.

Pp. 77-78: Will of James Collins of Winton County...to eldest son
    James Collins the plantation whereon I now live, 300 A and negro Bob...to daughter Elizabeth Toney, negro woman Tamar...to daughter Lydia Collins negro girl Pen...to son John Collins, negro man Sam...to son Major Croom Collins negro man Mingo..to daughter Mary Collins, negro Girl Vile...daughter Susannah Collins, negro Millia & stock of neat cattle...to son Daniel Collins 150 A purchased from Thomas Morris, adj. James Morris if Negro Tamar bares one more child, it shall be his...

to son William Winwright Collins, negro Girl named Phillis...hole estate into possession of Leven Collins, James Collins & Joseph Collins, my Executors and at the Term of 7 years from this date each child to receive their respective portions...James Collins (Seal), Wit: Daniel Odom, Ben Odom, Leven Collins. Will not dated. Prov. 2 Nov 1789, by Daniel Odom. Rec. 9 Jan 1790.

Page 79: S. C. Winton County: George Swicord of Burke County, Georgia, for Ł 300 lawful money of State aforesd., to Jacob Swicord, six Negroes (named), and cattle (marks given)... 3 Feb 1790...George Swicord (Seal), Wit: Willm Ashly, James Swicord. Prov. by James Swicord, 23 Feb 1790 before Wm Dunbar, JP. Rec. 26 Feb 1790.

Pp. 80-81: Daniel Bordeaux of Charleston, Merchant...whereas Pierce Butler Esquire stands bound unto Hercules Daniel Bize and divers other persons as securities, for the sd. Daniel Bourdeaux in the sum of Ł 15, 371 s 4 d 10 sterling, for the better securing of sd. sum deliver unto sd. Pierce Butler an undivided fourth part (with William Hill & Joseph Atkinson) of 60 negroes, belonging to the proprietor of the Aera (sic) Iron Works in York County, Cambden (sic) District, which said Negroes are now employed at the above mentioned works, also an undivided moeity with Robert McLewrath of 20 Negroes now employed under the sd. McLewrath at the Saw Mills at the Lower three Runs near Savannah River...20 May 1788... Daniel Bourdeaux (Seal), Wit: J. Payne, Wm. Payne. Prov. by Jonas Payne 19 Feb 1790, before S. Drayton. Rec. 4 Mar 1790.

Pp. 82-83: 19 May 1788, Daniel Bourdeaux of Charleston, Merchant, to Pierce Butler, for Ł 5 sterling, 1/4 part of 5000 A on Turkey Creek, waters of Broad River, purchased of Vardry McBee, also a third part of two tracts of land on Thickety Creek, waters of Broad River, surveyed for Daniel Bourdeaux, David Hopkins, and Francis Bremar, 14,583 A, also an undivided moiety of sundry tract of land at the lower three Runs, waters of Savannah River, also two tracts of 500 A each on Turkey Creek waters of Broad River, also one tract of land in St. Thomas Parish, 287 A, also 1/4 part with William Hill and Joseph Atkinson of about 10,000 A in York County, on which is a furnace known by the Aera (sic) Furnace, a Forge with four fires, a Sett of Steel Works and various other Improvements...also 100 A of Land on Savannah River and Tybee Creek in the State of Georgia... Daniel Bourdeaux (Seal), Wit: Jn. Payne, Wm. Payne. Prov. by Jonas Payne, 19 Feb 1790, before S. Drayton, JP.

Pp. 84-86: 20 May 1788, Daniel Bourdeaux of SC, Merchant, to Pierce Butler, Esqr., whereas the sd. Pierce Butler stands indebted to Hercules Daniel Bize and Divers other persons, for Ł 15,371 s 4 d 10, for Ł 5, 1/4 of 5000 A on Thicketty Creek waters of Broad River, purchased of Vardry McBee, 1/3 of 14,582 A on Thicketty Creek surveyd in two tracts surveyed for sd. Daniel Bourdeaux, Col. Davis Hopkins and Francis Bremar, adj. lands of Malacky Jones, Mathew Gatherly, Vardry McBee, Thomas Gordon & persons unknown, also a moiety of 16,569 A at the LowerThree Runs on Savannah River, whereon the Saw Mills are erected, a part of which was originally the property of Andrew Irwin, and sold by the Commissioners of Forfeited Estates, the other part being lands surveyed for Daniel Bourdeaux and Robert McLewrath, and for Pierce King, Jonathan Turner and William Green, also 2500 A Each on Turkey Creek waters of Broad River (two tracts), & 287 A on St. Thomas Parish adj. Thomas Harwin, Nathl Savineau, & William Wells... (the tract in St. Thomas Parish surveyed for John Benfield)...

also 1/4 part with William Hill and Joseph Atkinson of about 10,000 A in York County, Cambden District, one which is a furnace known as Aera Iron Works...100 A on Savannah River and Tybee Creek, opposite to the Island of Cocksput in the State of Georgia...Wit: J. Payne, Wm. Payne. Prov. in Charleston Dist. by Jonas Payne, 19 Feb 1790, sworn before S. Drayton, JP. Rec. 4 Mar 1790.

Pp. 86-87: Daniel Singleton of S. C., Winton County, for Ł 130 sterling, pd. by James Simms...forty Cowes & Calves, and Negroes Subina, Mingo and Isaac...24 May 1789...Danl Singleton (Seal), Wit: James Brabham, Samuel Bennit. Prov. by James Brabham before Thoms. Knight, JP 1 May 1790. Rec. 3 May 1790.

Page 87: 25 Jan 1787, Dan Bourdeaux of Charleston, Merch. to Esther Bourdeaux of St. Thomas's Parish, Widow, for s5, half of 15,169 A in detterent tracts in the Dist. of Orangeburg, at and near a Branch of Savannah River known as the lower three Runs whereon Saw Mills are erected, 2000 of which were originally the property of Andrew Irwin & sold by the Commissioners of forfeited Estates. Entered in the New Book of Mortgages No. 3 Book B page 115.
[entire entry stricken]

Page 88: John Galphin for Ł 100 sterling pd. by Thomas Galphin Hoomes, negro wench Beck and three Children (named), dated at the Rock Landing 20 Sept 1789...John Galphin (Seal), Wit: George Galphin. Prov. by George Galphin, 15 May 1790, before JOhn Wyche, JP. Saml Nunes sworn and saith that he new (sic) the sd. Girl Tenar to be the property of John Galphin, 17 May 1790 before John Wyche, JP. Rec. 18 May 1790.

Page 89: An Inventory & Appraisment of the Property of Aaron Gillett decd. Includes: 645 A of Land in Prince Williams Parish, 500 A on the head of Coosahatchee, 556 A on Jacksons branch, 500 A at Longs Bay, 92 A on Savannah River Swamp, 6050 Acres of Bogg Gutt with one half of the Mills &C thereon, 500 A on the Four Holes, 11 Negroes (named). 8 Mar 1790 by John Fitts, John Wickly, Willm Wickly. Rec. 19 May 1790.

Page 90: Willm Brown of Rose Hall, in the State of Georgia, for Ł 130 to Walter Robinson, three negroe Slaves York, Hagar & Child...dated at Savannah, 4 Nov 1788...Willm. Brown (Seal), Wit: J. Fox, Richd. Fortune. Prove. by Richd. Fortune before Jesse Winbourne, JP, 25 Feb 1790.
I do hereby certify that I have bargained, sold & Deliverd unto Mr. Willm Brown a certain Negro man York & Negro Woman Hagar. Saml Perrey, 24 Feb 1789. Thoams Greenwood (JP?). Rec. 4 May 1790.

Page 91: Owen Odom & John Stuart of South Carolina, County of Winton, planters, for Ł 55 pd. by Walter Robison, planter, of sd. county, a negro boy Jem about 11 years old... 23 May 1789... Owen Odom (O) (Seal), John Stuart (Seal), Wit: Daniel Green, JP. Rec. 4 May 1790.

Page 92: S. C. Winton County: Michl. Swicord of co. aforesd., for Ł 40 sterling pd. by William Robison of same, a negro wench slave Atty...8 Jan 1790...Michl. Swicord (Seal), Wit: George Swicord, Wm. Ashley. Prov. by George Swicord, before John Wyld, JP, 17 Apr 1790. Rec. 5 May 1790.

Pp. 93-94: 17 Apr 1790, Willm Brooker & wf Unity Brooker, both
of Winton County, for natural love and affection
and 35 shillings, Sd. William doth give to his wife Unity, all
stock of cattle, etc...22 Apr 1790...William Brooker (W) (Seal),
Wit: Wm. Robison, John Brooker. Unity Brooker acknowledge herself
fully satisfied for her third part of her husband's estate, 22
Apr 1790, Wit: Wm Robison, John Brooker. Prov. by William Robison
before Thomas Obannon, 3 May 1790. Rec. 5 May 1790.

Page 95: S. C. Winton County: 10 May 1786, Ann Moon to her
daughter Elizabeth Moon, for natural Love & affection,
three cows...Ann Moon (X) (Seal), Wit: Wm Robison, William
Brooker. Prov. by Wm Robison, who attested to his and the signature of William Brooker Jr., 20 Mar 1790, before Thoms. Obannon,
JP. Rec. 24 March 1790.

Page 96: Appraisment & Inventory of Jas Collins Estate by Danl
Odom, George Collins & Joseph Duncan, being first duely
sworn 4 Mar 1790. Includes four negroes (named), Total ₺ 542 8 4.
Rec. 10 May 1790.

Pp. 96-97: State of Georgia, Burk County: William Robison, Esq.
of S. C., for 100 guineas pd. by Lark Robison of Burk
County, Ga., negro Prymas...3 July 1790...Wm Robison (LS), Wit:
Nancy Robison, James Hammond. S. C. Winton County: Prov. by James
Hammond, 13 Jan 1790, before W. Dunbar, JP. Rec. 2 Feb. 1791.

Pp. 97-99: Will of David Edwards Sen. of Winton County, planter...
to my daughter Nancy one cow and calf...to my son Joshua the Smith
tools which I lent him some years ago and to his Son John one
cow & calf...to my son Richard one shilling sterling and I do
thereby disinherit him and his Heirs of any further part...to my
son David I give the Waggon and all that appertains thereunto...
to my son Victor two Cows and Calves...to son Theophilus, the House
& plantation I now live on with 350 A, leaving of it nevertheless
in full possession of my wife..remainder of my land be divided
between sons Davis and Victor...to grandson John Edwards, the son
of my son David Edwards...Joseph Turner, Agustus Williams and my
son David, Exrs., 14 June 1790...David Edwards Sen (Seal), Wit:
Jesse Winbourne, Jesse Rogers, Charles Carden. Prov. 1 Nov 1790
by Jesse Winbourne, before A. Smith. Rec. 16 Feb 1791.

Page 100: S. C. Winton County: Thomas Morris, for ₺ 45 sterling
pd. by Sarah Southwell, one negri girl Sharlot,
7 Oct 1790...Thomas Morris (LS), Wit: Mary Southwell, Edward
Southwell. Prov. by Mary Southwell (A), before William Buford, JP,
1 Nov 1790. Rec. 16 Feb 1791.

Page 101: Benjamin Toney of Winton County, to James Collins, for
₺ 40 sterling, negro woman Tamas about 40 years old &
her future increase, 22 Nov 1791, Benjamin Toney (X), Wit: Thomas
Wyld, Nathaniel Saunders (N). Rec. 16 Dec 1790. Prov. by Thomas
Wyld before Thomas Obannon, 14 Dec 1790. Rec. 16 Feb 1791.

Pp. 102-103: Will Lee of Orangeburg District, for ₺ 45 sterling
pd. by John Buford of Burk County, Georgia, negro
George age 7 and bay mare, two years old...29 Sept 1790...William
Lee (X), Wit: Peter Mathews, Samuel Shelly, Wm. Buford. Prov. in
Winton County by William Buford before John C. Smith, JP, 1 Nov
1790. Rec. 4 Mar 1790.

Pp. 103-104: Account of the Sale of the Estate of Thomas Castillow
decd sold 10 Apr 1790 by Joseph Miller, admr.

Buyers: John Bush Senr, Theophilus Baxter, Ezekiel Williams, Joseph Miller, William Green, Robert Ashley, Henry Castellow, John Green, James Jackson, Sampson Griffin, Ann Castellow, Jonas Griffin, Isaac Odom, Merrimon Cook, Stephen Write, Benajah Williamson, Isaac Bush Sen, William Dunbar, Robert Ashley, Isaac Bush Jun.
Items sold include several negroes (named). Rec. 14 May 1790.

Page 105: William Dunbar of Winton County, for Ł 165 s 10 sterling, pd. by George Robison, several negroes (named) and cattle...26 Nov 1790. W. Dunbar (LS), Wit: Joseph Jeter, William Price. Prov. by William Price before Thos. Obannon, JP 10 Dec 1790. Rec. 24 Feb 1791.

Pp. 106-107: Joseph Brook of Winton County, for divers causes, to William Brooker, son of John Brooker of sd. county, negroes (Named), 28 Sept 1790. Joseph Brooker (X) (LS), And for the better securing of the property for the sd. William Brooker my nephew, I constitute my friend Richard Creech an Executor. Wit: Bartholomew Roberts, Wm. Barker. Prov. by Bartholomew Roberts before William Buford, JP. Rec. 2 Nov 1790.

Page 107: Thomas Morris of Winton County, for Ł 36 sterling pd. by Thomas Knox of same, planter, wench named Manney... 10 Oct 1789...Thomas Morris (Seal), Wit: Wm. Hardin, Geo. Robison, Acknowledged in Court 1 Feb 1790.

Page 108: Nancy Collins of Winton County, to Thomas Morris, for Ł 50 sterling, negro slave Violett, 17 Aug 1790... Nancey Collins (N) (LS), Wit: Thomas Wyld, John BAtes Jun., Samuel Way. Prov. by Thomas Wyld before Thomas Obannon, 14 Dec 1790. Rec. 14 Dec 1790.

Page 109: Winton County: Abigail Williams of co. aforesd., Spinster, for Ł 74 s 3 d 4 sterling, to Richard Creech, all stock of cattle (marks given), also 235 A...25 Nov 1789... Abigail Williams (X) (LS), Wit: W. Buford. Prov. by William Buford before Walter Robison, JP 3 May 1790. Rec. 2 Nov 1790.

Page 110: James Collins of Winton Co., for Ł 82 sterling, to Thomas Morris, negro Bob about 20 years old...22 Nov 1790. James Collins, Wit: Thos Wyld, Nathl Saunders (N). Proved by Thos Wyld before Thomas Obannon, JP 14 Dec 1790. Rec. 14 Dec 1790.

Page 111: Winton County: James McKay of co. aforesd., for Natural love & affection to my son George McKay & s 5, negroes (named)...27 Aug 1790 James McKay, Wit: Thos Wyld, James Montgomery, Nicho Nobles. Prov. by Thomas Wylds, 28 Aug 1790, before W. Buford, JP. Rec. 28 Aug 1790.

Page 112: E. Gillett certifies that he sold to William Dunbar Esq., give negroes (named), sold by order of court to pay off a Writt of Attachment obtained in favor of Joseph Dick Exr. to the Estate of William Moss against Moses Cree, 12 Aug 1787, Testes: Benj. Allen. Prov. by Benjamin Allen 5 Feb 1791 before Jno. Carr Smith, JP. Rec. 5 Feb 1791.

Pp. 113-116: Daniel Bourseaux of Charleston, Merchant, for in consideration of a bond bearing even date with these presents, bound to Esther Bourdeaux of St. Thomas Parish, for Ł 4400 sterling for the payment of Ł 2200 like money, on or before 26 Jan next...negro slaves (Named) now at the Three Runs Saw Mills (Twelve men & one girl) whose names are not known... 26 Jan 1787...Daniel Bourdeaux (LS), Wit: Charles Bouchanneau. E. A. P. Radtbert. Prov. by Ernst Augustus Pillip (sic) Radtbert 26 Jan 1789. Recd. to be recorded 17 Feb 1790.

Page 117: Received this 17 May 1790 of Richard Kirkland of Winton County, Ł 55 for one Negro Wench named Tamar & her boy child Tom about 1½ years old, the wench about 18 years old...John Rains (LS), Wit: Joseph Crofts, Ethel Clary. Prov. by Joseph Crofts 21 Aug 1790, before Jno. Carr Smith, JP. Recd. to be Recorded 28 Aug 1790.

Page 118: State of SC, Orangeburgh District: Recd 4 Jan 1784 of Mr. Benjamin Odom Senr, Ł 100 sterling for Negro Isaac ...Edwrd Myles, Wit: Thos. Miles.
    Pricala Miles swears that the assigned wit. to be the hand of Thomas Miles decd, 3 Aug 1790, before W. Robinson, JP.
    Pricala Miles appeared and on her oath states that she believes the within mentioned name of Edward Myles as it is written to be the hand write of her Husband Edwd Myles decd, 25 Aug 1790, before Daniel Green, JP. Recd. the 3 Oct 1790 to be recorded. Rec. 6 May 1791.

Page 119: Wm Patterson of State of Georgia, for Ł 700 SC money, to Robert Hankinson, 2 negroes James & Mary...9 Mar 1783...William Patterson (Seal), Wit: George Golphin. Prov. by George Golphin before John Wyche, 21 July 1790. Rec. 6 May 1791.

Pp. 120-1: State of North Carolina, Dobbs County: Majr. Croom of the county aforesd., for natural love & affection to my granddaughter Mary Collins of Winton County, SC, negro Violete... 24 Jan 1791...Majr. Croom (Seal), Wit: Thomas Uzzell, Wm. Croom. Sworn in Dobbs County, by Majr. Croom that Wench Tamer said Violate and her increase is his right and that he never give up before but for the use and benafit of James Collins & Wife Caty's children, 24 Jan 1791, before Wm Croom, JP.
    Prov. in Winton County by Thomas Uzzell of Dobbs Co., NC, 8 Feb 1791, before William Dunbar, JP. Recd. to be recorded in Feby 1791. Rec. 6 May 1791.

Page 122: State of NC, Dobbs County: Major Croom do sell to James Collins of Winton County, SC, for Ł 100, negro Mingo 24 Jan 1791, Wit: Thomas Uzzell, Wm Croom. Prov. by Thomas Uzzell in Winton Co., 8 Feb 1791, before Wm. Dunbar, JP. Recd to be recorded in Feby. 1791.

End of Will Book 1.

(negro), Abraham 129
Adam 150
Agur 144
Ammoritta 150
Amos 146
Andrew 98
Atty 154
Bakus 145
Beck 154
Bella 143
Bob 129, 152, 156
Brister 150
Brutus 70, 81
Buck 146
Bucks 148
Butler 130
Caesar 21, 30
Cambridge 146
Ceasor 146
Cesar 16
Chima 146
Cork 143
Cornelia 144
Cuff 146
Daniel 146
Dave 146
David 143
Dick 62, 146, 150
Dido 145
Doll 143, 146
Dub 143
Dublin 143, 146
Eady 81
Edy 70
Fillis 5
George 152, 155
Hagar 129, 148, 154
Hannah 146, 148, 152
Hard Times 150
Ireland 144
Isaac 154, 157
Jack 145
James 146, 157
Jane 146
Jean 148
Jem 154
Jemimah 148
Jerry 129
Joe 129, 145
Juday 146
July 146
Lewis 146
Manney 156
Mary 157
Millia 152
Mingo 152, 154, 157
Minna 146
Moses 152
NEll 150
Nelly 98

Page 148
Patt 145
Pegg 146
Pen 152
Phillis 153
Primus 67
Prince 62, 146, 150
Priss 143
Prymas 155
Quauco 143
Rode 146
Rose 145
Saffo 129
Sal 152
Sam 152
Sambo 150
Sarah 17, 62
Saul 5
Seser 148
Sharlot 155
Silve 145
Simon 129
Solomon 143
Srah 146
Subina 154
Sylvia 129
Tamar 152, 157
Tamas 155
Tenar 154
Tinah 150
Tom 144, 157
Venos 129
Vile 152
Violate 157
Violet 145-46
Violete 157
Violett 145, 148, 156
Will 5, 146
York 154
, Dick 59
, Prince 59
, Sarah 59
---, Thos 6
ABETON, Elisha 56, 130
ABNER, Thos Graham 90
ABNEY, Dannet 59
  Lucy 21, 143
  Lucy (--) 32, 143
  Nathaniel 2, 4, 32, 74, 143, 145
ABSLOM, Elijah 119
ABSTON, Elij 104
  Elijah 34
  Elisha 65, 67, 70-71, 74
  John 34
ADAMS, Jacob 42, 85, 94, 119, 130, 152
  Jno 72
  Randolph 130

  Robert 42, 65, 75, 85, 130, 152
  Robt 86, 88, 94-95, 119
  William 71, 130
  Willm 84
  Wm 56, 66-67, 70, 74
ADDAMS, Willm 126
ADIS 47
ADKINS, Shadrack 85
ADKINSON, David 58
ADOMS, Robt 32
AIRS, John 130
ALDRICH, A P 102
ALDRIDGE 56
  Richd 54
ALEXANDER 40
  John Vincent 29
  Vincent Rene 13
  Vincent Rone 17
ALLEN, Benj 92, 96, 156
  Benjamin 156
  Benjm 8
ALLISON, Joseph 61
ALSTEN, Elijah 94
ALTMAN, Sarah 145, 145
  Sarah (--) 145
ANDERSON, John 149
ANTHONNY, Jno 95
ANTHONY, Joel 11, 15
  John 152
  Patience 85
  Queney 116
  Apprentice 46, 52, 77-78, 108
ARDIS 66, 73
  J 63
ARNAND, Winif 92
  Winifred 101
  Winniford 83
  Winiford 114
ARNAUD, Winstd 125
ARNES, Peter 103
ARNOLD, James 33, 36, 130
ARNOND 117
ASHLEY 79
  John 56, 110, 120, 130
  Robert 156
  Robt 108, 119
  William 65, 77, 83, 130
  Willm 49, 76-77, 93, 101-02
  Wm 9, 29, 55, 62, 65, 72, 75, 77, 79, 82, 88, 114-15, 154
  Willm 153

ATKINSON, Joseph 153-54
ATLMAN, John 145
BABCOCK, James 133, 135
BAILES, Charls 13
BALLINGER, John 148
BANNER 39-40, 44, 46
  Peter 62, 73, 80, 83,
  107, 126, 130
BARDOX, Anthony 98
BARFIELD, John 113,
  137, 140
BARKER, Elizabeth 149
  Frans 56
  Wm 156
BARNARD 122
  Timothy 121
BARRINGTINE, -- (--) 24
  James 24
BASS, Mrs 14
  Savannah 11
  Susanna 19
BASSET, Francis 27,
  103, 139
BASSETT 44, 47, 67
  Frances 40, 71, 130
  Francis 8, 133
  Frans 16, 27, 65, 135
  Fras 49, 56, 67-68,
  133, 141
  Sarah 22
  Trass 56
  Willm 34
BATES 27
  Andrew 29
  Jno 8, 90, 113, 121,
  123, 142
  John 3-4, 12, 18, 41,
  51, 67, 83-85, 91,
  96, 99, 100, 113,
  126, 130, 140, 156
  Joohn 111
  Rich 66
  Richd 29
  Sarah (--) 18
  Wm 18
BAXTER, Catherine 143,
  146
  Cathrine 25
  Proc 152
  Theo 116
  Theophilus 146, 156
  William 143, 146
  Willm 146
  Wm 25, 32
BEAUFORD, Jno 70, 114
  William 107
  Willm 48, 111
  Wm 49, 103, 114
BEAUFORT 91
BECK, Charles 50

Chas 32, 58, 60, 75,
  119
BECKHAM, Thos 115
BEDDINGFIELD 47
BEKC, --rles 130
BELCHER, --nis 130
BELLINGER, E 102
BENFIELD, John 153
BENNET, John 144
  Saml 118
BENNIT 116
  Samuel 154
BENTHEAN, James 101
BENTLEY 38, 40, 42,
  46, 54
  Edmd 36, 42, 49, 52,
  61, 85, 87, 105, 107
  Edmond 42
  Edmund 27, 95
  Edmunt 95
  Edwd 24
  James 16
  Martha 16
  Mathias 12
BENTLY, Edm 58
  Edna 35
  James 12
BERRY, Nancy 122
BEST, Absalom 13, 37,
  50, 69, 75, 89, 93,
  130
  Absalam 2
  Absolom 85, 127
  Elizabeth 127
  Henry 72, 81, 89,
  101, 114, 124
BILES, Chas 118
BINDOX, Anthony 101
BIRD, Benj 73
  David 152
BISSET 19
BIZE, Hercules
  Daniel 153
BLACK, Wm 61
BLACKMAN, Stephen 20
  Winnefred 148
  Winnefred (Lee) 148
  Zelpha 148
BLALOCK, Rich 97
  Richard 130
  Richd 41, 99, 119
BLAOCH, Richard 84
BLITCHENDON, Abraham
  245
  Lucretia 145
  William 145
BLOMETT, --arles 131
BLOUNT, Benja 149
  Jacob 87
  Marg 93

Mary 102, 112
BLUFORD 121
  Willm 119
BLUNT, Benj 56, 66-67,
  69-71, 74-75, 85-86,
  88-90
  Benjamin 131
  Mary 83
BLUNTIN, Margt 59
  Ruben 59-60
BOILES, Charles 56
BOILS 47
  Chas 119
BONDS, James 119
BORDEAUX, Daniel 153
BOUCHANNEAU, Charles
  157
BOUGH, Danl 97, 115
BOURDEAU, Anthl 112
BOURDEAUX 118
  Anth 92
  Anthn 113
  Antho 113
  Dan 154
  Daniel 146, 157
  Danl 115
  Esther 154, 156
  Esther (--) 154
BOURSEAUX, Daniel 156
BOUSH 96
BOUSH, Isaac 75, 85
  Isac 148
BOWERS 47, 51, 63, 66,
  73
  Patience 124
BOYD, Abram 64
  Willm 152
BOYENTON, --roh 131
  Jeriban 131
BOYET, Abram 54
  Josiah 108-09
  Josias 138, 140
  Saml 54, 64, 69
  William 23, 58, 95,
  108-09
  Willm 75, 87, 138,
  140
  Wm 61, 69, 84, 108,
  140
BOYETT 44
  Josiah 109
  Josias 87
  Saml 41
  Wm 116
BOYL-, Charles 41
BOYLE, Fras 55, 63
BOYLES, Charles 94,
  131
  Richd 94
BOYNENTON, Moses 104

BOYSTON, Aaron 104
BOYT 47, 49, 56
  Stephen 4
BRABHAM, James 4, 90,
  92, 98, 154
  Jas 89
  Jos 88
  Joseph 74, 85-86
BRADHAM, Joseph 65,
  126
  Josl 75
BRADLAM, James 130
BRADLAM, Joseph 130
BRADLEY, Rob 65
  Robert 25, 51, 130
  Robt 46, 53-54, 56,
  67-68, 94, 119, 123,
  149
BRANDLEY, Robt 53
BRANK, Fred 89
  Fredk 90
BRANT, Fred 42, 63, 75,
  80, 85-86, 88
  Frederick 3, 70, 74,
  130
BRAZEL, Jacob 76
BRAZIEL, Jacob 146
BREMAR, Francis 153
BRIANT, Simon 25
  William 65
  Wm 77
  Bridge 4, 12, 22, 45,
  49, 70, 105, 110,
  117, 121
BRINEY, Willm 149
BROCKER, Jo 125
BRONTON, Ruben 129
BROOK, Ann 108
  Joseph 156
  Thoms 108
BROOKER 117
  --liam 131
  --oseph 131
  Charles 121
  John 31, 155-56
  Jon 70
  Jos 54, 56, 64-65,
  69, 78-79, 92, 101,
  119-20, 139
  Joseph 3-4, 13, 49,
  51, 64, 67, 72, 83,
  93, 107, 114, 121,
  130, 156
  Leack 78
  Leah 54, 64, 67,
  69-70, 79
  Lear 29-30
  Shields 97
  Unity 155
  Unity (--) 155

Wiliam 50
William 155-56
Willm 155
Wm 24
BROW, Jas 82
BROWN 35, 39-40, 44,
  46-48, 61, 70, 87,
  90, 148
  --bert 132
  Barlet 149
  Bart 111
  Bartl 117
  Bartlet 111
  Bartlett 3-4, 10,
  13-14, 16, 21, 54,
  56, 60-62, 64-65,
  67-69, 71-72, 74-75,
  81, 83-84, 86-87,
  97, 99-101, 104,
  111, 126-27, 131,
  139
  Bartley 49
  Benj 29, 51
  Benja 149
  Benjamin 69, 100
  Charles 1, 3-4, 49,
  107
  Charles I 81
  Charles J 90, 103
  Chas 90, 120
  Chas Jones 82
  J G 102
  Jame 51
  James 11, 41, 75,
  84, 100, 126, 129,
  131, 149
  Jams 129
  Jno 69
  John 76, 149
  Jones 70
  Jos 15
  Robt 42-44, 46, 65,
  75-79
  Tarlton 4, 12, 24,
  32, 42-44, 46, 49,
  59, 67, 69, 71, 75,
  91, 103, 109, 113
  115, 118, 131, 136,
  139
  William 10, 37, 129,
  149
  Willm 75-77, 89, 112,
  154
  Wilson 101
  Wm 6-7, 13, 19, 46,
  56, 69, 82, 105, 111,
  116-17, 129
BROWNE, Robt 116
  William 149
BROWNSON, James 100

BROXTON, George 114
  Jno 114
BRUNTON, Jacob 129
  Margaret 129
  Marget 129
BRYAN, Ann 25
  Simon 9, 107, 131,
  150
  William 25, 131, 150
  Wm 9-10
BRYANT, Ann 25
  Simon 25, 41, 119
  William 25, 78, 94
  Willm 76
  Wm 75, 79, 82, 107
BUCH, Isaac 131
BUCHALOO, Garrat 75
BUCKALOO, Garrat 119
BUCKSTON, Benj 113
  Jacob 127
BUDD, Susannah 131
BUFORD B, 88
  Jno 55, 62, 64, 67,
  70-71, 114
  John 67, 129, 155
  W 21-22, 28, 32, 41,
  54, 56, 60, 65, 68,
  118, 121-22, 126,
  130, 146, 156
  William 4, 31-32, 34,
  36, 41, 43, 70-71,
  74, 101-02, 105,
  109, 121, 131, 141,
  155-56
  Willm 17, 46, 52, 54,
  60, 62, 68, 79, 133,
  135, 139
  Wm 2, 4-5, 7-9,
  12-13, 17-18, 21-22,
  24, 28, 45, 56, 58,
  93, 71, 80, 100,
  104, 109, 118-19,
  122, 129, 135, 138,
  140, 144, 155
BUFORT, William 2
BUNCH, Lovett 131
BURDEAU, Anthony 100
BURDEAUX 99
BURDEUX, Anthony 122
BURDOUX, Anthony 99
BURDOX, Anthony 101
BURFORD 110
  William 1, 129
BURNS, Thomas 62
BURTON 35, 37, 39, 59
  Benj 44
  Jacob 101
  Thomas 29, 47, 49,
  61
  Thoms 92

Thos 9, 34, 60-62,
  70, 96, 112
BUSH 112
  Adamus 51
  Isaac 50, 61, 76,
    85-86, 95, 150,
    152, 156
  Isaach 84, 150
  Jno 8, 84, 104-05,
    107, 117
  John 52, 76, 85, 94,
    108, 124, 148, 150,
    152, 156
BUSTON 64
  Benj 13
  Saml 72
BUTLER, Pierce 148,
  153
BUXTON 47
  Benj 46, 56, 108, 110
  Benjamin 103, 131
  Jacob 8, 131
  Nudon 131
  Saml 64
  Samuel 131
  Thel 46
  Theo 46
  Thomas 47
BYLES, Charles 131
  John 42, 94, 131
BYRD 81
  Benj 55, 60, 63, 74,
    88
  Benjamin 145
  Benjy 63
  Wm 55
CAIN, Nicholas 59
CAMPBELL, David 83
  Duncan 90, 101
CANADY, Alex 65
CANFIELD, David 130
CANNIERS, Margt 21
CANNON 38-40, 45-47
  H 16
  Henry 2, 5, 13-16,
    22, 24, 34, 37,
    55-56, 61-62, 70,
    73, 79, 130, 146
  Joshea 14
  Pugh 130
  Rudford 130
CAPERS, Richard 149
CAPPS 38, 48
  Wm 35
CARDEN 38
  Charles 130, 155
  Chas 55
CARDIN 48
  Charles 119
CARGILL 48

Thos 54-55
CARNES 105
  J P 23
  P 85
  Peter 23, 80, 83, 85,
    90, 97-99, 115
  Petre 120
  T P 52
  Thomas P 80, 85, 104,
    139
  Thomas Peters 43
  Thoms Peters 59
  Thos P 104, 133, 141
  Thos Peters 135
CARNEY, Jesse 15
  Jessee 11
CARR 38
  William 50, 58, 130
  Willm 56
  Wm 44, 63, 67-68, 73,
    107, 119
CARRELL 40
CARREY, Edw 100
CARROLL 46
  Jno 61
  Wilson 7
CARSON, Ths 129
  William 3
CARY, William 52
CASTELLOW, Ann 156
  Henry 156
  Thos 79, 84, 150
CASTILLO, Thomas 107
CASTILLOW, Thomas 155
CASTILOE, James 152
CATHORN, Sarah 77
CATO, Willm 75, 150
  Wm 106
CATRE, William 130
CAUSEY 38-40, 43, 46,
  48
  Absalom 6-7, 9,
    14-15, 17, 19, 41,
    44, 62-63, 81, 127,
    136, 149
  Absolam 16
  Absolom 70-71, 73
  Absom 38
  William 42, 130
  Wm 13, 30, 71
CAVE 29, 39
  Jno 108, 110, 116,
    141
  John 32, 51-52, 103,
    130, 136
  Jos 51
CAVES, Jno 13, 45
CAWSEY, Absalom 140
CAWSYE, Absalom 130
CAYTON, Isom 4

CHANDLER 146
CHAPMAN, Elender 146
  Frances 146
  Mary 146
CHARITY 47
CHAVERS, Jno 81
  John 76, 141
  Lettice 87, 136, 140
CHESTER, Davd 54
  David 51, 55, 63, 73,
    80, 88
  Davis 53
CHIRMAN, Eliza 86
CHISMAN, Eliza 59
CHISMANS, Eliza 140
CHRISTIE 37, 89-90
  William 1, 31, 143
  Willm 56, 62
  Wm 56, 58-59, 62, 64,
    73, 80, 88, 96, 115,
    117, 143
CHRISTY 45, 47-48
  William 45
  Willm 55
  Wm 32, 47
CLARK, James 37
  Jonathan 4, 12, 34,
    41-42, 92, 97, 113,
    130
  Lewis 56, 130
  Nich 64
CLARKE 31
  Elizb 25
  Elizb Olive 25
  Jonathan 2, 23, 143
  Wm 113
CLARY, Ethel 157
CLAYTO, Isham 96
CLAYTON 40, 45-47, 96
  Ishal 90
  Isham 67-68, 70, 72,
    74-75, 83-84, 90,
    119, 130
  Jno 12, 16, 20, 47,
    51
  Joham 56
  John 92, 99, 150
CLEATON, Isam 3
CLEMENS, Verdeman 25
CLEMENTS, --ement 131
  Clement 42
  Verdemon 56
CLEMONS, Verdamon 130
Clerk 1-2, 8, 17-18,
    22, 26, 32, 38, 65,
    68, 80, 85, 88, 135,
    148
COCHRAM, Jno 8
COCHRAN, John 41, 75,
    77

Willm 86
COCKER, Henry 58, 86,
    112, 149
    Nathan 107, 120
COCKERHAM, John 126
COCKRAN, John 131
COKER, Henry 3, 6, 16,
    21, 30, 72, 143,
    148-49, 152
    Nathan 42
    William 23
    Wm 28
COLE, Mathew 94
COLEING, Blanchard 42,
    131
COLEMAN, Hezek 81
    Hezekiah 59, 74
COLEY, John 149
COLLDEN, Blanchard 119
Collector 3, 21, 28,
    58, 60
COLLIN, Leven 120
COLLINS 37, 39-40,
    44-46, 118
    --ven 132
    Ann 24, 53, 133, 138,
        140
    Caty (--) 157
    Daniel 145, 152
    Elizabeth 152
    Geo 69, 90, 95
    George 3, 23, 28, 31,
        41, 50-51, 90, 131,
        155
    Hephen 71
    James 11, 15, 22-23,
        29-30, 38, 43-44,
        46, 95, 106, 131,
        145, 152-53, 155-57
    Jas 138, 155
    Jno 12-13, 16, 20,
        25, 56, 68, 81, 124
    John 2, 31-32, 51,
        58, 72, 79, 82,
        123, 131, 143-44,
        146, 149, 152
    Jos 43
    Joseph 3, 16, 31-32,
        41, 49, 51, 86, 131,
        145, 153
    Leavin 31
    Leven 51, 56, 105-07,
        121, 126, 153
    Levin 95, 129
    Liddia 74
    Lydia 152
    Major Croom 152
    Mary 145, 152, 157
    Moses 3, 23, 25, 51,
        53-54, 70, 75, 84,
        119, 131
    Nancey 156
    Nancy 145, 156
    Nancy (--) 145
    Phereby 148
    Step 96
    Stephen 10, 14, 18,
        69, 99, 112, 143
    Steven 31
    Susannah 152
    William Winwright
        153
COMINGS, Harmond 146
COMS, Peter 16
CONE, Jacob 63
    Jno 55, 62, 64, 70,
        90
    John 83
    Matthew 56, 131
CONNEY, Arthur 146
Constable 6, 17, 24,
    58, 60, 62, 67,
    74-75, 99, 107-08,
    112, 136
CONWAY 40, 46
    Arthur 152
    William 3
    Wm 5
CONYERS 39, 44
COOK 48
    --hn 132
    Abraham 132
    Abram 63
    Abrm 33
    Absolom 72
    James 92, 100
    Jno 78
    John 61, 75-77, 82,
        120, 146, 152
    Merrimon 156
    Robt 41, 117
    Wilson 51, 60, 103,
        108, 119, 145
COOKE, John 65, 79
    Wilson 145
    Wm 129
COOKER, Nathan 131
COOPEE, George 94
COPE, Geo 70, 74
    George 3, 67, 71
    Jacob 70, 74, 80
COPY 74
CORBAT, Judith 91, 101
CORBATT, Judith 106
CORBETT 125
    Benj 56, 65, 107,
        110, 123
    Benjamin 94, 131
    Danl 52
    Joseph 131
CORBIT, Benj 120
    Benjamin 120
CORBITT, Benj 67-68
CORCHER, Henry 95
CORD, Robert 129
    Robt 129
Coroner 1, 30, 49, 59,
    82, 105
CORSSLY, George 107
COSSEY, Absolom 72
COUPEE, George 56, 131
COURNEE, Jesse 49
COWLINS, Blanchard 94
COX, John 4
    Thomas 131
    Thos 6, 24
CRADDOCK, Barthl 123
    Jno 69, 71, 81
    John 72, 144
CRADOCK, John 104
CRAWFORD 38, 47
    James 45
    Thomas 52, 73
    Thos 63
CREACH, Richard 4
    William 49
CRECHER, John 92
CREE, Moses 13, 156
CREECH 69, 118
    --hard 130
    --n 130
    Ann 18, 22
    Henry 65, 75-79, 82,
        119, 130
    Kenny 75
    Ricd 13
    Rich 18, 22, 68, 71,
        75, 79, 89, 93
    Richard 3, 9, 72,
        104, 120, 122,
        145-46, 156
    Richd 4, 50, 54-56,
        60, 64, 67-68, 70,
        85-86, 88, 90, 112,
        117, 141
    Stephen 72
    W 129
    William 2, 72, 74,
        130, 144
    Willm 56, 101
    Wm 4, 64, 75, 84,
        129
CREEH, Richard 61
CREEK, --ohn 131
CREETCH, Ann 144
    Richard 130, 144
CRIMER, Barbary 99
CROBETT, Benj 120
CROCKER 78
    Henry 117

163

Jno 115-16, 125
John 69, 78-79, 93, 96, 102, 105, 133, 135, 138
CROCKET, Benj 84, 119
Danl 56, 107
Daniel 131
CROFTS, Joseph 157
CROKER, John 83
Nathan 121
CROOM 157
Wm 157
CROSLEY, --orge 131
George 66, 74, 92
CROSSEY, George 71
CROSSLE, Andrew 144
George 144
Henry 144
John 144
Mary 144
Molly 144
Rachael 144
Rachael (--) 144
William 144
CROSSLEY, Geo 70
George 56
CROSSLIE, George 80
CROSSLY, George 67
Henry 144
CROSTIE, William 37
CROW 39, 44
Jno 55
John 27
CUASEY, Absolam 10
CUNNINGHAM, Ann 18, 25
Patrick 54
CURRY 100
CUSHMAN, Simeon 45
CUTHBERD, Isaac 6
CUTHBERT 40, 46
DABNEY 34, 40
Sarah 130
DAIVS, Wm 70
DANIEL, William 31, 130
DARLINGTON, Job 152
DARRINGTON, Jno 95
Job 95
DAUGHTON, Thomas 130
DAVAIS, Wm 6
DAVE, Jno 112-13
John 112
DAVID, Geo 110
Jno 116
Mary 116
William 72
Wm 152
DAVIES, Wm 6
DAVIS 37, 39-40, 46-48, 51, 59, 70,

72, 77
Arthur 3, 65, 75, 84, 87, 130
Francis 11
Garderner 103
Gardner 109, 119
Geo 90
George 62, 69, 83
Hezekiah 75, 150, 152
Jacob 103
James 75, 96, 108
Jno 54, 79, 92, 112
John 16, 58, 60, 72, 88, 96, 101, 103, 114, 125
Joseph 52
Mary 27, 92, 96, 125
Mary (--) 52
Mary (--) (Williams) 27
Rebecca 87
Sarah 64, 74
William 2, 31, 47, 51, 58, 60, 64, 84, 97, 100, 130
Willm 63, 101-02
Wm 4-6, 21, 29, 34, 44, 47, 51-53, 55, 62-63, 69, 71-73, 79-80, 88-89, 94, 101, 104, 114, 116, 124
DAVISS 35-36
DEAN, Luke 22
DEAS 27
Henry 85
DEASON, Abraham 103
DEE, Mary 44
DEEN, --hn 130
Abnor 131
DEES, Needham 149
DEESE, Mary 144
DEESON, --aac 131
Abraham 126, 131
Abram 56
Isaac 42, 75, 126
DELON 48
Michl 41
DEMERY 104
DENNE, Samuel 131
DENNIS, David 26
Saml 56, 75, 107, 119
DePRUSHEE, Peter 42
DERISEE, Mrs 24
DeROACHE 113
James 101
Peter 72, 94
DeROUSHEE, Peter 107

DeROUSSEE 54
Peter 44, 55, 82
DeRUSHEE, Peter 43
DEWEESE, --ah 130
DIAS, Henry 76, 146
Wm 45
DICK, Jos 63
Joseph 13, 73, 156
DIESTO, Moses 63, 67, 81
DIKES, William 15, 132
DINGLETON, Danl 154
DISHAROON, John 53, 146
DISTO, Moses 45, 70, 72, 132
DISTOE, Moses 4
DIXON, John 90
DOAN 113
DOANE, James 97, 113
DOBBINS, Thomas 125, 146
Thoms 93, 102
Thos 84, 90, 93, 112, 115
DOWNS, Wm 83
DRAYTON, S 153-54
DRENNON 40
David 30, 35, 41-44, 75, 84
DRUMMON, John 23, 56
DRUMMOND 38
Jno 120
John 3, 28, 107, 121, 131
DUESTO, Mary 121
Moses 7, 143
DUNBAR 12, 47, 114, 116
Golphin 101
Jno 88
W 146, 150, 152, 155-56
WILLIAM 2, 4, 23-24, 102, 121, 131, 156-57
Willm 45, 66, 68, 87, 103, 109
Wm 8, 24, 32, 45, 58, 68, 72, 86, 103, 111, 114, 117, 123, 150, 153, 157
DUNBARR, William 111
Willm 108
Wm 53, 56, 80, 117
DUNCAN 68
Jos 54, 64, 69, 95, 107-08, 119
Joseph 34, 36, 49, 68-69, 92, 94, 110, 113, 135, 138, 155

DUNN, Docr 135
  Jno 107
  John 42, 131
  Newton 94
  Nuden 56
DYAL, Nathl 125
DYAS, Henry 9, 11, 15, 150
  Wm 150
DYCHE, William 42
DYCHES, Geo 55
  William 11
  Willm 38
  Wm 22, 43
DYES, Thos 66
  Wm 66
DYESS, Elizabeth 146
  Elizabeth (Everett) 146
  Henry 150
  Thomas 146
  William 146
  Willm 146
DYKES, George 64, 72, 79
  Wm 69, 71
EARL, Saml 54, 62, 70, 79
EAVES, --benjamin 131
  William 145
EDENFIELD, --am 130
  David 26, 69, 71
EDWARDS, -- (--) 155
  David 119, 155
  J D 102
  John 155
  Joshua 155
  Nancy 155
  Richard 155
  Theophilus 155
  Victor 155
  William 146
ELKINS, --hn 131
  John 26, 42, 132
  Shadrach 152
ELMORE, Phillip 54
ENECKS, Thomas 51
  Thos 53
ENICKS, Thos 119
ENOCK, Thel 42
  Thomas 130
ENOCKS, Thos 54, 108, 110, 113, 116
ENOX, Thomas 23, 28
  Thos 103
EUBANKS, John 131
EVANS 130
EVE-R--T, Wm 22
EVERET, Wm 66, 150
  Ann Dyes 66

William 66, 76
Willm 85, 150
EVERETT, Elizabeth 146
  Nancy 146
  Polly 146, 152
  Salley 146
  Suckey 146
  Tempe 146
  Willm 146
EVERITT, John M 146
  Nancey 146
  Nancey (--) 146
  Nancy 146
  Sally 146
  Tempe 146
  Thoms 146
  William 146
FAIR, James 2, 4, 51-52, 55, 63, 73, 80, 104, 145, 150
  Jas 55, 60, 63, 80, 88
  Jos 55, 63, 104
FAIRMAN, Arthur 7
FALLAS, Geo- 27
  George 27, 123
FARR 55
  James 1
FAUSE 130
FEASTERS, Andrew 146
FEBIGER, Levi 69
FERGUSON 148
  Sarah (--) 61
  Ferry 4, 9, 12, 42, 104
FIBIGER, Lars 17, 64
  Laurence 17
FIELD 40
  Reading 48
FIELDS 48, 99, 118
  Jno 99, 112
  John 92, 99-01, 122
  John S 98
  Redden 25, 30
FILPOT, Thos 17
FILPUT, Ann 150
  Ann (--) 150
  Daniel 150
  Danl 152
  David 150
  Elizabeth 150
  George 150
  Thomas 145, 152
  Thoms 150
  Thos 148, 150, 152
FITSS, John 136
FITTS, Jno 8, 62-64, 75, 84, 90, 97, 103, 113, 118-19, 124

John 23, 28-29, 55, 68, 71, 73, 83, 92-93, 100, 102, 112, 133, 135, 137-38, 140, 154
  Sarah 117
  Wm 103
FITTZS, John 132
FO--ER, Arthur 42
Foard 4, 9
Ford 49, 68, 77, 86, 93, 104-05, 110, 121
FOREMAN 40, 46, 148
  Ann 3, 5
  Arthur 9
  Jacob 76, 146
Fort MOORE 22
FORTUNE, Richd 154
FOX 47
  J 154
  Jno 42, 51
  John 49, 51
FRANCES 40
  Fred 38, 43
  Frederick 21, 129
FRANCH, Michael 25
FRANCIS, Fed 129
  Fred 36
  Frederick 30
  Fredk 16
FRANK, James 91
FRANSH, James 92
FRAZER, Arch 110
  Archd 108
  Archibald 110
  Lewis 108, 110, 117, 130
  William 130
  Willm 50
  Wm 110-11, 117
FRAZIER, Lewis 110, 117
  Wm 58, 60
FREDERICK, Henry 6
  Thomas 126
FREEMAN, william 65, 121, 130
  Willm 76, 78
  Wm 75, 77, 79, 82, 107, 119-20
FRENCH 118
  James 72, 98-99, 104, 106, 122
  Laurana 80, 83, 88, 117
  Looley 52
  Looly 63
  Lorana 50
  Lurana 90

Michl 104
Tooley 73
FRENEAU, Peter 146
FREY, John N 152
FROST, Judge 102
FRUGER, Archibald 131
    Arthur 103
FRYER, John 76, 146
    Mary 76, 146
FURGUSON, Henry 72
GALLAHER, Jno 118
    John 152
GALLEHER, John 152
GALLMAN, Hamman 149
GALPHEN, Thos 63
GALPHIN, George 154
    John 154
    Thomas 73
    Thos 86
GARBURROW, Charles 83
GARNER, James 74, 145
    Zachries 56, 148
GARNETT 47, 56
    Jos 112, 116, 149
    Joseph 112
    Thos 22, 56, 63, 116
GARRINGTON, John 28
GARVIN, D 146
    Robert 145
GATHERLY, Mathew 153
GAVIN, David 83
GEATER, Joseph 31
GEDDEN, James 71
GEDDINS, James 51,
    53-54, 90, 94, 121
    Jas 90
GEES, --ias 130
GEETER, Joseph 94
GELLETT, Elijah 33
GEORGE, Emanuel 34
GEST, Wm 113
GIBBONY, Hugh 96
GIBSON, David 4
GIDDINS, James 13
    Jas 70
GIDDONS, James 3
GIDEON, James 31, 46
GIDEONS, James 132
GIFFIN, William 132
GILBERT 40, 46
    Willm 53
    Wm 29, 53, 84
GILL 39, 56, 67, 70,
    77
    Jno 17, 54, 56, 66
    John 26, 37, 44,
    71-72, 133, 135-37,
    145
GILLET, Elijah 146
GILLETT 37, 39, 43-44,
    48, 118
A 2, 21, 24, 28-29,
    34, 36, 41, 44
Aaron 1-2, 4, 10-11,
    13-18, 21-24, 26,
    32-34, 36, 41, 45,
    55, 154
Doc 65
E 78, 103, 106, 111,
    114, 118, 135, 146,
    156
Elij 21, 35, 116
Elija 31
Elijah 36-37, 45-46,
    55, 62, 64-65, 69,
    72, 79-80, 82-83,
    88, 90-91, 93, 97,
    103-04, 109, 111-12,
    114, 117-18, 124,
    130, 133, 135, 139,
    141, 145-46
Elisha 79
Eliza 55, 72, 88
Eliza (--) 64
Elizabeth 45
Elizth 83
Garnishee 45
Olaron 47
GILLS, John 140
GINDRATT, Dorcas 100
GIPSON, David 132
GLASS, Jno 66
GLOVER, Abner 87
    Drury 152
    Graham 96
GOLIKELY, Reuben 12,
    58, 60, 78, 90,
    144, 150
    Rheubin 126
    Ruben 60
GOLPHIN 89, 114, 116,
    125
    Geo 115-16
    George 72, 104, 112,
    116, 157
    Jno 116
    Sarah 149
    Sarah (Smith) 149
    Thoms 149
    Thos 63, 81, 108,
    123
GOOD, William 42
    Willm 38
    Wm 34, 44, 69
GOODAN 44
GOODE, William 32, 34,
    103, 131
    Willm 31, 42
    Wm 10, 13-14, 19,
    33-34, 71, 110
GOODEN, John 149
GOODWIN, Charles 112
    Sheadrick 6
GOODWYN 39
    Frederick 16
    Sheadrick 9
    Thead 22
    Theadorick 21
    Threaderick 22
GOOGE, Wm 108
GORDON, Thomas 153
    Thos 119, 124
GORE, --annan 131
    Manning 72
    Nolly 131
GOSS 71, 82, 96, 115,
    125
    Jno 67, 84
GRADY, Jno 7
GRAHAM, Peter 87, 90
GRAVES 47, 56
    Humphrey 56
    Thos 56
GRAYHAM, Thos 87
GREEN 69, 71, 90
    D 29
    Dan'l 25
    Daniel 1-2, 4, 23,
    27-29, 31, 43,
    45-46, 48, 50, 52,
    84-85, 94-95,
    100-01, 126, 145,
    154, 157
    Danl 25, 27, 51-52,
    86-87, 96-97, 99,
    100-04, 107, 109,
    115, 121, 123, 149
    Elkana 129
    Elkanah 30, 86, 121
    Elknor 146
    Garnishee 77
    Jno 8, 11, 20, 46,
    51, 54, 61-64,
    69-70, 75, 79,
    81-82, 112, 115,
    121, 146
    John 15, 29, 32,
    46-47, 49, 54,
    60-61, 73, 81, 90,
    96-97, 114, 126, 156
    William 23, 27, 153,
    156
    Willm 145
    Wm 34, 87, 92, 104
GREENWOOD, Thoams 154
GREGG, James 100
GREGORY, John 66
    Jon 107
    Jonath 117
    Jonathan 56

GREGS, Jas 90
GRIFFEIN, Sampson 152
GRIFFEN, John 119
  Jonas 149
  Sampson 117, 152
  Samson 132, 148
  Sarah 138, 140
  Zachariah 132, 146
GRIFFIN, Jesse 69
  John 31, 84
  Jonas 156
  Mary (--) 76
  Samp 146
  Sampson 13, 22, 27,
    41, 76, 84, 90, 94,
    97, 99, 116, 118,
    149, 156
  Samson 83
  Sarah 106
  Thos 72
  William 132
  Wm 55, 63, 73, 80
  Zach 75
  Zachariah 65
GRIGOREY, Jonathan 132
GRIMER, Barbara 92
GRIMES, Barbara 120
  Jno 83, 91
  John 72
  Nathan 119, 121
  Willis 132
GRINER, Barbary 123
  Jacob 111, 117
GROSS 37
GRUBBS, John 131
GRYMES, Jno 82
GUEST, Wm 113
HALCOMB, James 2
HALL, Chris 80
  Christopher 54, 64,
    72, 74, 133, 135,
    138
  John 23, 146
  Thos 101
  William 52
  Wm 119
HALSEY, Silas 144
HAMMILTON, James 24
HAMMOND 10, 13-14, 19,
  39, 44
  James 155
  Jno 65
  John 103
HAMPTON 4
  Henry 72, 81, 89,
    101, 114
  Jno 12
HAMTON, Henry 124
HANCOCK, Wm 64, 72, 80
HANDKERSON, Robert 11

HANKERSON 10, 19, 36,
  39, 44, 97
  Robert 3, 10, 12,
    21
  Robt 16
HANKINS, Pattey 148
  Robt 66
HANKINSON 13-14,
  39-40, 115, 124
  Mary 148
  Patsey 148
  Richard 148
  Robert 4, 14-15,
    130, 148, 157
  Robt 16, 56, 58,
    148
  Sarah 148
  Sus 117
  Susanna 117, 148
  Susanna (--) 148
  Susannah 56
HAR-LE-Y 48
HARDEN, Willm 126
HARDIN, Jno 69
  William 95-96, 100
  Willm 91
  Wm 156
HARDING, Ezekiel 63,
  74
  Wm 105, 114-15
HARGROVE 39, 44
  Reuben 55
  Reubin 27
HARINGTON, John 108
HARLAM, Jacob 126
HARLER, Jacob 130
HARLEY 22, 37, 45, 47
  Jacob 50, 82, 84
  James 90
  Jos 8, 64, 90, 121
  Joseph 2, 4, 12, 18,
    32, 59, 73, 75, 82,
    89, 99, 105, 117
  M 70
  Thoms 112
  Wm 12
HARLING, Ezekiel 59
HARLOR, Jacob 58
HARRINGTON, John 23,
  41, 107
HARRIS, Benj 72, 78
HARRISON 40, 74
  Ben 63
  Burel 72
  Burr 34, 55, 73, 80,
    88
  John 30, 35, 41, 69
  Mary 35, 41
  Md 35
  Reuben 56

  Ruebin 130
HARRISS, James 149
HART, Jno 56
HARWIN, Thomas 153
HEATH, Benj 22
HENKERSON, Robert 30
HERINGTON, Ephraim 94
  John 94
HERRINGTON, --hn 130
  Ephraim 119
  Jno 119
HEYWARD, John 70
HICKS 47
  Armstead 85, 89
  Chris 95
  Christopher 152
  Jno 7, 9-10
  John 7, 14, 149
  Nathl 51
  Saml 42
  Wilmot 85
  Wm 85
HIDGCOCK, William 132
HILL 40, 46
  Jno 7
  Milly 10, 14
  William 153-154
  Wm 81
HITCHCOCK, William 42
  Wm 107
HOLLAND, Hugh 101
HOLLINGSWORTH, Timothy
  5
HOLLY, Jos 6
  Joseph 7
HOLMES 1, 26, 47, 51,
  63, 73
  William 4, 148
HOMES 66
HOMMER, Wm 56
HOOMES 89, 115
  Sally 124
  Thomas Galphin 154
  Wm 117
HOPKINS, David 153
  Davis 153
HORREMAN, John Casper
  149
HOUG, Sampson 138
HOUGH, Sampson 138
  Willm 138
HOURDAN, Isham 56
HOUSTON, George 123
HOWARD, Seth 37
HOWELL, Daniel 50, 84,
  132
  Danl 58
HUBBARD, Elijah 125
HUGHES, Henry 117
HUGHS, William 131

HUMPHREYS 46
  Joseph 50, 58, 131
HUMPHRIES 40
HUMPHRYES, Thos 152
HUTCHENSON, Jonn 131
HUTN, Mayes 126
ID 91-92
IDEM 91, 96, 112,
  114-17, 123-24
INGRAM, James 63
IRONMONGER, John 94
IRVIN, Wm 96
  Andrew 153-54
JACKSON 8, 39, 45, 154
  David 4, 42, 94,
    107, 130
  Edward 25, 32
  Edwd 32
  James 27, 32-33, 46,
    77, 84, 91, 94, 99,
    104, 110, 113,
    115-16, 119, 123,
    130, 156
  Jas 97, 105, 110,
    112-13, 117, 124
  Jos 96
  Ricd 103
  Richard 3, 25, 50,
    59, 130, 150
  Richd 54, 60, 83,
    90, 93, 108, 110,
    113
JACOB 126
JEETER, Joseph 49
JENKINS 37, 39, 44, 88,-91
  --rthur 130
  Ad 99
  Arth 55
  Arthur 4, 11, 14,
    16, 19, 24, 43, 54,
    56, 59, 63, 67, 74,
    84, 92-94, 97-99,
    101, 144
  Elias 118
  Fras 152
JETER 131
  Joseph 56, 156
JINKINS, Arthur 129
JOHNSON 40, 46, 48
  --rlevant 131
  Abra 75
  Abraham 56
  Ann (--) 106
  Bartholomew 94
  Derrell 48
  Derrl 35, 38
  Jno McKnight 67, 106
  Jno McKnight 56
  John McKnight 68,
    108, 131
  Joseph 52, 61, 95
  Levi 94
  Moses 35, 63, 73,
    136
  Nathan 103
  Parlevient 94
  Purl 92, 101
  Purlevant 119
  Purlivan 42
  Saml 68, 148
  William 32
  Zadock 140
JOHNSTON, --aham 132
  Lewis 14, 126
  Moses 28
  Purl 14
JOICE, --ams 131
  James 33, 75, 85-86
    88-90
  Jno 111
  John 94, 107, 126
JOINER, Jeremiah 5
JONES 121
  Gibbion 120
  Gideon 98
  James 63, 72, 158
  Malacky 153
  Owen 36, 97, 115
  Saml 93, 102, 115,
    124
  Samuel 83
  Thomas 55, 150
  Thos 63, 72, 116
  William 94, 132
  Willm 56
  Wm 4, 119
JORDAN 131
  --sham 132
  Isham 71, 74, 94,
    97, 99
  Robert 94
  Robt 74
  Robert 4
JOURDAN, Isham 67, 70,
    84, 119
  Job 97
  Robt 32
JOURDON, Rob 34
JOYCE, James 25
  Jno 13
JOYNAR, Jeremiah 143
JOYNER, Jeremiah 24
JUMAND, Joshua 10
Justice 103
KEE 113
  Wm 112-13
KELLY 45, 99, 110
KENNADAY 39, 44
  --ander 130
  Alex 75, 84
KENNEDAY, Alex 75
KENNEDY 96
  Alexander 3, 6
  Alexandr 6
KERNEY, Jesse 97
KERSH 48, 102
  --hn 130
  --rge 130
  Geo 65
  George 3, 9, 24, 75,
    84, 94, 97, 99, 146
  Geroge 76
  John 31, 55, 60, 97
KERSHE, Rich 54
KERSHEE, Richd 64
KEY, William 104
KIMBERHID, Martin 129
KIMBERHIDE, Martin
  129, 144
KIN, Grederick 144
KING 40, 46, 96
  Milley 87
  Pierce 153
  Rich 87
  Richard 144
KIRBY, Richd 55
KIRDLAND, Richd 120
KIRKLAND 65
  Benj 65, 89, 122
  Benjamin 4, 132
  Cid 125
  Geo 51, 107, 119-20
  George 25, 41, 121,
    132
  James 16, 22, 50,
    54, 58, 66, 103,
    110, 132-33, 139
  Jas 34, 108, 113,
    135, 152
  John 136
  Jos 117
  Ricd 13
  Rich 75, 78, 107,
    125
  Richard 9-10, 22,
    121, 125, 127, 132,
    157
  Richd 4, 13-14,
    76-77, 119, 121,
    125
KNIGHT 35, 47-48
  Benja 149
  Danl 27
  Jacob 146
  Thomas 1-2, 4, 9-10,
    14, 26-27, 31-32,
    34, 41, 43, 46,
    52-54, 58, 71,
    76-77, 103, 132

Thoms 154
Thos 2, 4-5, 8-9,
  12, 18, 21-22,
  27-28, 32, 34, 36,
  41, 43, 45, 52, 56,
  60, 66, 70, 74, 76,
  90, 95-96, 99-100,
  113, 118, 146
KNOX, Thomas 156
KOKER, Henry 8
  Nathan 9
KOOPE, Jacob 103
LAIN, Drewry 103
LAMAR, Thoms 82
LAMAX 45
  Willm 45
  Wm 41
LANCASTER, Jesse 107
  Joseph 42, 107, 130
  Robert 130
  Robt 51, 53, 65, 75,
  94, 107
LANE, Downy 41
  Drury 108, 110, 113,
  119, 130
LANIER, Benjamin 100
LANKERSTER, Robt 126
LARD, Adam 31, 119
  Joseph 75, 85, 150
LARK, Adam 94
  Robert 3, 143, 149
  Robt 32, 45, 58
  Rt 56
LATHAM, George 126
LATIERS, John 52
LAURENCE, Bartholomew
  106
LAW, Arthur Turner 29
LEACH, Anth 85
  Anthony 85, 94, 126,
  131
LEARS, Jno 11
  John 15
LEAVER, G 149
LEE 37, 48
  Benjamin Odum 148
  Elizabeth 148
  Elizabeth (--) 148
  Frederick 131
  Godfrey 8, 104, 146,
  148-49
  James 65, 75-78, 82,
  107, 130
  Lewis 148
  Linoel 103
  Lionel 65, 75, 119,
  130
  Richd James 79
  Robert 68, 129, 148
  Robt 75, 146

Sarah 148
Will 155
William 155
Winnefred 148
LEECH, Richd 65
LEESTER, Duke 130
LEGEAR, Benjamin 101
LEROCHE, --n 130
LEVERMAN, Mathias 105
LEVINGSTON, Henry 96
LEWIS 46
  James 18, 21
LIGHTFOOT, Jno 80
LIIKELEY, Reuben 132
LIKELY, Reuben 50
LITTLE, William 96,
  125
  Willm 116
  Wm 92
LIVERMAN, Mathias 105
LOE, Lott 72
LOMPRIERE, Clement 146
LONG, --omas 131
  Henry 123
  Levi 9, 36, 131, 150
  Luke 117, 123
  Thomas 73
  Thos 51, 53-55, 62
LOWE, John T 98
  John Tolson 97
  Lott 81
LUCAS, Randal 108, 117
LUCUS, Randall 110
MACKLEMURRY, Patrick 11
MAISE 102
  Robt 93
MALLETT, -- (--) 55
  Jno 55, 64
  John 72, 79
MARBURY 99
  Leonard 97-98
MARCH, Celia 54
MARK, Thoms 146
MARSH, Celia 64, 122
MARTIN, W E 102
MASH, James 108-09,
  138, 140
  Jas 108-09
MASON, William 3, 130
  Willm 103, 126
  Wm 9, 41
MATHENEY, Chas 123
MATHENY, Chas 71
MATHES 4
MATHEWS, James 27
  Peter 155
  Thos 28
MATTHEWS 40, 46, 93
  Benjm 10
  Emelia 32

James 23, 28, 65,
  130
Jas 75
Micajah 60, 84, 94,
  97, 99, 119, 130
Mocajah 42
Thomas 23, 41, 130
Thos 103
William 50, 130
Wm 58, 60
MAYERS 93, 102
MAYES 115
  Robt 84
  Robt A 84
MAYS, Robt 90, 96, 100
McBEE, Vardry 153
McCAIN, John 130
McCANE, Jno 56, 75
McCARRAL, John 60
McCARROL, Jno 69
McCLENNON, Pricilla 84
McELHANEY, Elizabeth
  (Filput) 150
McELHANY, Jno 124
  John 114
McELHENNEY, John 150,
  152
McELHENNY, John 148
McELMURRAY, Patrick
  19, 27
McELRATH, R 97
McELWORTH, Robert 2
McFAIL, Jno 54, 64, 69
McGREGORY, Rachael 112
McKAY, George 156
  James 127, 156
  Jennet 64
McKEELY 46
McKENSIE, Wm 5
McKINLEY, Wm 54, 64
McKOY, Jas 116
  Jennett 72
McLAMMURAY, Patn 5
McLEHANEY, John 56
McLEHANY, John 36, 86
McLEHENEY, Jno 115-16
McLEMMURRAY 39
McLEMURRAY, Patrick 45
McLEMURREY, Pat 22
McLEMURRY 22, 38
  Patrick 10, 33,
  43-44, 46
McLEOD, Eneas 96, 115
McLEWARTH 39
  Robt 56
McLEWORTH 37, 44
  Robt 37
McLEWRATH 48, 67
  Richd 114
  Robert 130, 153

Robt 54, 91, 93,
  102, 112-17, 125
McLINTO, Priscilla 93
McLINTON 102, 115
McMILLAN 47
  Alex 47
  Henry 67, 70, 77,
  107
McMILLEN, Alexander
  130
McMILLIAN, Henry 3,
  136, 140
McNEALY, Adam 7
McNEELEY 37
  Adam 56, 61, 75, 77,
  79, 82, 112, 123
McNEELY 37, 40, 47,
  118
  Adam 35, 51, 53, 64,
  70, 82
  Mary 33
McNEILLEY, Marey 143
  Marey (--) 143
McNELEY, Adam 72
McPHERSON, Isaac 117
McELMURRY, Parbuck 94
MERCER, James 128
MERRET, Fara 97
MERRIS, Joseph 34
MERRITT, Phar 115
MICHELL, John 132
MILES 37, 48
  Edmd 96
  Edward 4, 9, 13, 15,
  20, 132
  Edwd 20, 25
  Edwrd 157
  Pricala 157
  Pricilla (--) 25
  Thomas 157
  Thos 157
  William 31, 99, 132
Mill 69
MILLEDGE, John 148
MILLER 96, 112, 148
  Edwd 96
  Geo 54, 60, 64, 72,
  85
  George 51, 53-54,
  64, 66, 75, 81,
  132, 150
  Jno 85, 119
  Joh 123
  John 75
  Jos 78, 105, 107,
  117
  Joseph 52, 79, 150,
  155-56
  Nash 46
  Nathaniel 61

Nathl 46
MILLIDGE 47
MILLS 37, 40, 46, 48
  Baldock 36
  David 31, 37-38,
  132-33, 135, 139
  H 38
  Henry 2, 6-8, 17,
  22, 24, 26, 28-29,
  35, 43
  Rob David 34
MINER, William 11, 72
  Wm 129
MINERS, Robt S 83
MINKY, Shadrack 61
MINOR 87, 118
  William 15, 152
  Willm 81, 86, 89,
  152
  Wm 82-83, 87, 114,
  116, 129, 144
MIRES, John 94
MIRICK, James 6
MISTO, Moses 121
MITCHEL, James 21, 31
  Jno 129
  John 25
MITCHELL 47
  J P 95
  James 22, 31, 33,
  50, 54, 65, 74, 86,
  113, 133, 135-36,
  140, 143
  Jas 115
  Jno 53, 69, 71, 74,
  118, 133, 139
  John 36, 49, 56, 88,
  103, 111, 126, 135,
  139
  Mary 115, 129
MITCHELLS, James 41,
  43
MITHELL, John 28
MIXON, John 133, 135
  Reuben 42, 132
  Rheubin 103
MONTGOMERY 47
  James 2, 5, 11, 15,
  17, 21, 29, 49, 56,
  58, 60-61, 69, 83,
  92, 99, 101, 115,
  156
  Jas 69, 81, 84, 90,
  125
  John 17
  Jos 70
  Robt 72, 81, 91, 101,
  105
MONTGOMRY, James 131
MOODY 39

--mes 131
MOON, Ann 155
  Elizabeth 155
MOONEY, John 92, 145
  William 103
MOOR, Willm 149
MOORE 77
  Rachael 14
  Thomas 146
  Thos 55, 91, 101,
  106
  William 131
  Wm 9
MORRIS 38-39, 44,
  48-49, 68, 86, 110
  -- 131
  Edward 132
  James 23, 28, 33,
  42-44, 107, 120,
  126, 131, 145, 152
  Jos 54, 64
  Joseph 42, 131
  Mary 110
  Tho 143
  Thomas 3, 23, 30-31,
  34, 131, 143, 145,
  150, 152, 155-56
  Thoms 78, 116, 145
  Thos 22, 46, 55, 64,
  67, 81, 86, 91, 94,
  100, 111, 119
  Wm 87
MORRISS, Thomas 24
MOSES, Thos 14
MOSS, William 156
MOUNTS, Willm 126
MUCCLEROYTH 84
MULKEY, John 131
MUNSON, Robt 149
MURCOUCK 78
MURDOCK, Josiah 89
MURPHEY, Dennis 25
  James 7
  James A 24
  James C 7, 9, 37,
  144
MURPHY, Dennis 35
  James 78
  James C 78-79, 96
  Jas C 115
  Matthew 131
MURRAY, Wm 72
MYERS 115
  Jno 119
  John 41, 94, 131
MYLES, Edward 100, 157
  Edwd 13, 81, 91-92,
  101, 107, 150, 157
  Priscilla 107
  Teagle 91

William 45
Willm 92, 101, 113
Wm 91
MYRCIK, James 118
MYRICK 35, 39, 49
  Amyu 38
  Eli 38
  Eliza 48, 62, 133
  Elizabeth 25-27
  Elizb 25
  James 9, 23, 27-28,
    34, 45, 50, 78,
    133, 135-37, 140,
    150
  Jas 46, 66, 124
  John 25, 38, 62
  Lany 25
  Mary 25, 27, 38
  Sarah 25, 38
MYSER, John 146, 150,
  152
  Wm 61
MYSERS, John 76
MYSSER, Jno 75
  John 146
NASH, Jno (Thos?) 136
  Thos 136, 141
NAT---CHER, Joseph 25
NATURES, Joseph 143
NEAL, --mes 130
  James 60
NEALE, James 50, 58
NEATHER, Joseph 18
NED, C 84
NEISLER, Jno Adam 81
NEISTER, John Adam 68
NELSON, John 130
NEWM 46
NEWMAN 44, 47-48, 51,
  59-60, 63, 66, 73
  A 39, 152
  Alex 33, 47, 53,
    55-56, 58, 64-65,
    69-70, 72, 83-84,
    86, 90, 92, 96, 101,
    107-08, 114-15, 121,
    144
  Alexander 3, 32, 53,
    72, 98, 106, 121-22,
    129-30, 144, 149,
    150
  Alexandr 23
  Alexn 13, 16, 25
  Alexr 129, 138
  Avr 5
  Geo 123
  Jno 55, 78, 98
  John 32, 50, 78, 94,
    131, 149
  Reub 54-56, 64-65,

69
Reuben 32, 53-54, 72,
  130, 144
Reubin 3
Thomas 86, 98, 107
Will 144
William 3, 25, 72,
  131
Willm 42, 81, 133,
  141
Wm 13, 17, 47-48, 55,
  59-60, 64, 72,
  82-83, 91, 135, 144
NEWTON, Wm 108
NIBBS, William 30
NICHSON, Jno 113
NICKS 48
  Charles 50
  Edwd 107
  Littleberry 122
  Susannah 56
NICKSON 124
  Jno 115
NIGHT, Thomas 22, 83,
  94
  Thos 13, 17, 19, 21
NIMMONS, And 31, 34
  Andrew 51, 89, 106,
    126, 132
  Jno 58
  John 132
NIX 37
  Charles 31, 50, 132
  Chas 58, 75
  Edward 23, 28, 132
  Edwd 65, 75, 119
  George 132, 146
  Robert 31, 132
NIXON, Jno 93
  John 96, 102, 125
  Joshua 126
  Reuben 108, 110, 113
  Robt 83
  Thos 84
NOBLES 39, 44
  Hezekiah 32, 143
  Nich 99, 101, 118
  Nichk 49
  Nichl 42-44, 46
  Nicho 156
  Nicholas 14, 18, 131
  Nichs 92
  Nickl 56
  Nicholas 10
NUNES, Saml 154
O'BANNON 29
  Thomas 4, 23
  Thos 71
O'BRIAN, Thomas 2
O'DOM, Whitmil 13

Oath 43, 45, 52, 85,
  88-90, 95, 99,
  103-04, 106-08, 110,
  114, 119, 122
OBANION, Thomas 5
OBannon 37, 39, 45,
  48, 88, 101, 115
OBANNON, --homas 131
  J 35, 63
  Jno 72, 82, 89
  John 75, 82, 85-86,
    88, 94, 141
  John Ambrose 32
  Jos 63, 75
  Joseph 31, 62,
    73-74, 94
  Sampson 54, 62
  Thomas 36-37, 43, 46,
    48, 50, 58, 60-61,
    65, 71, 74, 84-85,
    89, 104, 107, 109,
    145-46, 155-56
  Thoms 88, 111, 150,
    155
  Thos 48, 50, 54, 56,
    61, 66, 70, 74, 76,
    81, 83, 86-87, 89,
    91-92, 106, 109,
    113-14, 119, 121,
    123, 134-35, 138-39,
    143, 146, 152, 156
  Turner 125
ODAM, Sabard 53
ODOM 35, 37, 39-40,
  44, 46, 48-49, 74,
  125
  A 43
  Ann 38
  B 48, 139
  BanJa 139
  Ben 153
  Benj 5, 19, 35,
    42-44, 46-47, 49-51,
    53-56, 63-65, 72-74,
    80-81, 83, 89-92,
    95, 101, 105,
    107-08, 110, 112-14,
    116
  BenJa 125
  BenJamin 3-4, 10, 12,
    14, 31, 103, 157
  BenJm 13, 18
  BenJy 48
  Daniel 31, 45, 132,
    145, 150, 153
  Danl 25, 51, 69, 75,
    82, 85, 89-90,
    95-96, 150, 155
  David 24
  Isaac 85, 145, 150,

171

156
M 38
Mcl 7
Mical 72
Michl 19, 81, 101, 114
Micl 7
Moses 7, 10-11, 13-15, 19, 55, 64, 131, 149
Owen 29, 105, 129, 154
Powell 74
Priscilla 118, 120, 123
Rachl 150
Sabard 40, 53, 60, 63, 86
Sabart 93, 102, 112
Sabert 73, 80, 83
Sabrad 12, 16
Sally 129
Tal 13
Tamar 46
Uriah 129, 131
Whitmill 9, 22
OFFORD 40
OHerd, John 28
OLFORD 46
OODOM, Sabert 82
OWEN, --lomon 131
  Solomon 41, 133, 135
  Thomas 41, 131
OWENS, Solomon 3, 8, 13, 24, 39, 76, 93, 146
  Thomas 3
  Willm 75, 126
OWIN, Solo 96
OWINGS, Thomas 94
OWNE, Solomon 137
OWNES, Solom 92
OWNES, Solomon 107
PACELY, John 96
PADGET, Elijah 115
PADGETT, Ervin 145
  Henry 145
  James 145
  Selah 145
PALMER, Chas 116
  Mary 117, 123
PARIS, Francis 15
PARKENSON, John 143
PARKER 4
  Bunell 52
  Burrel 89-90, 133, 139
  Burrell 75, 85-86, 88, 135
  Burrill 49

William 16
PARKERSON, John 33, 130
PARKINSON, Jno 8, 53, 65, 67, 80, 101, 114-16, 122, 124-25
  John 2,23-24, 37, 58, 68, 92, 101, 106, 122-23, 143-44, 146, 149
  Walter 109
PARRIS, Francis 29
Patrole 68
PATTERSON, A 102
  William 157
  Wm 157
PATTISON, Jno 77
PAYNE, J 153-54
  Jn 153
  Jonas 153-54
  Wm 153-54
PDGET, Liddea 145
  Sarah 145
PEACOCK, --braham 131
  Abraham 152
  Lewis 131
PECHMAN, Charles 41
PELOT, James 15
PEMBERTON 63
PENDERGAST 35, 39
PENDERGRASS, James 97
PENDLETON, Henry 51
PEOPLES 69
  Henry 17, 21, 69, 148
  Jno 115
  John 146
  Sarah 148
  Sarah (Lee) 148
PERKINS 9
PERREY, Saml 154
PERRY, Saml 105
PETERS, Elijah 77
PETTER, Jno 47
PHILPOT, Dal 74
  Daniel 50, 71, 87, 89
  Danl 58, 67, 70, 75, 78, 85-86, 88
  Thomas 56
  Thos 45, 86, 91, 96
PHILPOTT, Daniel 132
  Thomas 45, 132
PICKET, Ephrai 31
PILOTE 38-39
  Elizabeth 19
  Henny 19
  James 19, 45
PINCKNEY, Charles 107
PINEY, Lue 144, 144

PINKNEY, Charles 84
  Thomas 67
PITOTE, James 10-11
PLATT 110
  Ebenez 71
  Ebenez S 91, 96
  Ebenezer 81
  Jno 56, 67, 70-71
  John 66, 130
PLATTS, Jno 119
  John 145
PLUMMER, Mer 60
  Moses 9, 32, 37, 50, 58, 64, 66, 80, 103, 131, 143-44
  Sarah 143
POWELL 35
  --alekiah 131
  --homas 131
  Dorcas 46-49, 53, 56
  Eliza 74
  Jacob 65, 132
  Malachy 92, 118
  Malcha 96
POWERS, Nathen 75
  Nehem 119
  Nehemiah 41, 50, 58, 96, 132
  Nehemiar 48
PRAWLEY, Robt 53
PRENDARGAST, James 17
PRICE, Daniel 132
  Danl 33
  Jacob 149
  Jno 48
  William 31, 132, 156
  Willm 42, 126
  Wm 33, 42, 94, 107
PRIESTER 118
  Adam 117
PRINCE, Anna (--) 146
  Charles 146
PRINGLE, John J 146
  John Julius 146
PROCTER, Thomas 84
PROMMUNGER, John 72
PUCKETT, Ephream 99
PULLEY, Thomas 72
  Thos 55, 63, 82
  William 82
PULLY 48
  Thos 53
PURVIS, Jesse 148
PUTMAN 37
QUINLEY, Shadrach 132
  Shadrack 65
QUINLY, Shadrach 131
RADTBERT, E A P 157

Ernst Augustus
  Phillip 157
RAINEY, James 83, 90
RAINS, John 157
RANDAL 40, 115
  Jno 82, 92, 115
  John 61, 83, 94, 96,
    124-26
RANDALL 47-48, 115
  Jno 34, 66, 71, 75,
    82-83, 115
  John 93, 102, 109
RANDOLL, John 65
RANDOLPH, John 130
  Peter 13, 17
RANDON 40
  Peter 29
RATLIF, Mark 145
RAWLS 96
  Silas 85
READ, John 140
  Willis 130
RED 96
  Jno 20, 69
  John 15, 125
  Joseph 94, 131
  Tob 24
REDD 82, 115
  Jno 63, 71, 83
  Job 31, 63, 73
  John 28, 35, 63, 73,
    102-03
  Jos 119
  Joseph 65, 75-77,
    146
  Thos 124
REDDING, Eliza 97
REED, --adrach 130
  Charity 32, 45, 80
  Hardy 31, 130
  Jno 66
  Shaderick 31
  Shadrack 45
REESER, Michl 47
REEVES, --avid 130
  David 50, 58, 107
RENEW 71
RIBOSIN, George 148
RICE, Micajah 66
RICHARDSON 132
  Abraham 32
RICHISON, Moses 86
RICHMOND, Charles 107,
    121, 132
  Chas 120
RIFH 65
RIVER, Jacob 94
RIVERS, Jacob 65, 75,
    126, 132
  Jno 58, 63

  John 4, 50, 132
  Mary 64, 83, 90
ROACHE, James D 92
Road 4, 8, 12, 25, 45
ROBERSON, Henry 94
ROBERT 113
ROBERTS 47-49, 93,
    102, 115
  --ames 131
  Barth 68
  Barthl 119
  Bartho 67
  Bartholomew 46, 49,
    131, 156
  Bath 65
  Bathl 56
  Frans 31
  Fras 34
  Hez 115, 123
  Hezek 112, 144
  James 9, 51, 53, 75,
    77, 84, 86
  Jas 121
  Jonah 62
  Rowland 41, 110,
    113, 119, 131
  William 34, 130-31
  William 49
  Willm 42, 93, 126,
    139
  Wm 4, 12, 54, 56,
    62, 75, 85-86,
    88-90, 129
ROBERTSON, Geo 77
  George 65, 73, 126,
    132
  Henry 41, 69
  James 72, 91, 101,
    105
  Lark 83
  Walker 51, 96, 103
  Walter 73, 105-06,
    126
  William 96, 99, 122,
    131
  Wm 83
ROBETS, Rawlin 103
ROBINSON 5, 44, 47
  --rk 131
  Geo 106, 119
  George 2, 67, 103,
    126, 131
  Henry 64
  Lark 143
  W 157
  Walter 43, 45, 49,
    103-04, 121-22, 127,
    133, 138, 140, 154
  William 12, 31, 34,
    43

  Willm 126
  Wm 4-5, 7, 9, 13,
    28-29, 31, 33-34,
    140
ROBISON 23, 40, 47,
    111
  Allen 126
  G 80
  Geo 55-56, 63, 68,
    75, 78-80, 84,
    92-93, 101, 113-14,
    116, 156
  George 42, 56, 63,
    75-76, 78-82, 84,
    93, 110, 127, 150,
    156
  Henry 54
  Lark 10, 13, 16-17,
    92, 95, 101, 129,
    133, 135, 155
  Nancy 155
  W 52
  Walker 51, 113
  Walter 107, 109,
    111, 119, 121, 123,
    135, 140, 154, 156
  William 22-23, 32,
    41, 50, 54, 56,
    61-62, 71, 99,
    126-27, 129, 154-55
  Willm 52, 54, 65-66,
    68, 70, 89-90, 92,
    96, 99, 101, 115,
    150
  Wm 8, 12, 17-18,
    21-22, 24, 29, 32,
    34, 42-43, 52, 54,
    56, 60-62, 65-68,
    70-71, 77, 91, 99,
    106, 116, 129, 143,
    150, 155
ROBTSON, Walter 125
RODGERS, Andrew 72
ROGERS, Andrew 81
  Jesse 25, 32, 50-51,
    58, 60, 103, 109,
    119, 132, 155
  Reuben 51
ROLES, Silas 71
ROLLS, --ilas 132
  Silas 50, 58, 66,
    70, 74
ROUDNTREE, Job 75
ROUDTREE, Reuben 56
ROUNDTREE, --cob 131
  Jacob 58, 94
  Job 32, 53, 60, 84,
    145-46
  Reub 74
  Reuben 65, 67,

70-71, 145-46
Rubin 145
Rueben 131
ROUNTREE, Jacob 50
  Reuben 32
  Reubin 3
ROUSE 47, 56
ROUSEE 48, 104
ROUSER 77
ROUSHAM, James 80
ROUSHAR, Absolom 106
ROWLS, Silas 67, 71, 75
RUNNS 65
RUTHLEDGE, John 51
RUTLEDGE 45
SADLER, Geo 152
SAMPSON 141
SANDERS, Nathaniel 23, 103, 130
  Nathnl 122
  Reuben 68
SANDRES, Nathanel 143
  Nathaniel 143
SAP, Henry 25
SARBROUGH, Wm 124
SAUNDERS, Nath 109
  Nathaniel 145, 155
  Nathl 24, 31, 34, 108, 111, 156
  Reuben 148
SAVAGE, Parker 118
SAVINEAU, Nathl 153
SCARBORIGH, Wm 129
SCARBOROUGH, William 32, 103
SCARBROUGH 48
  Willm 112
  Wm 116
SCHIVER, Justice 83
SEELY, David 143
  Jonathan 103
SHADRACK 32
SHAW 3, 23, 27
  Dal 149
  Danl 54, 62, 70-71, 79, 81, 83, 90-91, 96-97, 101, 112, 114, 119, 124
  John 49, 146
  William 1, 42, 59
  Willm 36, 41-43
  Wm 20-21, 56, 64
SHEEK 83
SHELLEY, David 87
  Jno 116
SHELLY, Samuel 155
SHEPHERD, Martin 97, 115
  Sarah 149

Sheriff 1, 8, 10, 17, 21-22, 28, 31-32, 36, 38, 43, 46, 56, 59, 62, 67, 69, 71, 75, 78, 80, 85, 89, 109, 113, 120, 122, 130, 135-36, 141
SHERIFF, Thomas 58
SHIELD, Robt 58
  Thos 53
  Willm 101
SHIELDS 48, 70
  -- obert 131
  --omas 131
  Robert 36, 133, 137
  Robt 36-37, 55, 60
  Sarah (--) 71
  Sarah (Wallace) 71
  Thomas 50, 71, 75
  Thoms 92
  Thos 53, 56, 58, 67, 77, 94, 101
  Willm 92, 113
  Wm 124
SHILLIE, John 152
SHINGLETARRY, Danl 34
SHINGLETON, D D 26
  Daniel 26
  Danl 26, 34, 104
SHIPES, D 13
  Dav'd 13
  David 9, 33, 42-44, 46, 92, 94, 101, 106-07, 116, 119, 132, 149
  Ned 91
SHOEMAKE, Eliza 150
SIM, Tom 34
SIMM, Jas 34
SIMMONS, Richard 149
SIMMS 34, 118
  James 84, 92, 94, 112, 117, 132, 154
  Jos 98
  Saml 32, 119
  Samuel 67
SIMS, James 26, 31, 97, 99
  Saml 94
SINGLETARY 26
  David 26
SINGLETERRY 34
SINGLETON 35, 47-48
  Daniel 154
  Dl 35
SISSEN, William 43, 45
SISSON, William 50, 56, 58, 85, 94
  Willm 52, 84, 87, 89, 91, 98

Wm 47, 55, 58, 60, 86-87, 89, 91, 95-99, 115, 122
SKIRVING, Alex 116
SMELIN, John 130
SMITH 47-48
  A 30, 134-39, 143, 145, 155
  Aaron 1, 17, 19, 26, 30, 32, 37, 39, 53, 55, 61-62, 64-65, 82, 88, 97, 134, 136-39, 141-42
  Ann 149
  Aron 30, 74
  Caraway 88
  Elinor 149
  Henrietaa 149
  Hephen 58
  Jno 17
  Jno C 2, 13, 21, 23-24, 76-77, 79-82, 84, 87-88, 91, 103, 105, 109, 113, 115, 123-25, 138-39, 146
  Jno Car 106, 118, 126
  Jno Carr 156-57
  Jno Carraway 121
  Jno Co 13
  John C 2, 24, 33, 61, 63, 73, 88-89, 91-92, 96, 99, 101, 103, 109, 111, 114, 118-19, 143-44, 149, 155
  John Caraway 1
  John Carraway 26
  John P 80
  Joshua 41, 51, 94, 107, 126, 132
  Martha 56, 149
  Martha (--) 149
  Rob'n 24
  Robert 35
  Robt 24, 117
  Sarah 149
  Step 97, 122, 152
  Stephen 2, 4, 7, 9, 12-13, 16, 23, 41, 44, 51, 53, 56, 58, 66, 78, 106, 122-23, 129, 132, 144, 146, 149-50
  William 65, 110, 132
  Willim 78
  Willm 76, 140
  Wm 16, 22, 75, 77, 79, 82, 110, 136

Wm Jacamiah 21
SMITHD, McC 53
SNEAD, John 85, 89,
　　152
SNEALING, John 42, 84
SNELLING, -- (--) 52
　　John 52, 94, 97, 99
SOLOMON, Hos 106
　　Jas 116
　　Joseph 92, 101
SOMERALL, Henry 149
SOMERILL 31
SOMERLINE 42
SOUTHWELL 35
　　Edw 78
　　Edward 25, 78, 150,
　　　155
　　Edwd 78, 150
　　Jesse 25
　　John 150
　　Mary 27, 49, 133,
　　　150, 155
　　Sarah 24, 49, 62,
　　　78, 126, 131, 143,
　　　150, 155
　　Sarah (--) 150
　　Sarh 143
　　William 25, 150
　　Willm 133
　　Wm 20
SPEARS, Sarah 152
SPENCER, Geo 83
　　Geo B 152
SPILLIARDS, Higdon 125
STANLEY, Willm 150
STARK 118
　　R 47
　　Robt 23, 42, 69, 85,
　　　92, 96-98, 106,
　　　112, 115
STARKLEY, Robert 41
STEADMAN 44
STEDMAN 39
STEELE 131
STERLING, Isaac 87
STEWART, Charles
　　75-76, 94, 103,
　　146, 150, 152
　　Chas 85, 95
　　Hugh 152
　　Jno 95, 105
STINSON, Nathan 132
STOAKER, Randolph 72
STONE 40, 46
　　Francis 15
　　Frank 11
STOT, Abell 132
STRINGER 39, 44
　　Wm 6, 9-10, 21
STROZER, John M 120

　　John Martin 120
STROZIER, John Martin
　　26, 103
　　Mary 26
STUART, Chas 112
　　John 154
STURGESS, Willm 117
STURGIS, William 97
　　Willm 103
SUM 47
SUNN 48, 74
　　Doc 68
　　Docr 58
　　Dod 65
　　Fedt 72
　　Fred 55-56, 92, 101,
　　　117, 138
　　Frederick 72, 97,
　　　133
　　Fredk 96, 139
SURINOY, Jacob 33
SURRINCY, Jacob 131
Surveyor 152
SWEAT 48
　　Jno 55
　　John 38
SWICHERD, Michael 97
SWICORD 47, 89, 126
　　George 153-54
　　Gurge 126
　　Jacob 2, 53-54, 56,
　　　62, 64, 72, 82,
　　　106-07, 126, 132,
　　　153
　　James 153
　　Michael 17, 19, 84,
　　　95, 126, 132
　　Michl 41, 50-51, 55,
　　　58, 64-66, 94, 106,
　　　112, 119, 154
　　Micl 13
　　Ml 17
　　N B Jacob 53
SWOHACKER, Rudolph 64
SWYCARD, Micl 8
SWYCORD, Michael 131
SYKES 110
SYMES, James 56
SYMKINS, Arthur 24
SYMS, J 148
　　James 148
TABLE, Wm 51
TABOR, John 56
TALBOT, Matthew 97
TANNER 92
　　J 95
　　Noah 58, 69, 101,
　　　148
TARBER, John 94, 130
TAYLOR, Simeon 92, 101

　　William 55, 73
　　Wm 55, 60, 63, 80,
　　　88
TEASER, Laurens 65
TEASTER, --aurence 131
TEASTERS, Andrew 146
TELPUT, Thos 22
TESTER 40
　　Andrew 59, 146
　　Leandor 27
TESTOR 34
THOMAS, Gilshot 145
　　James 150
　　William 25
　　Willm 150
　　Wm 108
THOMMAS, Gill 55
THOMPSON, Wm 87, 119
THOMSA, William 97
THOMSON 47
　　Willm 34
THOWER, Levi 72
THRAVER, Levi 44
THREADAWAT, Ricd 24
THREADAWAY, Elijah 24
　　Ricd 13, 17-18, 23
　　Richard 18, 24, 28
　　Richd 4-5, 9, 13
THROWER, Levi 45, 54
THURSTON, James 107,
　　118
TILMAN, C 74
TIMMS 77
TINSLEY, Cornelious
　　132
TOBY 50, 68
TONEY, Abram 71
　　Benjamin 155
　　Elizabeth 152
　　Elizabeth (Collins)
　　　152
　　Susanna 150
TONY, Eliza 46
TOOL, --saac 132
　　David 132
　　Grace 63
　　Isaac 31, 51, 103-04,
　　　109, 122
　　Wm 34
TOOTEN, Willm 66
TOTEN, Wm 74
TOTTEN, Thos 65
　　William 56
TOWNSEND 47
　　Ruth 42, 49, 51,
　　　116, 122
TRADAWAY 63
　　Elijah 58, 83, 146
　　Mrs 30
　　Red 29

Rich 121, 127
Richard 29, 31-32,
  43, 58, 60, 65, 74,
  76-77, 79, 84-87,
  102, 126-27
Richd 4, 30, 32, 34,
  56, 59-62, 81-83,
  127
TRADAWY, Richd 86
TRADEAWAY, Rich 103
  Richard 41
  Richd 103-04, 119,
    121, 123
TRADEWAY 47
TRADEWELL 148
TREADAWAY, Richard 31
  Richd 8
TREADWAY, Richd 52
Treasurer 1, 43, 134,
  142
TREDAWAW, Richard 120
TREDAWY, Richard 36
TRONMONGER, Jno 82, 89
TROOP, John 101
TROVER, Jos Brooker 67
  Wm 117
TROWER 39, 40, 46
  Levi 58
TRUCK, James 131
TRYALL 56
TURNER 37, 47-48, 69,
  77, 115
  A 15
  Arthur 11, 37, 54,
    56, 59-61, 63-64,
    70, 73, 81, 83, 92,
    131
  Eliz 22
  Elizabeth 152
  James 152
  John 95, 152
  Jonathan 153
  Jos 63, 119
  Joseph 51, 84, 110,
    120, 131, 150, 155
  Noe 9
  Thom 152
  Vet 54
  Willm 41, 152
  Wm 54-55, 64, 69,
    77, 81
TUTEN 40, 46, 71
  Jos 87
  Joseph 56
  Thomas 56, 131
  William 131
  Wm 67, 75
TUTLE 71
  William 61
  Willm 64

Wm 54, 70-71
TUTON, William 23
  Wm 28, 140
TWINER 101
TWINING, Nath 83
  Nathaniel 99
  Nathl 91, 116
TYLER, Absalom 41, 51
  Absm 108
  Absolom 92, 110
TYLOR, Absm 113
  Absolom 103, 131
ULMORE, Philip 49
UZZELL, Thomas 157
VINCE 26
  -- 129
  Bid 13
  Jo 38, 65
  Jor 39
  Jos 32, 45, 53, 85
  Joseph 2, 4, 8, 19,
    22, 30, 34, 38,
    42-43, 45, 72, 75,
    86, 88, 106, 117,
    126, 129, 132, 143,
    146
  Rd 129
  Ricd 45, 78, 82, 85
  Richard 2, 31, 121,
    132
  Richd 65, 76-79, 91,
    98, 107, 120, 126,
    140
  W 22, 146
  William 1-2, 24, 42,
    94, 122-23, 132,
    141, 149
  Willm 42, 108, 117,
    135. 143, 146
  Wm 12, 24, 32, 34,
    38, 56, 113, 120,
    123-24
  Wm Willm 86
VINE, William 32
WADE, Hezekiah 149
WALKER, And 100
  Andrew 108
  Andw 92
  G 82, 126
  George 51, 85, 103,
    105, 130
  Isaac 51
  Israel 120
  Isreal 34, 49
  James 56, 107, 121,
    130, 152
  Jerad 120
  John 97
  Jonathan 34, 49, 51
  Joshua 53

Nathanael 150
Nathaniel 65, 73,
  130
Nathl 55, 63, 75,
  80, 88, 92, 110,
  150
Rachel 149
Richael 56
Roland 22
Willm 103
Wm 10, 104
WALLA-CE, Sarah 39
WALLACE 37, 39, 44,
  48, 67
  Jos 54, 56
  Josias 6, 16, 40,
    56, 71
  Michael 30
  Patrick 149
  Sarah 13, 19, 30,
    71
  Sarah (--) 30
WALLEN, Eliza 108
  Jno B G 129
WARD 39, 45
  Jno 17
  John 2, 133, 138
WARDEND, Elijah 108
WASDEN, Elijah 130,
  145
WASHINGTON 45
  Edwd 41
WATSON, Jno 72, 91,
  101, 105, 115
WAY 69, 124
  Amos 3, 12, 95,
    108-09, 143, 146
  Jas 117
  Sam 65
  Saml 13, 22, 33,
    55-56, 65, 67-68,
    75, 84, 113
  Samuel 3, 30, 72,
    130, 156
WEAKLEY, John 19
  William 49
WEATHERFORD, James 22
WEATHERSBY 37
  Lewis 13
  Thos 24, 59, 75, 84,
    86, 121
WEBB 40, 46
  Jeremiah 29
  Jos 59
  Joseph 53
WECKLEY, William 135
WECKLY, John 93
WEEKELY, William 130
WEEKLELY, John 36
WEEKLEY, Buford 129

George 130
Jno 17
John 56
Thos 119
William 49, 66, 130, 135, 137
Willm 65, 68, 103, 133, 136, 140
Wm 9, 67, 93, 130, 137
WEEKLY, Jno 62
 John 68, 74, 97
 Joseph 129
 William 33, 56, 110, 144
 Willm 140
 Wm 4, 13, 108, 119, 122, 129
WEEKS, Edwd 94
WELCH, Eleanor 52, 63, 73, 80, 88
 John 93
 Peggy 52
WELL, Widow 9
WELLS, --mes 131
 William 153
WELSH, John 83
WERT, Jasper 97-98, 115
WETHERSBY, Thos 119
WHEATLEY, William 2
WHEEKLY, John 41
WHEELER 39, 40, 44, 46
 Charles 2, 8, 12, 16, 27, 30, 49, 99, 133, 136, 140-41, 146
 Chas 58, 74, 81, 86, 136, 138, 141
WHEELR, Charles 59
WHELER, Charles 27
WHITE 40, 46
 John 132
WICKLEY, Jno 61, 69, 119
 John 32, 144
WICKLY 43, 47-48
 Cinthia 146
 Jno 60, 62, 64, 68, 72, 79, 81-83, 114
 John 4, 33, 50, 55, 58, 60, 65, 71, 88-91, 101-03, 105, 108, 112, 132-33, 135, 139, 144-45, 154
 Willm 90, 154
WIGGES, Willis 148
WIGGINS, Geo 96
 George 56, 149

Thomas 132
WIKLEY 90
WILEY, -- 100
WILKANSON, Willm 81
WILKINSON, William 90
 Wm 82
WILKSON, John 98
WILL, Jno 7
WILLIAM, Alen 100
 John 144
WILLIAMS 4, 39-40, 44, 46-49, 105
 Abigail 156
 Allen 91, 95-96, 100, 105, 112, 114-15
 Asa 51-52, 63
 Augustus 155
 Benajah 104
 Bera 97
 Eli 37
 Eliza 48, 62
 Eliza A 50
 Ezeh 84
 Ezekiel 3, 58, 126, 132, 156
 Hezekiah 15, 36, 42-43
 Jno 58, 94, 97, 104, 119
 John 50, 63, 66, 84, 99, 132, 144
 Jos 111
 Joseph 152
 Joshua 11, 15, 19, 65, 103, 119, 132
 Mary 32
 Nathan 27, 32, 56, 145
 Ow 54
 Owen 72, 104
 Rawley 132
 Richard 100
 Rolley 24
 Rowland 78
 Rowley 42, 94
 Thomas 128
 Widow 9, 93
 William 27, 42, 61, 120, 132
 Willm 46, 56, 126, 140
 Wm 18, 21, 69, 75, 95, 119
 Zacariah 94
WILLIAMSON, Benajah 108, 156
 Beray 115
 John 25
 Rebecca (--) 25

Willm 84
Wm 64, 83
WILLIS 38
 William 101
 Wm 43, 83, 114, 124
WILLISON, Saml 72, 91
WILLSON, Samuel 99
 William 125
WILSHER, Jno 55
WILSHITE, John 73
WILSON 47, 55
 -- (--) 55
 James 144
 Sarah 144, 152
 Sarah (--) 144
 William 90
 Wm 105
WILTSHIE, John 88
WILTSHIRE, Jno 116
 John 80
WIMBERLY, Edward 106
WINBERLY, Edwd 106
WINBORN, Jesse 86, 87
WINBORNE, Jesse 52, 53, 62, 65, 77, 86, 95, 100, 121, 127
WINBOURN, Jesse 56, 58, 60, 62, 76-77, 86, 94, 96, 99, 104, 106, 119, 132
WINBOURNE, Jesse 119, 154-55
WINBURN, Jesse 25, 30, 58, 65, 74-76, 84-85, 119, 121-22, 126-27, 138, 140, 145
WINDAM 47-48
 Isaac 56, 62
WINDBORNE, Jesse 50
WINDHAM 49
WISE, Wm 5, 16, 21
WISSON, Wm 88
WITHORSON, Wm 72
WOLEY, Zadock 11
WOMACK, Fred 117
 Wm 71-72
WOOD 149
 --exander 131
 --hro 131
 Alexn 149
 Alexr 149
 Henry 56, 66-67, 70, 75, 90, 132
 Jane 144
 Jesse 144
 Jethro 10, 14, 144, 150
 Jno 44, 129
 John 123, 144

Lucy 15-16, 19
Mary 144
Mary (--) 144
Susannah 61, 146
WOODCOCK, William 2, 25, 49, 99, 133, 141
 Willm 135
 Wm 6, 16, 58, 63, 73, 80, 101, 136, 152
WOODS, Alexander 149
 Henry 71, 74, 83
WOOLEY 124
 --adoch 132
 Lazarus 49, 121, 146
 Zadoc 136
 Zadock 20, 119, 122
WOOLLEY, Lars 15
 Xadock 25
 Zadock 15, 25, 51, 56, 75, 99, 103
 Zodack 115
WOOLLY, Zadoc 135
 Zadock 4
WOOLMERS 93
WOOTON, Thomas 36, 61, 134, 138-39
 Thoms 135
 Thos 64, 134-35, 138
WORKS, John 120
WREELEY 124
WRITE, Robt 112
 Stephen 156
WULD, John 131
WYCH, Jno 71, 82
 John 83, 96, 124
WYCHE 48, 92
 Jno 8, 43-46, 54-55, 58, 72, 81, 85, 90, 101, 111-12, 119, 124
 John 42, 44-45, 49, 58, 61, 72, 75, 79, 83, 85-86, 88-90, 92, 95, 99, 103-04, 107, 109, 111, 114, 119-21, 152, 154, 157
WYCHES, Jno 101
WYLD 39-40, 46, 53, 59-60, 77, 118
 C D 38-39, 48, 116
 Cleavers D 143
 Clevears D 55, 59, 103
 Clevers D 18, 21, 32, 47

Cleviers 30
Clw D 5
CVD 5
Jno 6-7, 13, 47, 53, 59, 63, 71-72, 78, 82, 84, 112
John 2, 4-5, 20, 24, 29-30, 43-46, 48, 50, 53-54, 68, 70-71, 73-74, 76-77, 79-81, 84-89, 91-93, 100-02, 143, 146, 149, 154
Lucy 59
T 137-38
Thom 104, 112
Thomas 32, 58, 61, 84-85, 88, 128, 133, 135, 139, 141-43, 145, 155-56
Thoms 103, 107, 137
Thos 17, 32, 53, 91, 102, 139, 143, 156
WYLDS, Thomas 156
WYNBOURN, Jesse 25
YARBROUGH, Charles 102
 Chas 91-92, 112
YOAN, Simon 67
YON, Simon 87
YONN, Sim 87
 Simon 87
 Willm 87
YOUNG, Jno 6
 John 77
 Sarah 96
YOUNGBLOOD, Jno 120
 Joseph 31, 41, 51, 107, 121, 132
YOWNS, Simn 140
 Simon 136
ZUBLY, David 149

Index prepared by
Shelley Viramonte
Wickenburg, AZ

Other Heritage Books by Brent H. Holcomb:

Bute County, North Carolina Land Grant Plats and Land Entries

*CD: Early Records of Fishing Creek Presbyterian Church,
Chester County, South Carolina, 1799–1859*

CD: Kershaw County, South Carolina Minutes of the County Court, 1791–1799

CD: Marriage and Death Notices from The Charleston [SC] Observer, *1827–1845*

CD: South Carolina, Volume 1

*CD: Winton (Barnwell) County, South Carolina Minutes of
County Court and Will Book 1, 1785–1791*

*Early Records of Fishing Creek Presbyterian Church, Chester County,
South Carolina, 1799–1859, with Appendices of the Visitation List of
Rev. John Simpson, 1774–1776 and the Cemetery Roster, 1762–1979*
Brent H. Holcomb and Elmer O. Parker

Kershaw County, South Carolina Minutes of the County Court, 1791–1799

Marriage and Death Notices from The Charleston Observer, *1827–1845*

*Winton (Barnwell) County, South Carolina Minutes of
County Court and Will Book 1, 1785–1791*

www.ingramcontent.com/pod-product-compliance
Lightning Source LLC
Chambersburg PA
CBHW070338240426
43665CB00045B/2203